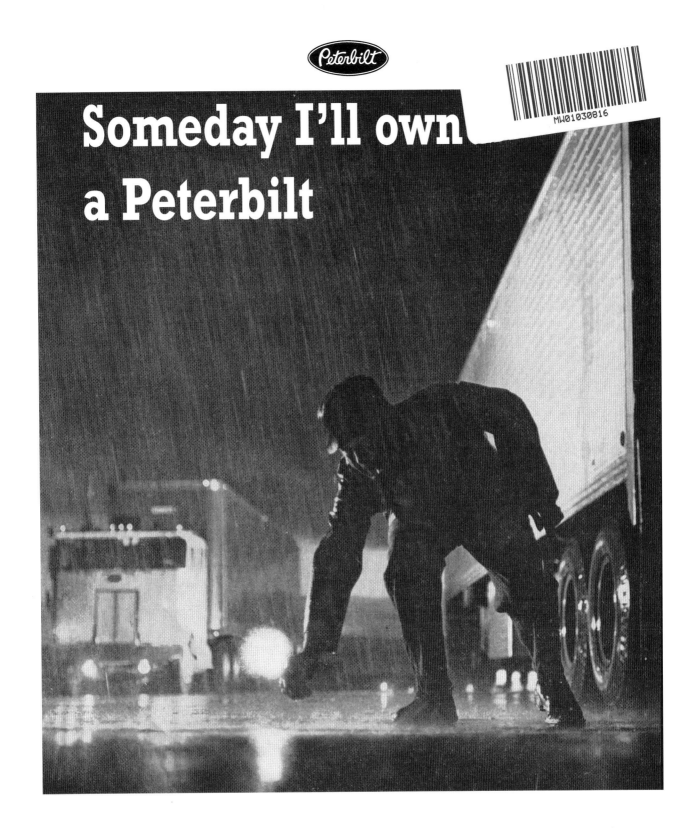

Someday I'll own a Peterbilt

THE EVOLUTION of CLASS

by

Warren Johnson

Table of Contents

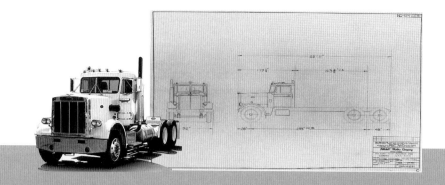

THE EVOLUTION of CLASS
by
Warren Johnson

Acknowledgement

I Wish To Thank.....

Bob Place for introducing me to collecting Peterbilt Literature.

Dave Bargren, John Lunde, and Henry Arthur of Lunde Peterbilt for their help in my collection and allowing me countless hours using their microfilm to research my data.

Todd Acker and Al Zwicky at Peterbilt Motors Company for their assistance.

Warner Hall for his assistance and contributions.

Glen Meuwissen of Allstate Peterbilt for his contribution.

Phil Sweeney for his assistance.

Sam Brown (retired) who provided several early pieces of literature and many hours of conversation that answered many questions.

Alan Garms of Houston Peterbilt for his contribution.

Clarence Levens of Denver Peterbilt for his contribution.

Jim Kliment whose contribution has been endless.

Jack Kopol and Stu Engs of Reno Peterbilt for their contribution.

Paul Allen of Peterbilt Motors Company for his guidance and contribution.

Barry Provorse of Documentary Book Publishers for the information he provided from the Oakland Tribune and PACCAR Inc. Archives.

Rick McClerkin of San Jose, California for his help and contributions.

Last, I wish to thank all the Peterbilt dealers and sales people who I have visited over the years which has given me the impetus to produce this book.

This book is dedicated to my wife Marcia, my daughter Molly and all the people who have supported me in this project.

1961 Peterbilt Model 351. Owner: Warren Johnson, Ashton, Illinois.

Forward

Peterbilt trucks have been in my life since 1956, when at the age of ten I rode in a cabover Pete hauling our cattle to market. I still can remember the driver jokingly reprimanding me for cleaning his license plate and tail lights assuring me that the DOT would pull him over; "Those clean lights will make DOT think I'm overloaded!" well, we got to market without incident. It was my first trip away from the farm, playing hooky from school with my parents permission, and sitting on top of the world in that cabover Pete. It is a memory I will never forget.

Over the years I have collected the usual, models, hats, tee shirts, a jacket, emblems, anything with Peterbilt on it. In 1996 I purchased a Model 351 Pete and began an earnest effort collecting literature, data sheets, sales brochures, engineer drawings, and anything relating to Peterbilt and its history. During the course of this collecting, I have come to discover that a lot is not known about the history of Peterbilt and all of the models that Peterbilt has produced. There are a few short articles in various publications, the book, "The Class of the Industry," but no single publication that shows the complete line of Peterbilt trucks by model that have evolved in the last sixty years. It is an interesting, if not intriguing, evolution that I wish to share with other Peterbilt enthusiasts.

While producing this book, I thought it best to let the literature portray Peterbilt's history. I have tried to avoid testimonials and personal views. I have included extraneous pictures, but again, I feel that the factory data and literature is the best source of an accurate portrayal of Peterbilt's history. I chose literature that would show all models, yet not be cumbersome and repetitive. I dwell on the earlier literature, it established the "Evolution of Class".

WARREN JOHNSON

Introduction

To understand the evolution of Peterbilt, several factors have to be explained. Peterbilt used two types of serial numbering systems for vehicle identification. The first, was a serial numbering system preceded with a letter, "L", "M", and "S", (Large, Medium, and Small). L's were 3 axle trucks, M's were 2 axle trucks, and S's were a 2 axle chassis, L-100, L-101, etc., M-100, M-101, etc., and S-100, S-101, etc. This system was discontinued in October 1959 with L4882 (S.O. 11388). The second, is the Sales Order (S.O.) numbering system. The sales order numbering system is a numbering system that began with the very first Peterbilt, S.O. 5001 (S-100). This is a number that is assigned when an order is received for a truck, not when the truck is built. Then in 1959, the sales order number was incorporated as the serial number with S.O. 11394. (S.O.11389 thru 11393 were cancelled orders, the reason for the gap between 11388 and 11394). Also, beginning in 1959,

if an order for a truck was cancelled before that truck was built, that sales order would be cancelled and that number never used. The sales order is not necessarily the order in which Peterbilt trucks are built. As an example, Mercury Freight Lines ordered nineteen Model 352's in early 1964, but did not take delivery until later in 1965, nearly one and one half years later. There are several reasons for this, among those are parts availability, planned inventory replacement, and tax/depreciation considerations.

Another system used for differentiating between 2 axle, 3 axle and 4 axle trucks was the use of the 200 series, 300 series, and 400 series model numbers. This system was discontinued with Models 289/359 in 1986.

The early Peterbilt Models 260, 334, 344, 345, 354, and 355 had a 2 letter suffix added to the model designation, example 334DT. The first suffix letter designated the type of fuel, "G" for gasoline or butane, and "D" for diesel. The second suffix letter would be a letter that designated a particular application or customers use for that truck. This suffix lettering was used until 1949. There were no prefix or suffix letters used with the Models 280/350, 360, 370, 380 and 390. With the introduction of the Models 281/351 thru the Models 282/352,

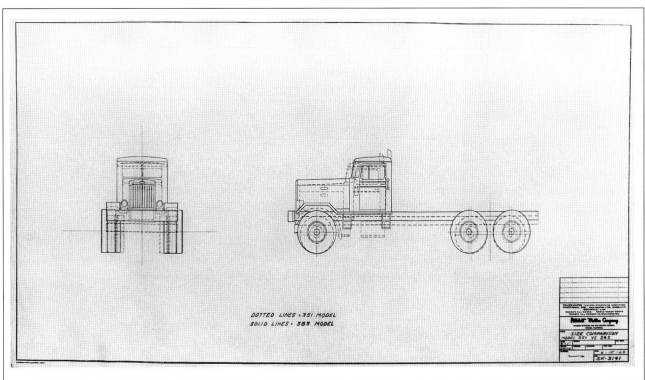

DOTTED LINES - 351 MODEL
SOLID LINES - 383 MODEL

Peterbilt engineer drawing dated June 5, 1962.

the suffix letters used were "A", "M", and "S" or "ST". The "A" was an all aluminum frame, the "M" was aluminum frame rails with steel cross members, and the "S" or "ST" was an all steel frame. If the suffix letters "RM" appeared after the serial number, that truck had been remanufactured at the Peterbilt factory.

Another prefix, and later suffix letter used was "K" for rebuild kits. The original rebuild kits were numbered K5000 thru K5894 with no reference to sales order numbers. This numbering system was used from November 1961 thru April 1968, at which time the kits were incorporated into the sales order of "serial number" system starting with 28080-K.

In 1969, with the Nashville, Tennessee plant opening, another suffix was added to identify which plant built a particular truck. The suffix letter "N" designated Nashville-built trucks, and "P" designated Newark-built trucks. It is suppositioned that "P" stood for Parent, the Newark factory. In September 1980, all vehicles were required to have a 17 digit serial or V.I. N. number. Now, the last 8 digits contain 2 prefix letters, example BP123456. The first prefix letter is the year of manufac-

ture: B-1981, C-1982, D-1983, E-1984, F-1985, etc. The second letter designated the manufacturing plant, N-Nashville, P-Newark, D-Denton, and F-Kenmex.

Peterbilt hood lengths were originally determined by the type of engine installation. The use of the terms "short hood" or "long hood" began appearing on a truck build sheet on a regular basis about 1969, and is a monicker that has remained since then. A long hood is typically a 127 inch BBC (bumper to back of the cab) and a short hood is usually the 119 inch BBC. These terms became popular with the Model 359, then the Model 379, although the earliest regular use was the short hood Model 351 with a Detroit 318 engine.

Historically, Peterbilt has custom-built trucks to an individual or fleet specification which virtually eliminates the cookie cutter or carbon copy truck. This along with body lines that date back to the first Peterbilt, ease of maintenance and repair, and rugged durability, maintains Peterbilt's popularity. A cross country ride will attest to this fact, count the number of older Peterbilts still on the road.

Peterbilt Model 334.

EVOLUTION OF CLASS

Fageol Model 10-66   Al Peterman's vision to fill his needs to move his timber.
Owner: Rick McClerkin, San Jose, California

L.H. Bill, the founder and first president of Fageol Motors Company, laid the foundation for an enduring company when he wrote, "We will never build to a standard lower than the highest. When we can buy better parts than we can make, we will buy them. When we can make better parts than we can buy, we will make them." Bill established the evolution of class when he vowed, "Utilizing superior engineering judgement, we will produce the best equipment or we will produce nothing." The company he created in 1915 became, in 1939, what is now internationally known as Peterbilt Motors Company.

Tacoma, Washington lumberman Theodore Alfred "Al" Peterman was a man known for his mechanical genius. Peterman's road to acquiring a truck company began in 1934, when he purchased 30,000 acres of forestland near Tacoma. Rather than build a railroad, he built

roads and acquired a small fleet of White trucks and modified them for his needs. While on one of his frequent business trips to San Francisco in 1938, he heard that Fageol Motors might be for sale, and 1939 he purchased the plant, its 13.5 acre site, parts and equipment for $50,000.00.

The first year was a year of redesigning and retooling. During the transition, employees were kept busy refurbishing and servicing all makes of trucks to generate cash. This refurbishing and rebuilding would continue for many years.

The first truck to be called a Peterbilt was a chassis built for Hirst Fire Truck Company, who added a hood, grille, fenders and fire apparatus. This unit was built in June 1939 and was sold to the Centerville (now part of Fremont) California Fire Department.

The first completed truck was a three axle "L" Model 334, L-100 SO (Sales Order) 5002. It was sold to Garrett Beckley of Stockton, California. The second completed truck was an "M" Model 260 M-100 SO-5003. It was sold to Pete Bordenave also of Stockton. Both units were completed in August of 1939 and sold through Connell & Garvey of Stockton. 1939 sales were 16 units, 2 Model 334's, 13 Model 260's and 1 Model 120.

In 1940 sales increased to 93 units, 41 Model 334's, 39 Model 260's, 2 Model 120's, and 1 Model 354. Peterbilt also built 10 Cabover chassis' for Freightways Mfg. of Salt Lake City. Freightways supplied the cabs, Peterbilt completed the trucks, installing pressure wipers, singletone airhorn and 16" diameter 4 shoe Tru Stop brakes.

1941 saw sales increase to 95 units; 11 Model 334's, 26 Model 260's, 32 Model 344's, 7 Model 270's, 15 Model 354's, 3 Model 120's, and 1 Model 364 for Snoqualmie Falls Lumber Company. This would be the only civilian style Model 364 built, with conventional cab, hood, fenders, radiator and headlight protectors, such as were available on the Model 354. The next 39 Model 364's would be built with "military style" hood, grille,

fenders, and open and enclosed cabs. A Model 270DD COE with no cab, hood, or fenders would be built for Lyon Van and Storage. Also, a Model 334 with no rear axles was supplied to Peterman Manufacturing of Tacoma, Washington where Peterman's chief mechanic Ed Valentine installed the Peterman designed Flex Axles, and the ribbed drums that Valentine himself had designed. The Models 270, 344, and 354 now sported an aluminum radiator style grille instead of the egg crate grille of the Model 260 and 334. The skirted fender was retained on the 270 and 344 while the 354 received a "flat" fender, stiffer suspension, and higher mounted radiator for off road work.

The Models 354/355 stood higher than the Models 344/345 which led to the axiom, "high mount" and "low mount". The increased height was due to the stiffer suspension, and raised cab and radiator. Later Model 354's and 355's would receive a larger radiator with the introduction of larger engines that carried over into the 280/350 series models. The high mount could be easily identified by the kick panel located below the door. Another argument for the high/low mount exists over the placement of the fan. The low mount had the fan bolted directly to the water pump, whereas on the

Model 334 with sleeper cab. Note hole in bumper. This was for a hand crank, that could be used to start the engine, set timing and adjust valves.

high mount, the fan was mounted on a pulley that placed the fan closer to the top of the radiator for better cooling. Peterbilt promoted this high mounting of the fan as a standard feature in their advertising.

1942 saw a downturn in sales because of the lack of availability of raw materials. Refurbishing and repair work generated as much revenue as new sales. New truck sales totalled 55 units; 1 Model 120, 1 Model 260, 1 Model 260 COE, 6 Model 270's, 11 Model 344's, 7 Model 354's, and 28 Model 364's built for military contractors. The COE was a 42" quarter cab mounted on a flat deck for Hall-Scott engine company.

1943 sales increased to 76 units; 2 Model 270's, 42 Model 344's, 21 Model 354's, and another 11 Model 364's for military contractors.

In 1944, sales tripled, jumping to 226 units, but on only 2 models; 60 Model 344's, and 166 Model 354's. In July,

Al Peterman would be diagnosed with cancer and died before the year's end. His widow, Ida, retained ownership, then in 1947, sold the company, but not the land, to a group of company managers, and outside investors led by Lloyd A. Lundstrom.

1945 saw sales break the 300 mark, which would continue for the next four years. 1945 sales were 323 units; 85 Model 270's, 20 Model 344's, 77 Model 345's, 131 Model 354's, and 10 Model 344's. The 345 and the 355 were updated versions of the 344 and the 354, respectively.

1946 sales were 346 units; 81 Model 270's, 41 Model 344's, 153 Model 345's, 24 Model 354's, and 47 Model 355's.

1947 sales were 315 units; 64 Model 270's, 71 Model 344's, 108 Model 345's, 16 Model 354's, and 56 Model 355's.

Peterbilt engineer drawing SK184 April 15, 1942.

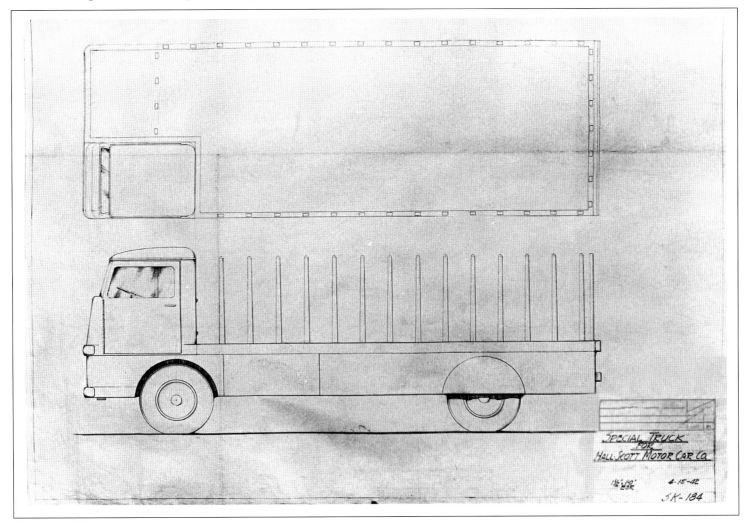

1948 sales were 319 units; 81 Model 270's, 64 Model 344's, 143 Model 345's, 10 Model 354's, and 21 Model 355's. Sales order #6823 would be changed from a Model 270 to a 345.

1949 would see a downturn in sales, but yet see the introduction of the first production cab overs and design changes in the conventional line. Over the next 5 years, Peterbilt would build the Models 280/350/360 in both cab over and conventional styles. 2 Model 360COE's were built with a trussed frame and a squared nose cab similar to Kenworth's cabover, the rest of the 360COE's would use the 280/350 style cab. Peterbilt would build 10 different models in 1949. Sales for 1949 were 214 units; 3 Model 270's, 3 Model 344's, 6 Model 345's, and 2 Model 355's. In the new series conventionals, there were 75 Model 280's, 55 Model 350's, 46 Model 360's, 5 Model 370's, 16 Model 380's, and 1 Model 390 sold.

1950 would see sales climb to 339 units, comprised of 9 different models. There were 74 Model 280's, 6 Model 280COE's, 112 Model 350's, 41 Model 350COE's, 55 Model 360's, 3 Model 360COE's, 18 Model 370's, 15 Model 380's, and 15 Model 390's.

1951 sales were 371 units; 62 Model 280's, 5 Model 280COE's, 104 Model 350's, 70 Model 350COE's, 67 Model 360's, 8 Model 360COE's, 15 Model 370's, 20 Model 380's and 20 Model 390's.

1952 sales were 411 units; 71 Model 280's, 20 Model 280COE's, 217 Model 350's, 54 Model 350 COE's, 19 Model 360's, 1 Model 360COE, 10 Model 370's, and Model 19 Model 380's.

1953 sales were 321 units; 48 Model 280's, 18 Model 280 COE's, 196 Model 350's, 34 Model 350COE's, 7 Model 360's, 1 Model 370, 15 Model 380's, and 2 Model 390's.

1954 saw the introduction of the 281/351/381 Models. The new models sported a new radiator grille, and eliminated the skirted fenders that had been around since 1939. Ironically, the Model 351 would be the model in production longest, the last 3 were built in 1976: one in March one in April, and one in May. 1954 sales were 276 units; 20 Model 280's, 30 Model 280COE's, 40 Model 281's, 58 Model 350's, 31 Model 350COE's, 80 Model 351's, 2 Model 360's, 2 Model 370's, 1 Model 380, and 12 Model 381's.

1955 would see the introduction of the 281/351 cabovers. Peterbilt would build 11 different models this year, with one customer ordering 2 Model 351 Peterbilts modified with Model 350 style hood, radiator, and grille. 1955 sales were 486 units;

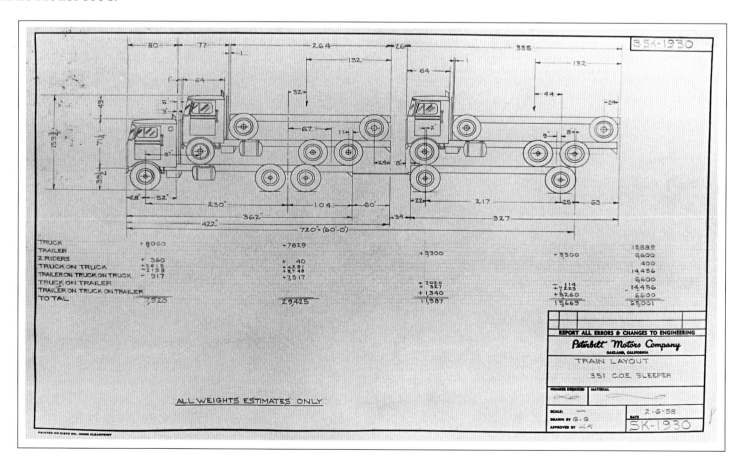

Peterbilt engineer drawing SK1930, Dated February 6, 1958.

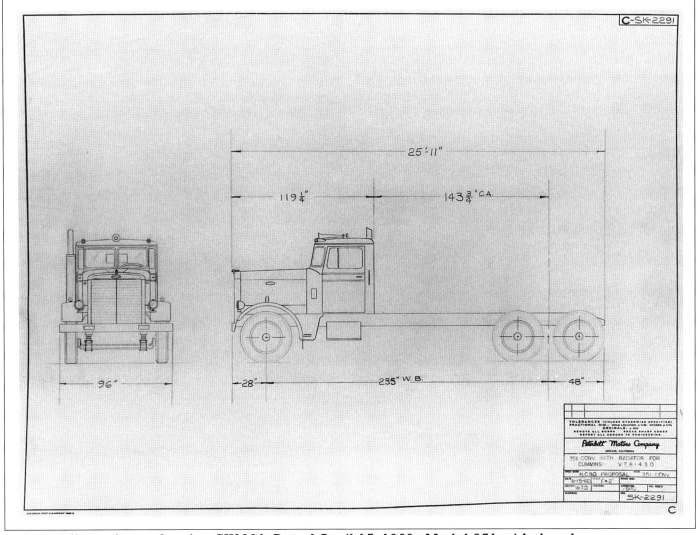

C-SK-2291

Peterbilt engineer drawing SK2291, Dated April 15, 1960, Model 351 wide hood.

13 Model 280's, 35 Model 280COE's, 81 Model 281's, 37 Model 350's, 56 Model 350COE's, 218 Model 351's, 10 Model 351COE's, 1 Model 360, 1 Model 361, 2 Model 370's, and 32 Model 381's. Incidentally the Models 280/350/360 and 281/351 would be the only models built as cabovers and conventionals.

1956 sales totalled 658 units and saw the introduction of an unusual dromedary, a Model 451COE with 2 steer and 2 drive axles, a horizontal 6 cylinder Cummins NHHT engine, and the sleeper mounted above the cab. This model was specially built for Ringsby Truck Lines, although engineer drawings show proposals of this model for Pacific Intermountain Express and Allyn Tank Lines. 1956 sales included; 15 Model 280's, 3 Model 280COE's, 117 Model 281's, 28 Model 281COE's, 33 Model 350's, 11 Model 350 COE's, 298 Model 351's, 68

Model 360

Model 351 COE's, 1 Model 360, 46 Model 381's, 38 Model 451COE's.

In 1957 Peterbilt built 1 more Model 451COE and builds 21 Model 356COE's for Ringsby. The 356COE had a single steer axle instead of the double steer axle of Model 451COE. Sales for this year are 492 units; 9 Model 280's, 107 Model 281's, 53 Model 281COE's, 35 Model 350's, 1 Model 350 COE, 186 Model 351's, 49 Model 351COE's, 21 Model 356COE's, 30 Model 381's, and 1 Model 451COE.

1958 sales drop to 395 units; 85 Model 281's, 31 Model 281COE's, 208 Model 351's, 60 Model 351COE's, and 11 Model 381's. This would be the year that Ida Peterman informs Peterbilt management that she intends to sell the land to a developer. The management, who by now is nearing retirement age and not wanting to acquire the expense of a new site, decides to sell the company. Peterbilt comes under the ownership of Pacific Car and Foundry (PACCAR).

1959 becomes the biggest year yet for Peterbilt. We see the introduction of the 282/352 cabover series, the Model 371 which is the off road version of the 351, the phasing out of the 281/351 cabover series, and the inclusion of the word "Class" in Peterbilt advertising. We would also see the end of the "L" and "M" serial numbering system, the last being L4882 (S.O. 11388), a model 381 sold in October,1959. Sales for 1959 are 780 units; 134 Model 281's, 11 Model 281COE's, 55 Model 282COE's, 1 Model 350COE, 390 Model 351's, 10 Model 351COE's, 149 Model 352COE's, 12 Model 371's, and 18 Model 381's. Interestingly, although the 350 COE had been out of production for 2 years, Otto Pirkle, who liked the 350COE so much, convinced Peterbilt to build one out of service parts.

1960 would see more use of the term "Class", not only in truck advertising, but also the use of elegantly adorned models posing with Peterbilt trucks. We would also see Peterbilt move from Oakland to Newark, California, with a Model 351 rolling off the assembly line in October. Sales for 1960 were 810 units; 167 Model 281's, 61 Model 282's, 332 Model 351's, 192 Model 352's, 24 Model 371's, and 34 Model 381's.

Sales for 1961 were 819 units; 219 Model 281's, 161 Model 282's, 220 Model 351's, 176 Model 352's, 38 Model 371's, and 5 Model 381's.

1962 sales pass the 4 digit mark, and saw the introduction of 2 new models, the 287 and the 341. There were 8 Model 287's built for P.I.E., primarily a light duty "local" tractor. The Model 341 was a small engine powered (weight savings) model for use as a dump or mixer chassis. Sales for 1962 were 1,210 units; 282 Model 281's, 147 Model 282's, 8 Model 287's, 2 Model 341's, 510 Model 351's, 211 Model 352's, 37 Model 371's, and 13 Model 381's.

1963 sales hit 1,528 units; 272 Model 281's, 93 Model 282's, 55 Model 341's, 555 Model 351's, 474 Model 352's, 20 Model 371's, and 59 Model 381's.

1964 would see 9 different models built this year. We would see the introduction of Peterbilt's STABILAIRE air ride suspension and the Models 343 and 383. The Model 343 was a partial cab and chassis. The 383 was an updated version of the Model 381 heavy duty off road truck. Sales for 1964 were 1,934 units; 407 Model 281's, 241 Model 282's, 31 Model 341's, 17 Model 343's, 673 Model 351's, 507 Model 352's, 8 Model 371's, 4 Model 381's, and 46 Model 383's.

1965 would see the introduction of the narrow nose tilt hood Models 288 and 358. Peterbilt offers a conversion kit for the Model 281/351 to a tilt hood. 1965 sales totalled 2,787 units; 410 Model 281's, 288 Model 282's,

1949 Peterebilt Model 360 COE, with trussed frame, (King Beef).

7 Model 288's, 100 Model 341's, 1,075 Model 351's, 841 Model 352's, 11 Model 358's, 1 Model 371, 26 Model 381's, and 28 Model 383's.

Sales for 1966 would be 2,682 units. There would be 9 models built this year. The 371 would be dropped this year and incorporated as a heavy duty 351. There were 272 Model 281's, 316 Model 282's, 101 Model 288's, 107 Model 341's, 801 Model 351's, 793 Model 352's, 248 Model 358's, 17 Model 381's, and 27 Model 383's sold this year.

1967 sees the introduction of Peterbilt's all time classic, the Model 359 and 289. Peterbilt is now building 11 different models. Sales for 1967 are 2,548 units; 57 Model 281's, 256 Model 282's, 117 Model 288's, 4 Model 289's, 75 Model 341's, 299 Model 351's, 934 Model 352's, 674 Model 358's, 61 Model 359's, 31 Model 381's, and 40 Model 383's. The early Model 359's had a 2 bar screen (grille) based on the Model 358's 2 bar screen. Because of the wider hood of the Model 359, this screen was susceptible to failure and was replaced with a 3 bar screen. The 2 bar screen was still available through parts for some time afterward.

The popularity of Peterbilt as an east coast truck becomes more evident in 1968, a market dominated by cabovers because of strict length laws. Peterbilt Models 282/352 surpass the 281/351, 288/358 and 289/359 series of conventionals. Sales for 1968 are 3,645 units; 46 Model 281's, 295 Model 282's, 108 Model 288's, 72 Model 289's, 150 Model 341's, 5 Model 343's, 275 Model 351's, 1,514 Model 352's, 418 Model 358's, 701 Model 359's, 12 Model 381's, and 49 Model 383's.

1969 sees Peterbilt expanding in the eastern markets with the opening of the Madison (Nashville) Tennessee plant. For the first year, only cabovers are built in Madison. Peterbilt begins using a suffix letter in the serial number, "P" (Parent) for Newark built trucks and "N" for Nashville trucks. Peterbilt is now building 12 different models. Sales for 1969 are 4,780 units; 39 Model 281's, 360 Model 282's, 90 Model 288's, 135 Model 289's, 137 Model 341's, 7 Model 343's, 364 Model 351's, 1,681 Model 352's, 472 Model 358's, 1,477 Model 359's, 9 Model 381's, and 9 Model 383's.

1970 would see the introduction of the low cab forward (LCF), models' CB200 and CB300. These trucks would be built at the Sicard factory in St. Therese, Quebec and were branded both Peterbilt and Kenworth. These trucks were originally developed for the short haul delivery and refuse industry. We would also see the introduction of the Model 348, a fiberglass tilt hood built

to replace the Model 341. There are now 14 models in Peterbilts line-up, with 3,435 total units sold this year. They are 3 Model CB200's, 41 Model 281's, 243 Model 282's, 77 Model 288's, 131 Model 289's, 1 Model CB300, 101 Model 341's, 1 Model 348,134 Model 351's, 1,621 Model 352's, 290 Model 358's, 771 Model 359's, 9 Model 381's, and 12 Model 383's.

1971 again would see 14 different models with a total 4,881 units sold. They were; 29 Model CB200's, 8 Model 281's, 326 Model 282's, 67 Model 288's, 104 Model 289's, 28 Model CB300's, 17 Model 358's, 115 Model 348's, 110 Model 351's, 2,816 Model 352's, 188 Model 358's, 1,056 Model 359's, 14 Model 381's, and 3 Model 383's. In 1971, Peterbilt would begin a transition of their recording medium from the Eastman Kodak "RECORDAK" to microfiche.

1972 hits a peak of 17 models, 18 if you consider the 2 experimental Model 352's built with jet turbine engines. We also see the introduction of the Model 346 with 90 or 106 inch axle setback, built as a cement mixer or dump chassis, and the Model 349. There is 1 model 1100 built in November 1972 that is a Model 359 with rounded bottom corner doors and the new style big window cab, (referred to as the 1100 cab). I believe this is the transition point from the small or narrow window to the big window cab. Sales for 1972 are 5,836 units; 42 Model CB200's, 5 Model 281's, 411 Model 282's, 38 Model 288's, 105 Model 289's, 45 Model CB300's, 4 Model 341's, 2 Model 346's, 189 Model 348's, 3 Model 349's, 116 Model 351's, 3,359 Model 352's, 212 Model 358's, 1,298 Model 359's, 4 Model 381's, and 3 Model 383's. Of the 2 experimental Model 352's, 1 had an Allison GT404 Gas Turbine engine, Allison HT740 automatic transmission and 10 inch diameter exhaust pipes standing 12'3" tall. The other turbine 352 had a Ford Motor Company Gas Turbine engine. Their biggest disadvantages were, the lack of engine braking and the length of time it took to spool up or down, . At 100% power, the N1 gas producer rotor rotates 50,940 RPM, the power turbine rotor rotates 33,420 RPM, and the power output shaft rotates 6,016 RPM.

Peterbilt Model 360.

Peterbilt Model 350 COE.

1973 thru 1976 would see the demise of the Models', 281, 288, 341, 346, 351, 358, 381, and 383. The last Model 351 would be built in May of 1976. Model 353, the heavy duty version of the Model 359, and the replacement for the heavy duty Model 351, would be introduced in 1974. Peterbilts' early Model 387, a heavy duty off road model would be introduced in 1974. 1 Model 253, a single axle version of the Model 353, and 1 Model 248, a single drive axle version of the Model 348, would be built in 1976.

The first Model 359 day cab. built at the new Denton, Texas factory.

Sales and build count for 1973 thru 1976 were 124 Model CB200's, 1 Model 281, 1,251 Model 282's, 80 Model 288's, 506 Model 289's, 564 Model 300's, 8 Model 346's, 575 Model 348's, 1 Model 349, 245 Model 351's, 13,721 Model 352's, 284 Model 353's, 260 Model 358's, 8,844 Model 359's, 5 Model 381's, 26 Model 383's, and 9 Model 387's. The Model 351 would yield 7,089 trucks in its 23 year run.

1976 Peterbilt would introduce an "H" version of the model 352. The cab height was raised to allow the installation of a larger radiator, 1,512 square inches worth. This would allow for the accommodation of the Cummins KTA525, KTA600, and the Cat 3408.

In 1977, Peterbilt would replace the Model 300 with the Model 310.

1978 Peterbilt introduces the "Corvette Style" dash to the already legendary Model 289/359, the truck that would be consistently identified in *Road King* Magazine's annual survey as the most preferred conventional on America's highways.

1980 Peterbilt opens its third factory in Denton, Texas. The first truck to roll off the assembly line is a Model 359 day cab, painted white. 1986, Peterbilt would discontinue manufacturing in Newark, but

engineering and corporate offices would remain. Then in 1992, we would see the entire shutdown of the Newark facility, with corporate offices moving to Denton.

1981 Peterbilt would experiment with its largest truck, the Model 397. This truck had triple steel rails placed 40 inches apart, measured 10 feet wide, 137 inch BBC, power including the KTA600, capable of 500,000 pounds gross combination weight, and had a price tag of $204,755. 1981 would also see the introduction of the Model 362, currently still in production.

In October 1985, Peterbilt would replace the Model 310, which had a production run of 1,097 units, with the Model 320.

In July of 1986 Peterbilt issued a press release stating their intent to build 359 model "Classic 359" trucks. These trucks would be equipped with TRW HBF Power Steering, Peterbilt Air Leaf Suspension, Dual Vortox Stainless Air Cleaners, Dual Exhaust, Polished Aluminum Air Tanks, Goodyear Tires, Peterbilt Polished Aluminum Wheels, Dual 29" 150 gallon Fuel Tanks, Step Light Under Cab Aluminum Tool Box, 63" Standard Height Sleeper Box, Classic II Interior (Gray/Black), Air Conditioning, Polished Outside Visor, Dual Grover 1042 Air Horns, Panasonic CQ-

Dual Round Headlights w/ Polished Shell, Bus Type Marker Lights, Perlux 200T Driving/Fog Lights, Aluminum Hood and Fenders, 119 or 127 inch BBC, "Classic 359" Emblem, "Classic 359" Numbered Brass Dash Plate, "Classic 359" Mudflaps, and choice of color per Peterbilt supplied paint chips.

1986 would also be the year Peterbilt introduces a series of trucks called the successors. They were the long haul Model 379 with a 119 or 127 inch BBC and aluminum hood; the high performance Model 377 with a 122 or 120 inch BBC, fiberglass hood, set forward or set back front axle; the short to medium haul Model 375 with 114 inch BBC and fiberglass hood; and the construction Model 357. Model 357 would be available with either a 119 inch fiberglass or a steel butterfly hood. Two other trucks that would be introduced would be the 378, a fiberglass hood version of the 379. The absence of the rivets on the fiberglass hood is quickest and easiest way to differentiate between the 378 and the short hood 379.

By 1987 we would see a total run of the Models 282/352, 56,300 units, Models 348/349, 5,152 units, Model 353, 1,843 units, Models 289/359, 64,858 units, and Model 387, (1st version) 181 units.

The fuel crunch of the seventies had left its mark on the trucking industry. In 1988 Peterbilt would introduce another aerodynamic model, the Model 372. It would be a truck that was great on fuel economy but short on driver appeal. By now the length law restrictions had been eased, and now was the era of the long hood conventionals. The Model 372 had a production run of 6 years, with 772 total units built. Peterbilt would also introduce the Model 376, a 2 axle version of the Model 375.

1989, Peterbilt released two special editions, Models 377 and 379. The trucks were painted regent red and metallic gold Imron paint. They were branded with a 50th anniversary logo on their sides, red and gold Peterbilt emblems, a 50th anniversary dash plaque, and 50th anniversary mud flaps.

In the medium duty range, the CB200 would be discontinued, its evolution would be the 13-210, the 224, the 227, and the 265. In 1992 the 224 would be replaced by the 200-30, and the 200-33 would replace the 227.

1995 Peterbilt introduces the Model 385, an aerodynamic short to medium haul fleet tractor, and the medium duty Model 330.

1999 would see the introduction of the new Model 387, a new premium aerodynamic conventional

Frontal view, Peterbilt Models 270/344/345.

model completely redesigned from the ground up. The Model 270, a medium duty cabover, a replacement for the Models 200-30 and 200-33 would be introduced in 1999 and in production early 2000.

Class. What is it? Just a pretty face?

The extensive use of CLASS appears to begin with the move to Newark, California in 1960. The next 4 pages show the earlier use of elegantly dressed models posing with highly polished and detailed trucks. Planning, site selection and the choosing of a model, who is beautiful and sophisticated, can take up to six months. This planning, coordinating and organizing process is still used today.

Class. What is it? Just a pretty face?

You know it when you see it. Nobody needs to tell you.
It speaks for itself, unmistakably. Class. Some people have it.
So do some trucks. But not very many.

Peterbilt Motor Trucks are now available throughout the U.S.
For nearest distributor, and literature,
write to Peterbilt Motors Company,
38801 Cherry Street, Newark, California 94560.

CLASS

Not Expensive.

Priceless.

A DIVISION OF PACCAR

Class. You either have it or you don't.
It's true of both owner/operators and fleets.
We know because half our sales are to owner/operators
And half are to fleets.
Obviously it's true of trucks. *Peterbilt*

It may look like the same Class
Conventional you're used to. But
it's changed dramatically. For
information please write to Peterbilt
Motors, 38801A Cherry Street,
Newark, California 94560.

MODEL 334

(DUAL DRIVE)

FRAME— Pressed chrome and manganese heat-treated steel channel, $1/4$ inch thick, $3 1/2$ inch flange, $10 3/8$ inches at deepest section.

MOTOR— (Model 334-GP and 334-GT) Waukesha Model 6SRKR; "L" type head, six cylinders; bore $4 5/8$ inches; stroke $5 1/8$ inches; piston displacement 517 cubic inches; develops 127 H.P. at 2400 R.P.M.

MOTOR— (Model 334-DP and 334-DT) Cummings Model HB 600; valve in head, six cylinders; bore $4 7/8$ inches; stroke 6 inches; piston displacement 672 cubic inches; develops 150 H.P. at 1800 R.P.M.

COOLING SYSTEM— Deep tubular type radiator core; cushioned to frame by thermoid rubber pad; core protected by cast aluminum grille; water circulated by pump; controlled by thermostat and fan driven by "V" type belts (thermostatically controlled air operated radiator shutter standard on Model 334-DP and 334-DT).

FRONT AXLE— (Model 334-GP and 334-GT) Timken 26450-N series, drop forged "I" beam section; Timken roller bearings; tread $70 3/8$ inches.

FRONT AXLE— (Model 334-DP and 334-DT) Timken 27452-N series, drop forged "I" beam section; Timken roller bearings; tread $75 3/8$ inches.

REAR AXLE— (334-GP and 334-DP) Two Peterbilt Timken axles with special alloy aluminum two-piece radius rods and larger bronze bushings. Timken 65700 worm drive differentials, full floating; Timken bearings; tread 72 inches; ratios to suit operating conditions. Axles connected with torque tube. (66700 series differentials can be supplied at extra cost.)

REAR AXLE— (334-GT and 334-DT) Timken SW-352-W series worm drive; full floating; Timken bearings; tread $72 1/4$ inches; ratios to suit operating conditions; radius rods (SW-452-W series can be supplied at extra cost.)

TRANSMISSION— Unit Power transmission four speeds forward, one reverse; direct on 4th.

CLUTCH— Two plate, dry clutch; ball thrust release bearing.

COMPOUND— Three-speed auxiliary transmission mounted amidship; speedometer drive.

DRIVE SHAFT— Three-piece tubular with six-needle bearing, oil lubricated, universal joints.

STEERING GEAR— Cam and lever type gear, steering post set to give maximum driving comfort; 22-inch diameter steering wheel.

TIRES— 9.75-20 balloon tires, single front and dual rear.

WHEELS— 10-hole Budd steel disc (spoke type); spare wheel included.

SPRINGS— (Model 334-GP and 334DP) Chrome manganese steel throughout; front, fourteen leaves, 48x3 inches; rear, sixteen leaves, $48x3 1/2$ inches.

SPRINGS— (Model 334-GT and 334-DT) Chrome manganese steel throughout; front, fourteen leaves, 48x3 inches; rear, eleven leaves, $55 3/4$ x 5 inches.

BRAKES— Four rear wheel, Westinghouse air, separate diaphragms, operated on each wheel with moulded lining; cast alloy drums; $7 1/4$ cubic foot compressor with unloaded head and governor; 16-inch diameter Tru-Stop disc type parking hand brake on drive line. Brake size $17 1/4$ x $5 1/2$ inches rear. (Front wheel brake $17 1/4$ x3 inches can be furnished at extra cost.)

FUEL SUPPLY— Two fuel tanks, mounted, one each side of frame; capacity 40 gallons each.

CHASSIS LUBRICATION— Alemite high pressure system.

CONTROLS— Gear shift and parking brake levers at center; accelerator with foot rest on toe boards; motor controls on dash; electric horn button at center of steering wheel; dimmer switch.

ELECTRICAL SYSTEM— (Model 334-GP and 334-GT) Delco-Remy generator and starter; 6-volt heavy duty truck type battery; sealed beam electric headlights and tail light.(12-volt system cam be furnished at extra cost.)

ELECTRICAL SYSTEM— (Model 334-DP amd 334-DT) Delco-Remy generator and starter; four 6-volt heavy duty truck type batteries sealed beam electric headlights and tail light.

INSTRUMENTS— Instruments indirectly lighted; includes speedometer, motor miles tachometer, ammeter, oil gauge, heat indicator and fuel gauge.

CAB— Fully enclosed Peterbilt deluxe all steel construction electrically welded back top and cowl constructed separately; fully lined with waterproof fir plywood affording insulation against heat, cold and eliminating vibration noises; grained interior finish; bucket or full width seat fully upholstered in genuine leather; safety glass throughout two cowl ventilators and rear window with sliding frame.

EQUIPMENT— Front bumper, spring steel; hood; full curved type fenders; dual electric horns; two pressure windshield wipers; two rear view mirrors with braces; approved type hand signal; tool kit in roll; wheel and axle wrenches; heavy duty hydraulic jack; grease gun; oil can; one tow hook and one tow yoke mounted on front; spare tire carrier, rear of frame.

NOTE: Spare tire carrier not furnished on dump or tractor trucks. These specifications are subject to change as often as additional proven refinements may be perfected.

A Quality Truck to Meet Every HEAVY DUTY Requirement

Model 334 (Dual Drive) Body Builders Dimensions

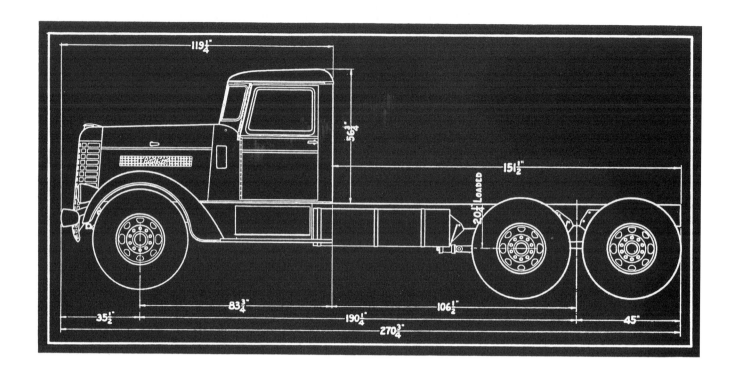

WEIGHTS

MODEL	GROSS VEHICLE	CHASSIS WITH CAB
334-GP	42000	12600
334-GT	42000	13600
334-DP	44000	13900
334-DT	44000	14900

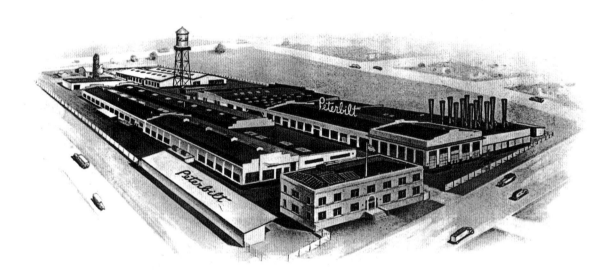

Peterbilt Motors Company

107th Avenue and Hollywood Blvd.
Oakland, California

HEAVY DUTY TRUCKS   MacDONALD LOW - BODY TRUCKS   MacDONALD LIFT TRUCKS

MODEL 260
(CHAIN DRIVE)

FRAME— Pressed chrome manganese heat-treated steel channel, 1/4 inch thick, 3 1/2 inch flange, 10 3/8 inches at deepest section.

MOTOR— (Model 260-GC) Waukesha Model 6SRKR; "L" type head, six cylinders; bore 4 5/8 inches; stroke 5 1/8 inches; piston displacement 517 cubic inches; develops 127 H.P. at 2400 R.P.M.

MOTOR— (Model 260-DC) Cummins Model HB 600; valve in head, six cylinders; bore 4 7/8 inches; stroke 6 inches; piston displacement 672 cubic inches; develops 150 H.P. at 1800 R.P.M.

COOLING SYSTEM— Deep tubular type radiator core; cushioned to frame by thermoid rubber pad; core protected by cast aluminum grille; water circulated by pump; controlled by thermostat and fan driven by "V" type belts (thermostatically controlled air operated radiator shutter standard on Model 260-DC).

FRONT AXLE— (Model 260-GC) Timken 35000-H series, drop forged "I" beam section; Timken roller bearings; tread 70 1/4 inches.

FRONT AXLE— (Model 260-DC) Timken 27452-TW series, drop forged "I" beam section; Timken roller bearings; tread 75 5/8 inches.

REAR AXLE— Timken T-18000-H series, tubular type; Timken bearings; tread 76 1/4 inches; adjustable radius rods; cast alloy brake drums.

JACK SHAFT— Special alloy housing, Timken 59000 series differential, bevel gear, full floating, Timken bearings, 1 3/4 inch pitch sprockets and chains, ratios to suit operating conditions.

TRANSMISSION— Unit power transmission four speeds forward, one reverse; direct on fourth.

CLUTCH— (Model 260-GC) single plate, dry clutch; ball thrust release bearing. (Model 260-DC) two plate, dry clutch; ball thrust release bearing.

COMPOUND— Three-speed auxiliary transmission mounted amidship; speedometer drive.

DRIVE SHAFT— Two-piece tubular with four-needle bearing, oil lubricated, universal joints.

STEERING GEAR— Cam and lever type gear; steering post set to give maximum driving comfort; 22 inch diameter steering wheel.

TIRES— 9.75-20 balloon tires, single front and dual rear.

WHEELS— 10-hole Budd steel disc (spoke type); spare wheel included.

SPRINGS— Chrome manganese steel throughout; front, 14 leaves, 48"x3"; rear, 14 leaves, 60 5/8"x3 1/2"; overload, 7 leaves, 37"x3 1/2".

BRAKES— (Model 260-GC) Four wheel, hydraulic, with vacuum booster, internal expanding type, fully protected by dust shields; operated on moulded lining; cast alloy drums; 16 inch diameter Tru-Stop disc type parking hand brake on drive line. Brake sizes 16x2 1/4 inches front and 17 1/4x5 inches rear. (Westinghouse four wheel air brakes with 7 1/4 cubic foot compressor can be supplied at extra cost.)

BRAKES— (Model 260-DC) Four wheel, Westinghouse air, separate diaphragms, operated on each wheel with moulded lining; cast alloy drums; 7 1/4 cubic foot compressor with unloading head and governor; 16 inch diameter Tru-Stop disc type parking hand brake on drive line. Brake size 17 1/4x3 inches front and 17 1/4x5 1/2 inches rear.

FUEL SUPPLY— Two fuel tanks, mounted, one each side of frame; capacity 40 gallons each.

CHASSIS LUBRICATION— Alemite high pressure system.

CONTROLS— Gear shift and parking brake levers at center; accelerator with foot rest on toe boards; motor controls on dash; electric horn button at center of steering wheel; dimmer switch.

ELECTRICAL SYSTEM— (Model 260-GC) Delco-Remy generator and starter; 6-volt heavy duty truck type battery; sealed beam electric headlights and tail light. (12-volt system can be furnished at extra cost.)

ELECTRICAL SYSTEM— (Model 260-DC) Delco-Remy generator and starter; four 6-volt heavy duty truck type batteries; sealed beam electric headlights and tail light.

INSTRUMENTS— Instruments indirectly lighted; include speedometer, motor miles tachometer, ammeter, oil gauge, heat indicator, and fuel gauge.

CAB— Fully enclosed Peterbilt de luxe all steel construction electrically welded; back, top and cowl constructed separately; fully lined with waterproof fir plywood affording insulation against heat, cold and eliminating vibration noises; grained interior finish; bucket or full width seat fully upholstered in genuine leather; safety glass throughout; two cowl ventilators and rear window with sliding frame.

EQUIPMENT— Front bumper, spring steel; hood; full curved type fenders; chain guards and oilers; dual electric horns; electric windshield wipers (pressure wipers standard when air brakes are installed); two rear view mirrors with braces; approved type hand signal; tool kit in roll; wheel and axle wrenches; heavy duty hydraulic jack; grease gun; oil can; one tow hook and one tow yoke mounted on front; spare tire carrier; rear of frame.

NOTE: Spare tire carrier not furnished on dump or tractor trucks. These specifications are subject to change as often as additional proven refinements may be perfected.

A Quality Truck to Meet Every HEAVY DUTY Requirement

Model 260 (Chain Drive) Body Builders Dimensions

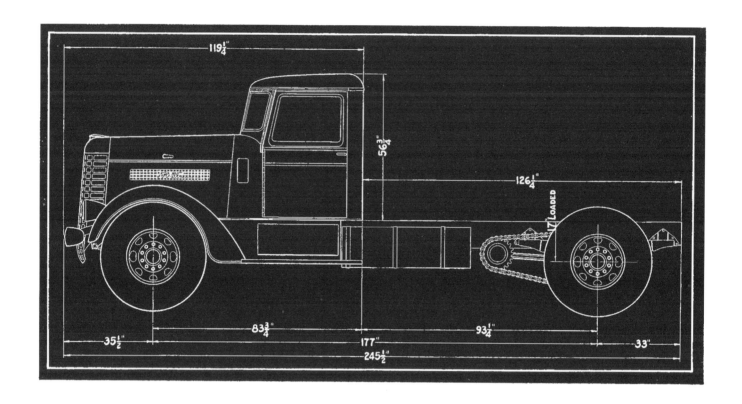

WEIGHTS

MODEL	GROSS VEHICLE	CHASSIS WITH CAB
260-GC	32000	10250
260-DC	37000	11700

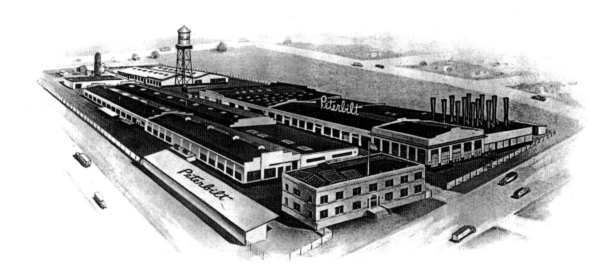

Peterbilt Motors Company

107th Avenue and Hollywood Blvd.
Oakland, California

HEAVY DUTY TRUCKS	MacDONALD LOW - BODY TRUCKS	MacDONALD LIFT TRUCKS

MODEL 344
(DUAL DRIVE)

FRAME— Pressed chrome and manganese heat-treated steel channel, 9/32 inch thick, 31/2 inch flange, 103/8 inches at deepest section. Reinforcement over rear axles. (Double frame optional at extra cost.)

MOTOR— (Model 334-GT) Waukesha Model 6SRKR; "L" type head, six cylinders; bore 45/8 inches ; stroke 51/8 inches; piston displacement 517 cubic inches; develops 127 H.P. at 2400 R.P.M.

MOTOR— (Model 344-DT) Cummings Model HB 600; valve in head, six cylinders; bore 47/8 inches; stroke 6 inches; piston displacement 672 cubic inches; develops 150 H.P. at 1800 R.P.M.

COOLING SYSTEM— Heavy duty cast aluminum radiator frame with deep tubular type radiator core; cushioned to frame by thermoid rubber pad; water circulated by pump; controlled by thermostat and fan driven by "V" type belts; thermostatically controlled air operated radiator shutter.

FRONT AXLE— (Model 344-GT) Timken 26452-N series, drop forged "I" beam section; Timken roller bearings; tread 737/8 inches.

FRONT AXLE— (Model 344-DT) Timken 27452-N series, drop forged "I" beam section; Timken roller bearings; tread 753/8 inches.

REAR AXLE— Timken SW-3000-H series; worm drive; full floating Timkin bearings; tread 721/4 inches; ratios to suit operating conditions; radius rods (SW-452-W series can be supplied at extra cost.)

TRANSMISSION— Unit power transmission four speeds forward, one reverse; direct on fourth.

CLUTCH— Two plate, dry clutch; ball thrust release bearing.

COMPOUND— Three-speed auxiliary transmission mounted amidship; speedometer drive.

DRIVE SHAFT— Three-piece tubular with six-needle bearing, oil lubricated, universal joints.

STEERING GEAR— Cam and lever type gear; steering post set to give maximum dviving comfort; 22-inch diameter steering wheel.

TIRES— 10.00-20 balloon tires; single front and dual rear.

WHEELS— 10-hole Budd steel disc (spoke type); spare wheel included.

SPRINGS— Chrome manganese steel throughout; front, 14 leaves, 481/2 x3 inches rear, 12 leaves, 521/4' x4 inches.

BRAKES— Four rear wheel, Westinghouse air. separate diaphragms. operated on each wheel with moulded lining, cast alloy drums; 71/4 cubic foot compressor with unloading head and governor; 16-inch diameter Tru-Stop disc type parking hand brake on drive line. Brake size 161/2 x 6 inches rear. (Front wheel brakes 171/4 x 3 inches can be furnished at extra cost.)

FUEL SUPPLY— Two fuel tanks, mounted, one each side of frame; capacity 40 gallons each.

CHASSIS LUBRICATION— Alemite high pressure system.

CONTROLS— Gear shift and parking brake levers at center; accelerator with foot rest on toe boards; motor controls on dash; electric horn button at center of steering wheel' dimmer switch.

ELECTRICAL SYSTEM— (Model 344-GT) Delco-Remy generator and starter; 6-volt heavy duty truck type battery; sealed beam electric headlights and combination tail and stop light. (12-volt system can be furnished at extra cost.)

ELECTRICAL SYSTEM— (Model 344-DT) Delco-Remy generator and starter; four 6-volt heavy duty truck type batteries; sealed beam electric headlights and combination tail and stop light.

INSTRUMENTS— Instruments indirectly lighted; includes speedometer, motor miles tachometer, ammeter, oil gauge, heat indicator and fuel gauge.

CAB— Fully enclosed Peterbilt deluxe all steel construction electrically welded; back, top and cowl constructed separately; fully lined with waterproof fir plywood affording insulation against heat, cold and eliminating vibration noises; grained interior finish; bucket or full width seat fully upholstered in genuine leather; safety glass throughout two cowl ventilators and rear window with sliding frame.

EQUIPMENT— Heavy duty 6 inch channel with hardwood insert bumper; full curved type fenders; dual electric horns; two pressure windshield wipers; two rear view mirrors with braces; approved type hand signal; tool kit in roll; wheel and axle wrenches; heavy duty hydraulic jack; grease gun; oil can; one tow hook and one tow yoke mounted on front; spare tire carrier; rear of frame.

NOTE: Spare tire carrier not furnished on dump or tractor trucks. These specifications are subject to change as often as additional proven refinements may be perfected.

A Quality Truck to Meet Every HEAVY DUTY Requirement

Model 344 (Dual Drive) Body Builders Dimensions

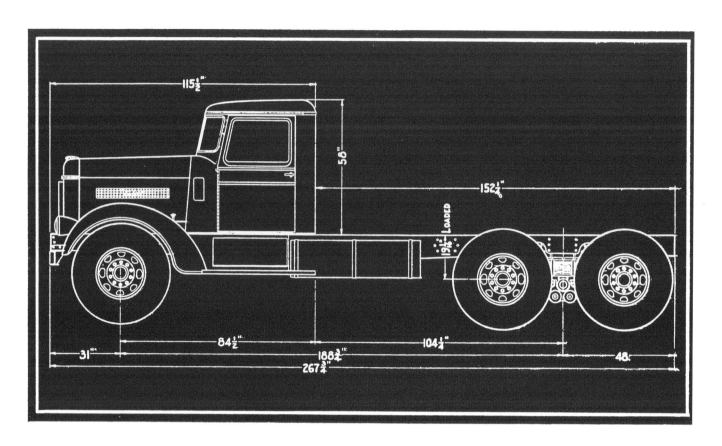

WEIGHTS

MODEL	GROSS VEHICLE	CHASSIS WITH CAB	CAPACITY
344-GT	42000	13750	28250
344-DT	44000	15150	28850

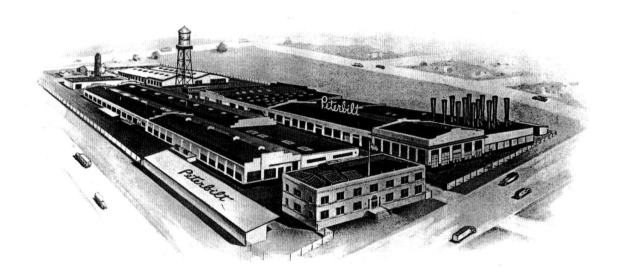

Peterbilt Motors Company

107th Avenue and Hollywood Blvd.

Oakland, California

HEAVY DUTY TRUCKS   MacDONALD LOW - BODY TRUCKS   MacDONALD LIFT TRUCKS

MODEL 270
(ENCLOSED DRIVE)

FRAME— Pressed chrome manganese heat-treated steel channel, 9/32 inch thick, 31/2 inch flange, 103/8 inches at deepest section.

MOTOR— (Model 270-GD) Waukesha Model 6SRKR; "L" type head, six cylinders; bore 45/8 inches ; stroke 51/8 inches; piston displacement 517 cubic inches; develops 127 H.P. at 2400 R.P.M.

MOTOR— (Model 270-DD) Cummings Model HB 600; valve in head, six cylinders; bore 47/8 inches; stroke 6 inches; piston displacement 672 cubic inches; develops 150 H.P. at 1800 R.P.M.

COOLING SYSTEM— Heavy duty cast aluminum radiator frame with deep tubular type radiator core; cushioned to frame by thermoid rubber pad; water circulated by pump; controlled by thermostat and fan driven by "V" type-belts (thermostatically controlled air oper-ated radiator shutter. Standard on Model 270-DD.)

FRONT AXLE— (Model 270-GD) Timken 35000-H series, drop forged "I" beam section; Timken roller bearings; tread 701/4 inches.

FRONT AXLE— (Model 270-DC) Timken 27452-TW series, drop forged "I" beam section; Timken roller bearings; tread 753/8 inches.

REAR AXLE— (Model 270-GD) Timken 65743-H series, worm drive or 75743-H series herringbone double reduction rear axle; full floating; Timken bearings; tread 70 inches; ratios to suit operating conditions. Radius rods. (66700 and 76000 series axles optional at extra cost.)

REAR AXLE— (Model 270-DD) Timken 66796-W series, worm drive or 76800-W series herringbone double reduction rear axle; full floating; Timken bearings; tread 72 1/4 inches; ratios to suit operating conditions. Radius rods.

TRANSMISSION— Unit power transmission four speeds forward, one reverse; direct on fourth.

CLUTCH— (Model 270-GD) Single plate, dry clutch; ball thrust release bearing. (Model 270-DC) Two plate, dry clutch; ball thrust release bearing.

COMPOUND— Three-speed auxiliary transmission mounted amidship; speedometer drive.

DRIVE SHAFT— Two-piece tubular with four-needle bearing, oil lubricated, universal joints.

STEERING GEAR— Cam and lever type gear; steering post set to give maximum driving comfort; 22 inch diameter steering wheel.

TIRES— 10.00-20 balloon tires, single front and dual rear.

WHEELS— 10-hole Budd steel disc (spoke type); spare wheel included.

SPRINGS— Chrome manganese steel throughout; front, 14 leaves, 431/2" x3"; rear, 14 leaves, 605/8" x31/2"; overload, 7 leaves. 37" x31/2".

BRAKES— (Model 270-GC) Four wheel, hydraulic, with vacuum booster, internal expanding type, fully protected by dust shields; operated on moulded lining; cast alloy drums, 16 inch diameter Tru-Stop disc type parking hand brake on drive line. Brake sizes 16x21/4 inches front and 171/4 x5 inches rear.(Westinghouse four wheel air brakes with 71/4 cubic foot compressor can be supplied at extra cost.)

BRAKES— (Model 270-DD) Four wheel, Westinghouse air, separate diaphragms, operated on each wheel with moulded lining; cast alloy drums; 71/4 cubic foot compressor with un-loading head and governor; 16 inch diameter Tru-Stop disc type parking hand brake on drive line. Brake size 171/4x3 inches front and 171/4x51/2 inches rear.

FUEL SUPPLY— Two fuel tanks, mounted, one each side of frame; capacity 40 gallons each.

CHASSIS LUBRICATION— Alemite high pressure system.

CONTROLS— Gear shift and parking brake levers at center; accelerator with foot rest on toe boards; motor controls on dash; electric horn button at center of steering wheel; dimmer switch.

ELECTRICAL SYSTEM— (Model 270-GC) Delco-Remy generator and starter; 6-volt heavy duty truck type battery; sealed beam electric headlights and combination tail and stop light. (12-volt system can be furnished at extra cost.)

ELECTRICAL SYSTEM— (Model 270-DD) Delco-Remy generator and starter; four 6-volt heavy duty truck type batteries sealed beam electric headlights and combination tail and stop light.

INSTRUMENTS— Instruments indirectly lighted; includes speedometer, motor miles tachometer, ammeter, oil gauge, heat indicator and fuel gauge.

CAB— Fully enclosed Peterbilt de luxe all steel construction electrically welded; back, top and cowl constructed separately; fully lined with waterproof fir plywood affording insulation against heat, cold and eliminating vibration noises; grained interior finish; bucket or full width seat fully upholstered in genuine leather; safety glass throughout two cowl ventilators and rear window with sliding frame.

EQUIPMENT— Heavy duty 6-inch channel with hardwood insert bumper; full curved type fenders; dual electric horns; two pressure windshield wipers; two rear view mirrors with braces; approved type hand signal; tool kit in roll; wheel and axle wrenches heavy duty hydraulic jack; grease gun; oil can; one tow hook and one tow yoke mounted on front; spare tire carrier; rear of frame.

NOTE: Spare tire carrier not furnished on dump or tractor trucks. These specifications are subject to change as often as additional proven refinements may be perfected.

A Quality Truck to Meet Every HEAVY DUTY Requirement

Model 270 (Enclosed Drive) Body Builders Dimensions

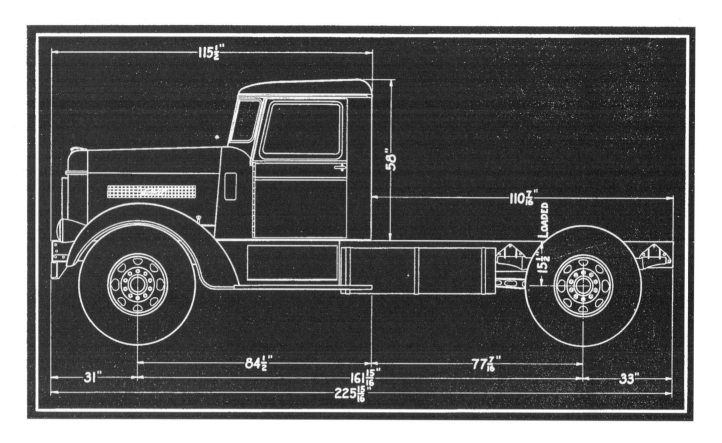

WEIGHTS

MODEL	GROSS VEHICLE	CHASSIS WITH CAB
270-GD	26300	9950
270-DD	37000	11200

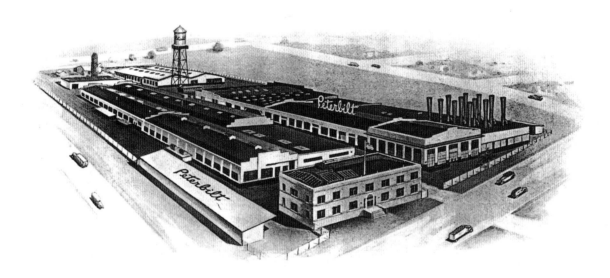

Peterbilt Motors Company

107th Avenue and Hollywood Blvd.

Oakland, California

HEAVY DUTY TRUCKS   MacDONALD LOW - BODY TRUCKS   MacDONALD LIFT TRUCKS

Peterbilt

TRUCKS

DEPENDABLE   TRANSPORTATION

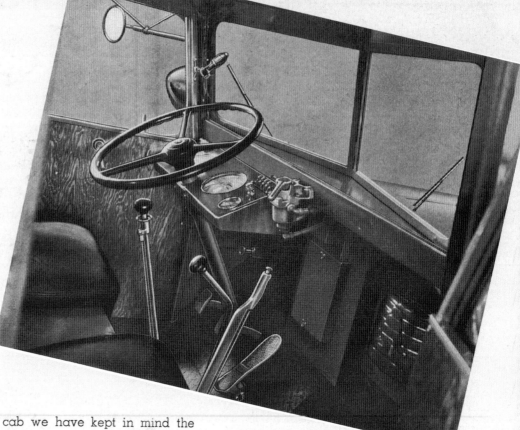

In designing the PETERBILT cab we have kept in mind the factors which influence the comfort, safety and convenience of the driver. A choice of either a full-length seat or bucket seats, upholstered in heavy duty, hand buffed genuine leather, and Marshall coiled springs, afford long life and driving comfort.

Side ventilators, as well as a sliding window in the back of the cab, afford ample circulation of air without the lowering of the door windows.

Smooth-working heavy-duty window regulators are provided, as well as heavy plate shatter-proof glass throughout. Locking type door handles and a large, heavy metal tool box are furnished as standard equipment.

PETERBILT cabs were designed to afford the driver maximum visibility, not only of the highway, but of all instruments and controls incident to the proper operation of a motor truck.

The three-spoke steering wheel presents the least interference with the visibility of the entire instrument panel. The panel, as well as the instruments thereon, is so positioned that the operator can observe the entire group without turning his head. The entire instrument panel is illuminated with indirect lighting.

All switches and controls are conveniently placed at the driver's finger-tips, affording ease of operation and safe control at all driving speeds.

The fuse terminal block, which connects all lighting and electric wiring is located inside the cab, and not under the hood of the engine, making it accessible for quick fuse replacements and repairs, and also keeping it entirely free from oils, grease, and dirt.

FACTORY AND EXECUTIVE OFFICES OF
PETERBILT MOTORS COMPANY
OAKLAND, CALIFORNIA

The PETERBILT plant, pictured above, is the largest factory on the Pacific Coast devoted exclusively to the manufacture of heavy-duty motor trucks.

Ever alert to changing conditions in motor trucking, PETERBILT engineers continue to set the pace for advanced design and rugged construction in heavy-duty motor trucks. Always abreast or in advance of the times, the new PETERBILT incorporates ample safety factors, smart appearance, greater flexibility and durability than has been heretofore known in the trucking world.

The PETERBILT plant covers an area of 13½ acres, and all buildings are of fire-proof construction.

With complete metal fabricating, machining, woodworking, upholstering and painting departments, PETERBILT offers the Western truck owner the finest in service facilities for repairing, rebuilding and servicing their equipment, in addition to carrying a very large stock of replacement parts to properly maintain heavy-duty motor truck equipment.

Peterbilt Motors Company

107th AVENUE AND HOLLYWOOD BOULEVARD · OAKLAND · CALIFORNIA

The PETERBILT cab incorporates many exclusive features. It is all steel, electrically welded, very rigidly braced and reinforced throughout, and still very light in weight.

The top cowel, back and doors are all separately made over fixtures and jigs which assures absolute accuracy in manufacture. In the event of damage to any part of the cab, sections can be replaced without the necessity of buying an entirely new cab.

This light-weight, all steel construction makes a very rigid cab and quite different from the usual composite type of wood and steel. This all-steel construction eliminates all rattles and squeaks, making a tight, sound, and sturdy cab at all times.

The interior of the PETERBILT cab is lined with a grained waterproof plywood, all sections having been formed to a perfect fit. This plywood lining not only eliminates the drumming noises, but it also provides air-space between the steel exterior and the plywood lining which affords effective insulation against heat and cold, adding much to the comfort of the driver.

The cab is equipped with a dome light as illustrated, which is operated by an independent switch.

When bucket seats are installed, an ample-sized metal tool box is provided. When straight seats are furnished, tool space is provided under the seat, and small emergency tool compartments are built in at each end of the seat.

The running board, as well as the floor and toe boards of the PETERBILT cabs, are furnished in diamond plate metal, assuring long life as well as cleanliness in the cab.

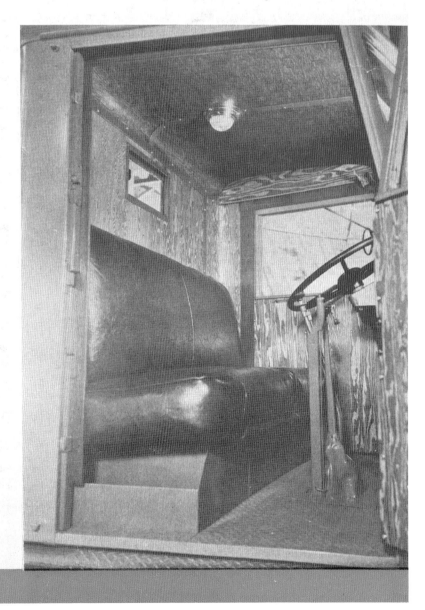

270 SERIES

344 SERIES
345 SERIES
(DUAL DRIVE)

354 SERIES
355 SERIES
$\left(\begin{array}{c}\text{HEAVY DUTY}\\\text{DUAL DRIVE}\end{array}\right)$

A Quality Truck to Meet Every HEAVY DUTY Requirement

Peterbilt Motors Company

107th AVENUE AND MacARTHUR BOULEVARD · OAKLAND · CALIFORNIA

Peterbilt Motors Company

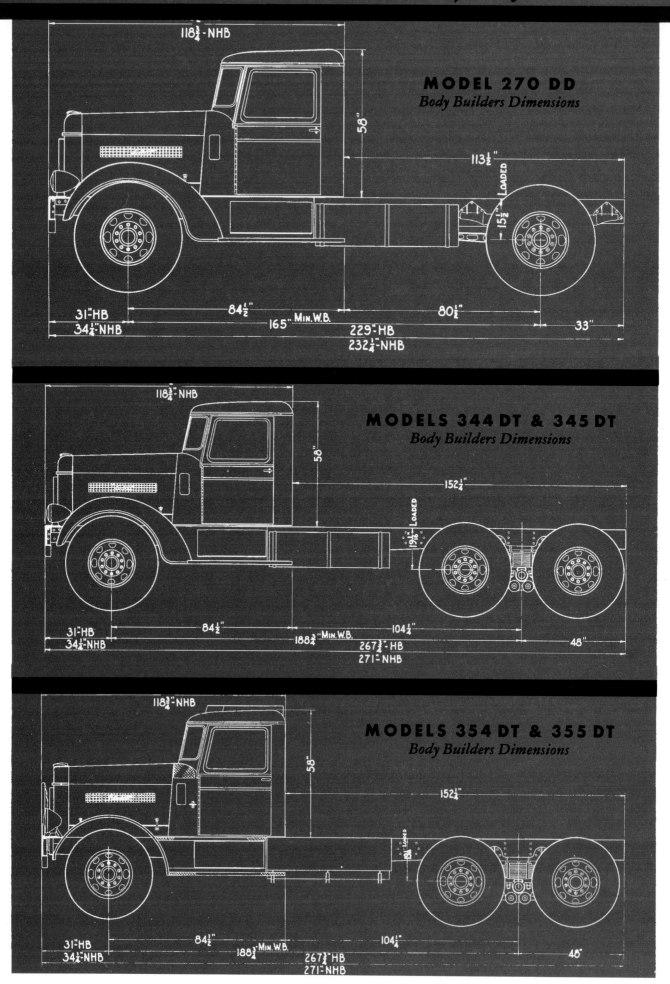

MODEL 270 DD
Body Builders Dimensions

118¾"-NHB
58"
113½" LOADED
15½"
31"-HB
34¼"-NHB
84½"
165" MIN.W.B.
229"-HB
232¼"-NHB
80½"
33"

MODELS 344 DT & 345 DT
Body Builders Dimensions

118¾"-NHB
58"
152¼"
19¼" LOADED
31"-HB
34¼"-NHB
84½"
188¾" MIN.W.B.
267¾"-HB
271"-NHB
104¼"
48"

MODELS 354 DT & 355 DT
Body Builders Dimensions

118¾"-NHB
58"
152¼"
19¼" LOADED
31"-HB
34¼"-NHB
84½"
188¾" MIN.W.B.
267¾"-HB
271"-NHB
104¼"
48"

Peterbilt

Peterbilt Trucks

Dependable

RADIATOR MOUNTING

The Peterbilt radiator is of the assembled type with the cast aluminum sides, top and bottom tanks and core being bolted together as a unit, making any part replaceable and the entire unit easily serviced. The core is of the deep tubular type with a frontal area of 1050 square inches.

The radiator assembly is independently carried on the two rear shock absorbent Lord rubber mountings located on the tubular cross member.

The cast aluminum assembled type radiator shell with the thermostatically controlled air-operated vertical shutters is mounted independently of the radiator in the two front Lord mountings on the tubular cross member. The shell is attached to the cab through a wide top section of the hood so that the cab and radiator shell can move as a unit and allow the radiator to float without any stress.

ACCESSIBILITY

Of the many features built into Peterbilt trucks, one of the most important is "accessibility."

All electrical wiring is carried in loom conduits and connections between cab and chassis are through unit junction boxes accessibly mounted on the dash.

All oil, air and fuel lines are of large-sized copper tubing run in loom conduit and securely clipped to the frame to insure long life and to afford proper insulation from heat, cold and vibration. Lines between frame and engine and frame and cab are through flexible connections with lines running to an accessibly mounted common manifold. The use of junction boxes and manifold simplifies the removal of cab or engine by concentrating all connections at common points.

FRONT END CONSTRUCTION

The front end of all Peterbilt trucks carries a deep section channel crossmember, bolted in for easy removal of engine. A tubular crossmember is also used upon which are located the shock absorbent Lord rubber mountings that carry the radiator core and radiator shell, and insulate these units from all stresses and strains. This tubular member is securely welded to the front spring frame brackets to form a rigid front end, eliminating frame weaving motion.

FRAME CONSTRUCTION

Peterbilt frames have been especially engineered, employing the finest of alloy steels to give toughness and durability without excessive weight. Their design incorporates the needs of highway operations with their accompanying weight restrictions as well as the ability to handle the larger and heavier loads carried in off-highway service.

Frames are deep section fish belly type, $10\frac{1}{8}$" deep at center, 9/32" thick with $3\frac{1}{2}$" flanges and tapered both front and rear. Material is chrome manganese heat-treated steel with a tensile strength of 105,000 pounds per square inch. For off-highway service, a full frame insert or two full inserts are used, giving double or triple frame construction, depending upon the type of operation. Ample cross members are installed for rigidity and all frames are cold riveted to insure permanent tightness of rivets and proper drawing up of metal to metal contact surfaces.

Below is a center section of the frame with two arch type cross members, one at the top of the frame and one at the bottom to make a box construction and keep the frame in alignment under the most severe operating conditions. The top member carries the rear of the cab which is centrally mounted on a rubber cushion.

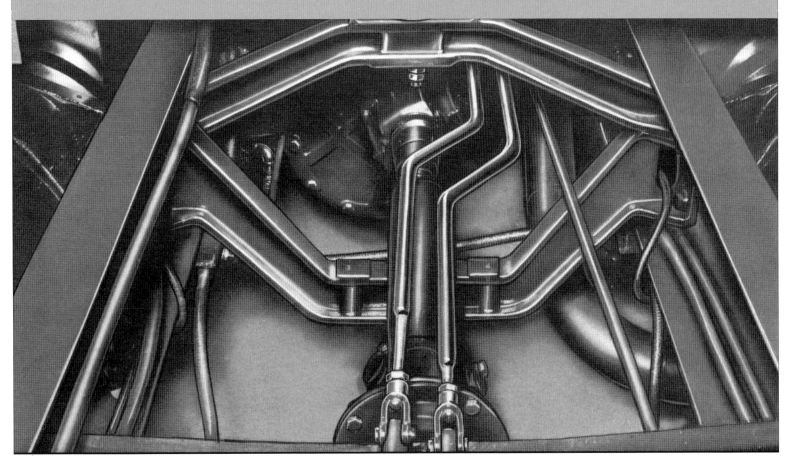

PETERBILT HEAVY

PETERBILT TRUCKS are engineered and built in the West to handle every transportation requirement of heavy-duty trucking, whether it be on or off highway operation.

All Peterbilt trucks contain the same basic fundamentals of design such as driver comfort and ease of handling as well as built-in long life, which is a requisite in dependable transportation. However, each truck is specifically engineered to perform the required functions of the operation in which it is to work after a careful survey has been made covering the conditions prevailing in such operation.

The application of these proven basic fundamentals plus the individual engineering for each specific job result in a truck which has already built up an excellent reputation in the heavy-duty transportation field.

Peterbilt trucks are daily proving their worth in long-distance hauling where uninterrupted schedules must be maintained and where a failure would mean the loss of perishable cargo. These operations are just a few where Peterbilts prove their dependability.

TY MOTOR TRUCKS

For highway operations light alloy metals of greatest tensile strength are used throughout the truck, reducing dead weight to a minimum, affording greater payloads. On off-highway operations such as the logging and construction fields where weight restrictions are not a factor, double and sometimes triple frames, as well as heavy-gauge steel for cab, hood and fenders are used. Fuel tank guards, radiator guards, lamp guards, and many other reinforcements are built into Peterbilt trucks, insuring longer life and reducing loss of time to a minimum for maintenance and repairs.

Careful consideration is also given to axle and transmission requirements. A selection of these units as to sizes, types of drives, and gear ratios suited to the operation is made, as well as wheel and tire size requirements. Large, fast-acting air brakes on all wheels, with a maximum number of square inches of braking area, a limiting valve conveniently located in the cab for control of front wheel brakes in operation under snow and ice conditions, make Peterbilt the safest truck in heavy-duty truck operations, which all adds up to "DEPENDABLE TRANSPORTATION."

DELUXE ALL-STEEL SAFETY CAB

The new all-steel deluxe safety cab on all Peterbilt trucks is the result of many years of painstaking research work by Peterbilt engineers among drivers and owners under every known operating condition. A cab combining all features necessary for all types of heavy duty hauling, both on and off highway, are built into this new Peterbilt cab. Safety, comfort, visibility, accessibility, cleanliness, appearance, and many other features make up this new and larger cab.

CONTROLS

The panel control board, directly in front of the driver, and within easy reach, carries the latest type of electric toggle switches, front wheel brake limiting valve, cigar lighter, ash tray, compression release emergency stop, cab heater control, and trailer brake hand valve. The instrument panel contains all of the necessary instruments, grouped and mounted on a hinged panel, with non-glare indirect lighting mounted directly in front of the driver. The unique hinged mounting of the instrument panel makes adjustments and repairs convenient. A large, well positioned steering wheel, treadle pedal brake and accelerator controls, transmission, compound transmission, and emergency brake controls are within easy and comfortable reach of the driver. Three-point suspension on Lord rubber mountings makes riding a pleasure.

COMFORT

The new all-steel Peterbilt safety cab is wider and deeper than previous models, allowing plenty of leg room, and allowing seat adjustments for tall and short drivers. A selection of adjustable bucket or full cushioned seats is available. All are upholstered with the finest coil springs, covered with foam rubber and genuine hand-buffed Spanish leather. Quickly removable seat risers and floor boards are other features of accessibility. A heavy duty, insulated rubber mat adds to cab comfort.

Many specially designed accessories, such as defroster fan, heater, visor, spot light, fog lights, I.C.C. lights, etc., all especially adapted for Peterbilt trucks, are available at extra cost.

VENTILATION

In the design of the new all-steel Peterbilt cab, great attention has been given to access and ventilation. The doors of the new cab are wider, making it much easier to get in and out, and they are equipped with ventilating windows. Cowl ventilators admit fresh air when the truck is in motion, and the full-opening rear window allows full circulation of fresh air. The double-sealed doors keep out drafts and dust and the spacious windshield affords full visibility. All around, the new Peterbilt cab was well planned to be cool and airy during the summer; tight and warm during the winter months.

FUEL TANKS

Two 50 gallon fuel tanks for gasoline and Diesel fuel, are standard equipment on all Peterbilt models. Larger capacity tanks are available at extra cost. Gasoline and Diesel fuel tanks are equipped with large filler openings; snap locking caps for fast fuelling; are securely attached to the frame at the rear of the cab; concave heads and center baffle plate insure greater tank strength; replaceable end covers protect the rear of each tank; and all tanks have large cast brass sumps with drain cocks mounted on the bottom. On all butane powered trucks, two 100 gallon fuel tanks are standard equipment.

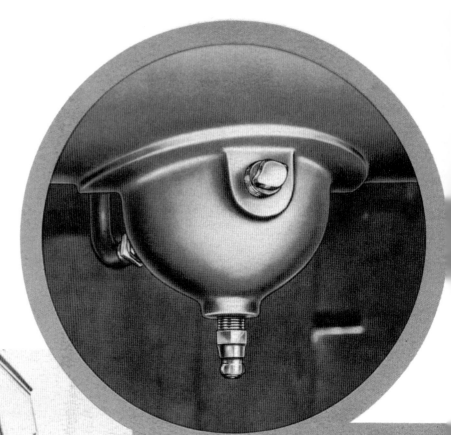

BATTERY BOX AND AIR CLEANER

A large accessible, well-ventilated battery box with quick removable cover is attached to the frame on the right side of the cab and makes battery servicing fast and easy. This location, the closest possible to the starting motor and solenoid switch, permits the use of extremely short battery cables.

All Peterbilt trucks carry a large oil bath air cleaner mounted on the outside of the cab, insuring clean, fresh air to the motor. The vertical exhaust stack and muffler with protecting shield are mounted on the right corner of the cab and flexibly connected to the exhaust pipe.

Peterbilt Motors Company

Factory and General Offices

10700 MacARTHUR BOULEVARD · OAKLAND, CALIFORNIA

Peterbilt

Model 364

Model 364 Snoqualmie
Falls Lumber Company

Model 364's built for
military contractors

Model 364

Model 364's
built for
military
contractors

MODEL 280

CAB— Cab manufactured by Peterbilt and completely new, using the time proved Peterbilt construction and designed for maximum driver comfort after an extensive survey of requirements and desires. Fully enclosed, deluxe all steel welded construction. Fire wall and toe boards are insulated, balance of cab is lined for reduction of heat transfer and noise. Two cowl ventilators, large sliding rear window and adjustable wind wings in the doors insure controlled ventilation. Doors are completely weather stripped and mounted on piano-type hinges. Cab dimensions 70" wide, 61 1/2" high, 59" long. Choice of de luxe bucket seats, or straight seat cushion and lazy back, all upholstered in genuine leather, using foam rubber cushions. Large tool box with cushion pad alongside driver's seat. Easily removable floor boards covered with heavy insulated rubber mat. Junction blocks for electrical and tubing connections facilitate removal of cab or engine. Flexible connections used on all lines between engine and chassis.

INSTRUMENTS— Heavy duty individually mounted instruments grouped in panel with non-glare indirect lighting and rheostat control. Instruments include speedometer, motor-mile recording tachometer, water temperature indicator, oil pressure gauge, air pressure gauge, electrical fuel gauges and ammeter. Instrument panel hinged to tilt out permitting easy access to switch controls and connections. Toggle switch controls for lights, electrical accessories and ignition. Automatic circuit breakers located in panel on fire wall inside of cab with wiring diagram showing all electrical circuits involved.

CONTROLS— Matched treadle pedals for foot brake and throttle controls. Hand brake and shifting levers in center of cab. Electric horn button in center of steering wheel. Air horn and arm signal controls in upper forward left hand corner of cab for easy access. Foot controlled high-low beam switch with beam indicator on dash. Hand trailer valve and front brake limit valve (when specified) accessibly mounted on dash.

COOLING SYSTEM— Deep tubular type core with 1,050 square inches frontal area. Assembled type radiator with top and bottom tanks and side plates bolted together with core to make a complete unit. No soldered joints. Tanks and side plates replaceable. Radiator supported independent of shell on two rubber mountings for freedom from cab and frame movement. Radiator shell mounted independent of core on two rubber mountings. three piece hood with wide center section bolted to shell and cowl permits cab, hood and radiator shell to move as a unit without any stresses on core. Shutter is mounted on radiator shell and is thermostatically controlled and air operated.

STEERING GEAR— Cam and lever type with ball bearings. Steering post set at proper angle for maximum driver comfort. 22-inch diameter steering wheel, dual steering ratio.

FRAME— Fish-bellied type, pressed chrome manganese, heat-treated steel channel 9/32" thick 3 1/2" flanges, 10 3/8" at deepest section. Cast steel frame brackets, full double channel frame available for exceptionally heavy-duty operation. Extruded aluminum frame with aluminum brackets and crossmembers available. Channels 10 1/2 deep with 1/2" web, flanges 3 1/2" wide and 3/4" thick.

FRONT BUMPER and TOW EYES— Heavy duty, deep sectional steel, securely fastened to front frame bracket, with recessed towing eyes.

FRONT AXLE— Manufactured by Timken, equipped with timken tapered roller bearings, Westinghouse air brakes, and 10 stud Budd hubs.

REAR AXLE— Manufactured by Timken, equipped with timken tapered roller bearings, Westinghouse air brakes, and 3/4 tapered liners. full floating axles, 10 stud Budd hubs and cast alloy brake drums. Adjustable radius rods are used to insure correct axle alignment at all times.

SPRINGS— Chrome manganese steel, front and rear. Front springs 48" x 3 1/2" insuring riding comfort and better handling.

MOTOR— Optional motors available diesel, butane or gasoline (See specification sheet.)

CLUTCH— Two-plate dry type with ball thrust release bearing.

TRANSMISSION— Unit power type transmission, four of five forward speeds, available in either steel or aluminum case.

COMPOUND— Three speed mounted amidships. Available in steel or aluminum case.

DRIVE SHAFT— Tubular with Spicer needle bearing universal joints.

BRAKES— Westinghouse air brakes on front and rear axles with front wheel brake limit valve available if desired. Molded, tapered linings, cast alloy drums, treadle pedal foot brake. Two air storage reservoirs of ample capacity. Tru-stop disc type parking brake mounted behind compound operating on drive line.

WHEELS— Budd ventilated disc type with wide base rims. Spare wheel supplied.

TIRES— Heavy duty type, of suitable size for both on and off highway operation; available in standard and premium types.

ELECTRICAL SYSTEM— Sealed beam head lights, combination stop and tail lights with reflector lens. Heavy duty generator with voltage regulator. Six (6), 12-24 volt systems. All batteries accessibly mounted in covered campartment on right hand running board.

FUEL SUPPLY— Two 50-gallon fuel tanks, mounted one each side of frame. Larger capacity tanks available at additional cost. Large filler openings, brass sump on bottom with drain cock. Electric fuel gauges. Two butane tanks, 100 gallons each, supplied on butane-powered trucks.

CHASSIS LUBRICATION— Alemite high pressure system.

ACCESSORIES— Standard accessories include cigar lighter and ash tray on dash, cab dome light, electric horn, large single tone air horn on roof of cab, adjustable rear view mirrors externally mounted on each side of cab, Dual air operated wind shield wipers, manually operated illuminated arm signal mounted on driver's side of cab, tool kit, 12-ton hydraulic jack, wheel wrench, Alemite lubricator, oil can and parts book.

Additional accessories available include spotlight, fog lights, heater, defroster fan, I.C.C. lights on cab, tachograph, sanders and radiator guard.

NOTE: For detailed specifications of component units see Specification sheet.

A Quality Truck to Meet Every HEAVY DUTY Requirement

Model 280 Body Builders Dimensions

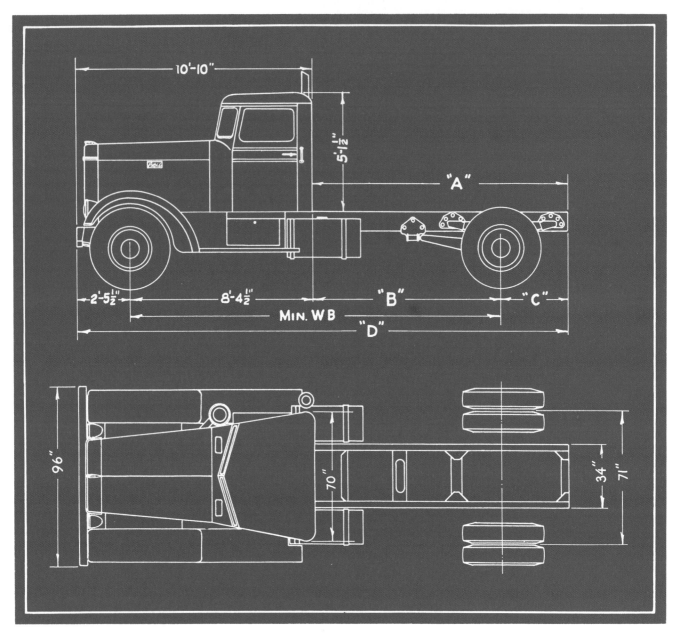

WHEEL BASE	A	B	C	D
175''	9'-1½''	6'-2½''	2'-11''	19'-11½''
189''	12'-3''	7'-4½''	4'-10½''	23'-1''
202''	15'-3''	8'-5½''	6'-9½''	26'-1''
227''	18'-3''	10'-6½''	7'-8½''	29'-1''

NOTES

Minimum wheel base shown above with standard equipment, standard size tires, and fuel tanks.

Special wheel base, load distribution, tire size and fuel tanks subject to factory approval.

If axle attachment is used, minimum wheel base with standard equipment becomes 187''.

Peterbilt Motors Company

10700 MacArthur Boulevard
Oakland, California

HEAVY DUTY TRUCKS   MacDONALD LOW - BODY TRUCKS   MacDONALD LIFT TRUCKS

MODEL 360

CAB— Cab manufactured by Peterbilt and completely new, using the time proved Peterbilt construction and designed for maximum driver comfort after an extensive survey of requirements and desires. Fully enclosed, deluxe all steel welded construction. Fire wall and toe boards are insulated, balance of cab is lined for reduction of heat transfer and noise. Two cowl ventilators, large sliding rear window and adjustable wind wings in the doors insure controlled ventilation. Doors are completely weather stripped and mounted on piano-type hinges. Cab dimensions 70" wide, 61 $1/2$" high, 59" long. Choice of de luxe bucket seats, or straight seat cushion and lazy back, all upholstered in genuine leather, using foam rubber cushions. Large tool box with cushion pad alongside driver's seat. Easily removable floor boards covered with heavy insulated rubber mat. Junction blocks for electrical and tubing connections facilitate removal of cab or engine. Flexible connections used on all lines between engine and chassis.

INSTRUMENTS— Heavy duty individually mounted instruments grouped in panel with non-glare indirect lighting and rheostat control. Instruments include speedometer, motor-mile recording tachometer, water temperature indicator, oil pressure gauge, air pressure gauge, electrical fuel gauges and ammeter. Instrument panel hinged to tilt out permitting easy access to switch controls and connections. Toggle switch controls for lights, electrical accessories and ignition. Automatic circuit breakers located in panel on fire wall inside of cab with wiring diagram showing all electrical circuits involved.

CONTROLS— Matched treadle pedals for foot brake and throttle controls. Hand brake and shifting levers in center of cab. Electric horn button in center of steering wheel. Air horn and arm signal controls in upper forward left hand corner of cab for easy access. Foot controlled high-low beam switch with beam indicator on dash. Hand trailer valve and front brake limit valve (when specified) accessibly mounted on dash.

COOLING SYSTEM— Deep tubular type core with 1,050 square inches frontal area. Assembled type radiator with top and bottom tanks and side plates bolted to-

gether with core to make a complete unit. No soldered joints. Tanks and side plates replaceable. Radiator supported independent of shell on two rubber mountings for freedom from cab and frame movement. Radiator shell mounted independent of core on two rubber mountings. three piece hood with wide center section bolted to shell and cowl permits cab, hood and radiator shell to move as a unit without any stresses on core. Shutter is mounted on radiator shell and is thermostatically controlled and air operated.

STEERING GEAR— Cam and lever type with ball bearings. Steering post set at proper angle for maximum driver comfort. 22-inch diameter steering wheel, dual steering ratio.

FRAME— Fish-bellied type, pressed chrome manganese, heat-treated steel channel $9/32$" thick 3 $1/2$" flanges, 10 $3/8$" at deepest section. Cast steel frame brackets, full double channel frame available for exceptionally heavy-duty operation. Extruded aluminum frame with aluminum brackets and crossmembers available. Channels 10 $1/2$ deep with $1/2$" web, flanges 3 $1/2$" wide and $3/4$" thick.

FRONT BUMPER and TOW EYES— Heavy duty, deep sectional steel, securely fastened to front frame bracket, with recessed towing eyes.

FRONT AXLE— Manufactured by Timken, equipped with timken tapered roller bearings, Westinghouse air brakes, and 10 stud Budd hubs.

REAR AXLE— Manufactured by Timken, equipped with timken tapered roller bearings, Westinghouse air brakes, and $3/4$ tapered liners. full floating axles, 10 stud Budd hubs and cast alloy brake drums. Adjustable radius rods are used to insure correct axle alignment at all times.

SPRINGS— Chrome manganese steel, front and rear. Front springs 48" x 3 $1/2$" insuring riding comfort and better handling.

MOTOR— Optional motors available diesel, butane or gasoline (See specification sheet.)

CLUTCH— Two-plate dry type with ball thrust release bearing.

TRANSMISSION— Unit power type transmission, four of five forward speeds, available in either steel or aluminum case.

COMPOUND— Three speed mounted amidships. Available in steel or aluminum case.

DRIVE SHAFT— Tubular with Spicer needle bearing universal joints.

BRAKES— Westinghouse air brakes on front and rear axles with front wheel brake limit valve available if desired. Molded, tapered linings, cast alloy drums, treadle pedal foot brake. Two air storage reservoirs of ample capacity. Tru-stop disc type parking brake mounted behind compound operating on drive line.

WHEELS— Budd ventilated disc type with wide base rims. Spare wheel supplied.

TIRES— Heavy duty type, of suitable size for both on and off highway operation; available in standard and premium types.

ELECTRICAL SYSTEM— Sealed beam head lights, combination stop and tail lights with reflector lens. Heavy duty generator with voltage regulator. Six (6), 12-24 volt systems. All batteries accessibly mounted in covered campartment on right hand running board.

FUEL SUPPLY— Two 50-gallon fuel tanks, mounted one each side of frame. Larger capacity tanks available at additional cost. Large filler openings, brass sump on bottom with drain cock. Electric fuel gauges. Two butane tanks, 100 gallons each, supplied on butane-powered trucks.

CHASSIS LUBRICATION— Alemite high pressure system.

ACCESSORIES— Standard accessories include cigar lighter and ash tray on dash, cab dome light, electric horn, large single tone air horn on roof of cab, adjustable rear view mirrors externally mounted on each side of cab, Dual air operated wind shield wipers, manually operated illuminated arm signal mounted on driver's side of cab, tool kit, 12-ton hydraulic jack, wheel wrench, Alemite lubricator, oil can and parts book.

Additional accessories available include spotlight, fog lights, heater, defroster fan, I.C.C. lights on cab, tachograph, sanders and radiator guard.

NOTE: For detailed specifications of component units see Specification sheet.

A Quality Truck to Meet Every HEAVY DUTY Requirement

Model 360 Body Builders Dimensions

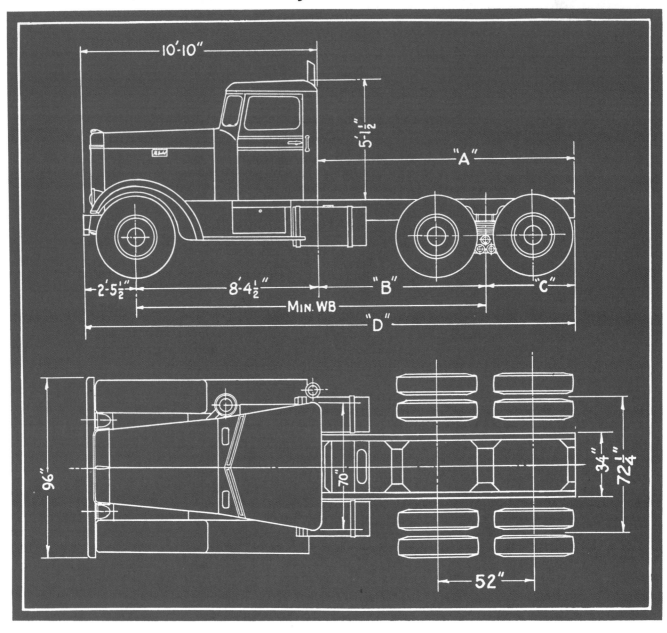

WHEEL BASE	A	B	C	D
198⅝''	12'-2⅛''	8'-2⅛''	4'-0''	23'-0⅛''
208''	15'-3''	8'-11½''	6'-3½''	26'-1''
227''	18'-3''	10'-6½''	8'-8½''	29'-1''
240''	20'-3''	11'-7½''	8'-7½''	31'-1''

NOTES

Minimum wheel base shown above with standard equipment, four speed transmission, standard size tires and fuel tanks.

If five speed transmission is used, minimum wheel base becomes 205⅜''.

Special wheel base, load distribution, tire size and fuel tanks subject to factory approval.

Peterbilt Motors Company

10700 MacArthur Boulevard
Oakland, California

HEAVY DUTY TRUCKS   MacDONALD LOW - BODY TRUCKS   MacDONALD LIFT TRUCKS

Peterbilt

COE
CAB OVER ENGINE
HEAVY DUTY
TRUCKS

A Modern Answer to Increased Pay Loads

Regulations and limitations of gross vehicle weights and train lengths in many states, together with decreasing per unit weight of commodities hauled thru the use of plastics and lightweight alloys, seriously handicap many truck operators in the conducting of their business on a profitable basis.

The Peterbilt cab over engine heavy duty truck is the answer to this problem. The long wheelbase unit for truck and trailer operation permits more pay load space in a given overall length. The short wheelbase two axle tractor allows the use of longer trailer and semi trailer or "doubles" in a given overall length, while the short wheelbase two axle or dual drive tractor will allow the use of a long semi trailer and still stay within the requirements of the states with minimum overall length laws. Each of these operations give the added pay load space so badly needed.

The weight saving in the Peterbilt truck through the use of lightweight, strong aluminum alloys further increases the pay load capacity, all of which assists in a profitable operation.

In addition to the increased load space and the increased pay load, the two most important features which will insure a profitable operation, are the **accessibility** and **dependability** built into the Peterbilt cab over engine truck. The minimum of time and expense required in servicing, adjusting, lubricating and repairing a Peterbilt cab over engine truck is the solution to the operator's problems.

In the picture at the left you will notice that the exhaust manifold is positioned below the floor line of the cab, where a clean sweep of air from the fan sends the hot air back and out, instead of permitting it to rise and heat the cab floor.

Engine and Steering Gear Accessible from Standing Position

A study of the illustrations on this page will indicate the extent to which PETERBILT engineers have gone to provide quick accessibility for servicing, repair, replacement and adjustment. To gain access to either side of the engine, where the mechanic can work close to the engine, standing on the floor level, with all parts within arms length, it is merely necessary to swing the fenders to the open position. This involves only the removal of one heavy duty cap screw and takes about the same amount of time as lifting the hood of a conventional truck.

The picture below shows the intake side of the engine, with fender swung open. Note the accessibility of the steering gear, air compressor, fuel pump, fuel filter, and fuel injection system.

Note particularly the splash skirt above the wheel which mates with a similar skirt built as an integral part of the fender. When the fender is swung into closed position these two skirts form an effective seal, protecting the engine from water and dirt, eliminating the need for a separate engine cover.

TILTING CAB PERMITS EASY ENGINE REMOVAL

The cab is carried on rubber mountings at the rear and rubber insulated hinges at the front and tilts forward 90°, where it is secured by two steel cables running from the frame to the rear of the cab. Tilting of the cab can be accomplished with a minimum amount of time and labor. It is not necessary to disturb or disconnect any electrical wiring or any fuel, air or water lines.

With the cab in the tilted position it is a simple operation to remove the entire power plant, including engine, clutch, transmission and controls. The only time the cab is tilted is to facilitate this operation (complete engine removal) as all other service functions, including removal of transmission, clutch and controls can be performed with the cab in its normal position.

The gear shift tower of the Peterbilt Cab Over Engine Truck is of Peterbilt's own design, with fewer working and wearing parts than found in other cab over engine trucks.

INSTANT ACCESSIBILITY FOR SERVICING

The front is carried on a full length piano type hinge at the top and is conveniently raised by unhooking two heavy duty hood hooks. A hinged rest is provided on each side of this panel to hold it in the raised position. With the front end in this raised position, complete accessibility is obtained for servicing the air cleaner, headlights, footbrake valve, radiator, shutters, electrical circuits and junction blocks, and fuel, oil and air lines which run to a common manifold.

The fenders are hinged at the rear and easily swing open to permit access to both sides of the engine for complete servicing of the steering gear and all units on the engine. The post type hinges allow the mechanic to lift the fender off when in the open position and store it out of the way to conserve space if so desired.

All service functions are performed with the mechanic standing on the floor, a position conducive to better workmanship and faster servicing than in the conventional type truck.

GREATER COMFORT AND SAFETY

The cab is constructed with the same rigid bracing and welded construction that has made the conventional Peterbilt cab so popular for its comfort, safety and long life. The ventilators in the cowl, the adjustable window wind wings in the doors and the sliding rear window give complete driver controlled cab ventilation for summer weather. The fully sealed doors and completely lined cab interior insure driver comfort in inclement weather.

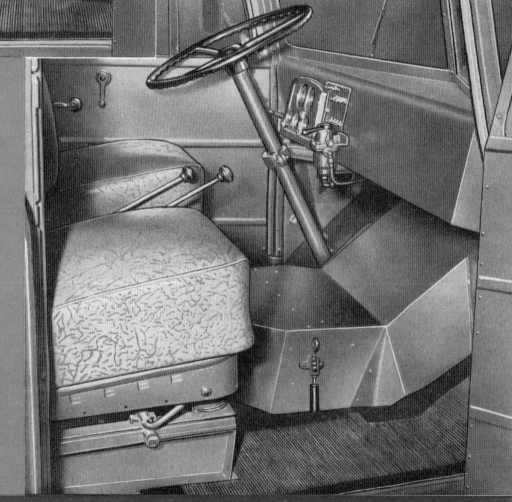

The wide cab (87½"), mounted 16" higher than the conventional type, is equipped with large, full view windshields, and door glasses to give exceptional driver visibility. The cab width places the driver where he has complete vision for backing and maneuvering. The added height puts his line of vision above the headlights of oncoming traffic and permits an unobstructed view over the cars in the traffic lane ahead.

Along with accessibility, dependability and simplicity, there is engineered into the Peterbilt cab-over-engine truck, the maximum in comfort and safety.

COE Dual Drive Body Builders Dimensions

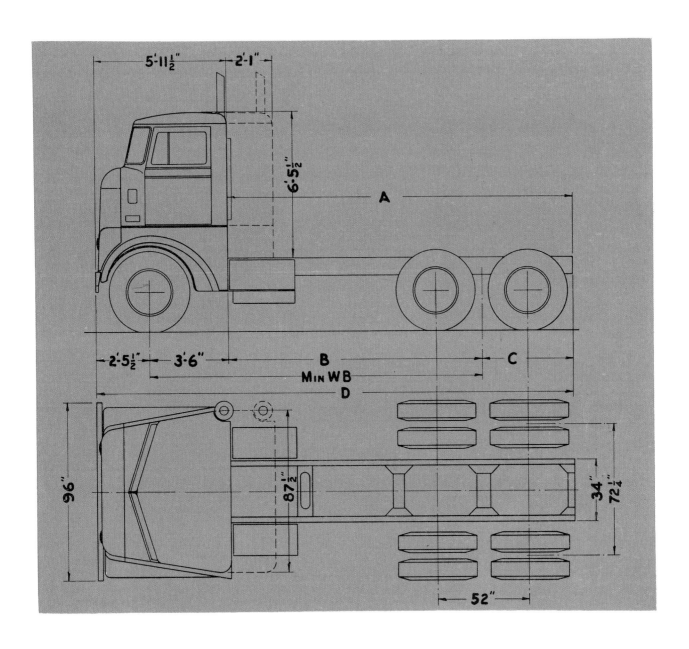

WHEELBASE	A	B	C	D	SPECIALS
135-3/16"	11'-9-3/16"	7'-9-3/16"	4'-0"	17'-8-11/16"	8 speed transmission—emergency brake on rear axle*
165"	18'-3"	10'-3"	8'-0"	24'-2½"	
178"	20'-3"	11'-4"	8'-11"	26'-2½"	
190"	22'-3"	12'-4"	9'-11"	28'-2½"	

NOTES:

Minimum wheelbase shown above with standard size tires and fuel tanks. *Where drive shaft brake is required add 4⅜" to the wheelbase. Sleeper cab is available and indicated by broken line. Special wheelbase, load distribution, tire sizes and fuel tanks subject to factory approval.

COE Two Axle Body Builders Dimensions

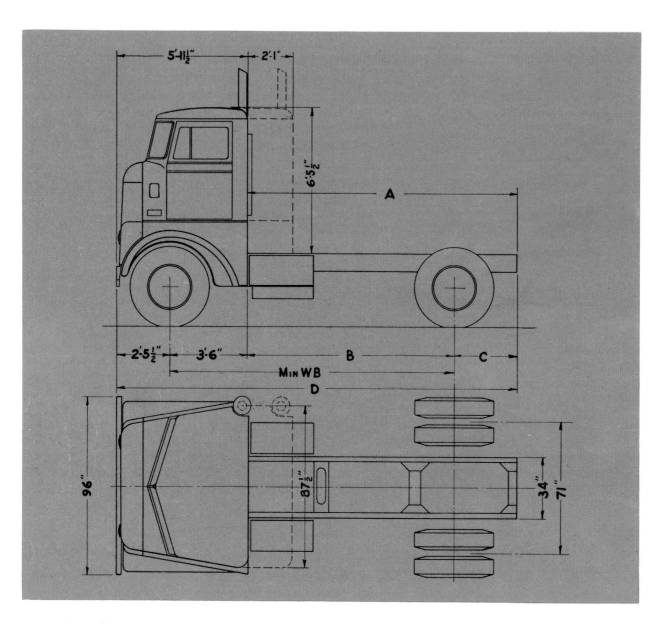

WHEELBASE	A	B	C	D	SPECIALS
111½''	8'-8½''	5'-9½''	2'-11''	14'-8''	4 speed transmissions—emergency brake on rear axle*
117¼''	9'-2¼''	6'-3¼''	2'-11''	15''-1¾''	5 speed transmissions—emergency brake on rear axle*
180''	18'-3''	11'-6''	6'-9''	24''-2½''	
194''	20'-3''	12'-8''	7'-7''	26'-2½''	

NOTES:

Minimum wheelbase shown above with standard tires and fuel tanks. *Where drive shaft brake is required, add 4⅜'' to wheelbase. 111½'' and 117¼'' wheelbase trucks only sizes available with main transmission and 2 speed rear axle. Sleeper cab is available and shown in broken line. Special wheelbase, load distribution, tire sizes and fuel tanks subject to factory approval.

MODEL 350

CAB— Cab manufactured by Peterbilt and completely new, using the time proved Peterbilt construction and designed for maximum driver comfort after an extensive survey of requirements and desires. Fully enclosed, deluxe all steel welded construction. Fire wall and toe boards are insulated, balance of cab is lined for reduction of heat transfer and noise. Two cowl ventilators, large sliding rear window and adjustable wind wings in the doors insure controlled ventilation. Doors are completely weather stripped and mounted on piano-type hinges. Cab dimensions 70" wide, 61 1/2" high, 59" long. Choice of de luxe bucket seats, or straight seat cushion and lazy back, all upholstered in genuine leather, using foam rubber cushions. Large tool box with cushion pad alongside driver's seat. Easily removable floor boards covered with heavy insulated rubber mat. Junction blocks for electrical and tubing connections facilitate removal of cab or engine. Flexible connections used on all lines between engine and chassis.

INSTRUMENTS— Heavy duty individually mounted instruments grouped in panel with non-glare indirect lighting and rheostat control. Instruments include speedometer, motor-mile recording tachometer, water temperature indicator, oil pressure gauge, air pressure gauge, electrical fuel gauges and ammeter. Instrument panel hinged to tilt out permitting easy access to switch controls and connections. Toggle switch controls for lights, electrical accessories and ignition. Automatic circuit breakers located in panel on fire wall inside of cab with wiring diagram showing all electrical circuits involved.

CONTROLS— Matched treadle pedals for foot brake and throttle controls. Hand brake and shifting levers in center of cab. Electric horn button in center of steering wheel. Air horn and arm signal controls in upper forward left hand corner of cab for easy access. Foot controlled high-low beam switch with beam indicator on dash. Hand trailer valve and front brake limit valve (when specified) accessibly mounted on dash.

COOLING SYSTEM— Deep tubular type core with 1,050 square inches frontal area. Assembled type radiator with top and bottom tanks and side plates bolted together with core to make a complete unit. No soldered joints. Tanks and side plates replaceable. Radiator supported independent of shell on two rubber mountings for freedom from cab and frame movement. Radiator shell mounted independent of core on two rubber mountings. three piece hood with wide center section bolted to shell and cowl permits cab, hood and radiator shell to move as a unit without any stresses on core. Shutter is mounted on radiator shell and is thermostatically controlled and air operated.

STEERING GEAR— Cam and lever type with ball bearings. Steering post set at proper angle for maximum driver comfort. 22-inch diameter steering wheel, dual steering ratio.

FRAME— Fish-bellied type, pressed chrome manganese, heat-treated steel channel 9/32" thick 3 1/2" flanges, 10 3/8" at deepest section. Cast steel frame brackets, full double channel frame available for exceptionally heavy-duty operation. Extruded aluminum frame with aluminum brackets and crossmembers available. Channels 10 1/2" deep with 1/2" web, flanges 3 1/2" wide and 3/4" thick.

FRONT BUMPER and TOW EYES— Heavy duty, deep sectional steel, securely fastened to front frame bracket, with recessed towing eyes.

FRONT AXLE— Manufactured by Timken, equipped with timken tapered roller bearings, Westinghouse air brakes, and 10 stud Budd hubs.

REAR AXLE— Manufactured by Timken, equipped with timken tapered roller bearings, Westinghouse air brakes, and 3/4 tapered liners. full floating axles, 10 stud Budd hubs and cast alloy brake drums. Adjustable radius rods are used to insure correct axle alignment at all times.

SPRINGS— Chrome manganese steel, front and rear. Front springs 48" x 3 1/2" insuring riding comfort and better handling.

MOTOR— Optional motors available diesel, butane or gasoline (See specification sheet.)

CLUTCH— Two-plate dry type with ball thrust release bearing.

TRANSMISSION— Unit power type transmission, four of five forward speeds, available in either steel or aluminum case.

COMPOUND— Three speed mounted amidships. Available in steel or aluminum case.

DRIVE SHAFT— Tubular with Spicer needle bearing universal joints.

BRAKES— Westinghouse air brakes on front and rear axles with front wheel brake limit valve available if desired. Molded, tapered linings, cast alloy drums, treadle pedal foot brake. Two air storage reservoirs of ample capacity. Tru-stop disc type parking brake mounted behind compound operating on drive line.

WHEELS— Budd ventilated disc type with wide base rims. Spare wheel supplied.

TIRES— Heavy duty type, of suitable size for both on and off highway operation; available in standard and premium types.

ELECTRICAL SYSTEM— Sealed beam head lights, combination stop and tail lights with reflector lens. Heavy duty generator with voltage regulator. Six (6), 12-24 volt systems. All batteries accessibly mounted in covered campartment on right hand running board.

FUEL SUPPLY— Two 50-gallon fuel tanks, mounted one each side of frame. Larger capacity tanks available at additional cost. Large filler openings, brass sump on bottom with drain cock. Electric fuel gauges. Two butane tanks, 100 gallons each, supplied on butane-powered trucks.

CHASSIS LUBRICATION— Alemite high pressure system.

ACCESSORIES— Standard accessories include cigar lighter and ash tray on dash, cab dome light, electric horn, large single tone air horn on roof of cab, adjustable rear view mirrors externally mounted on each side of cab, Dual air operated wind shield wipers, manually operated illuminated arm signal mounted on driver's side of cab, tool kit, 12-ton hydraulic jack, wheel wrench, Alemite lubricator, oil can and parts book.

Additional accessories available include spotlight, fog lights, heater, defroster fan, I.C.C. lights on cab, tachograph, sanders and radiator guard.

NOTE: For detailed specifications of component units see Specification sheet.

Model 350 Body Builders Dimensions

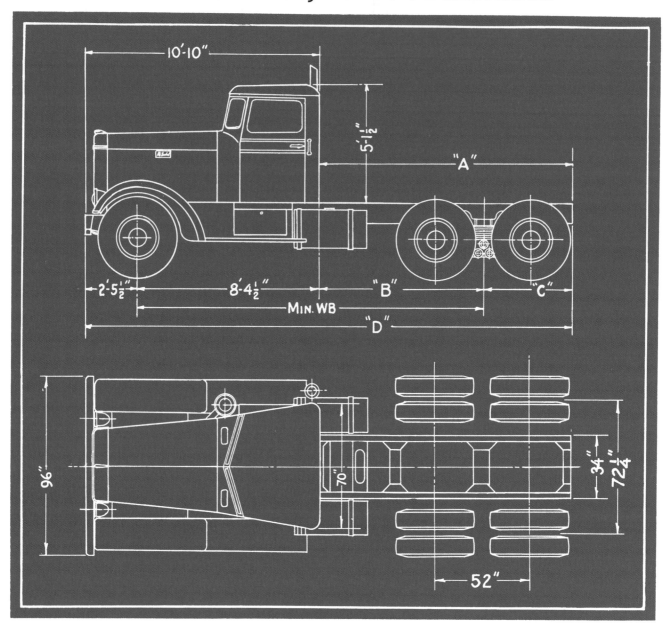

WHEEL BASE	A	B	C	D
193¼''	11'-8¾''	7'-8¾''	4'-0''	22'-6¾''
208''	15'-3''	8'-11½''	6'-3½''	26'-1''
227''	18'-3''	10'-6½''	8'-8½''	29'-1''
240''	20'-3''	11'-7½''	8'-7½''	31'-1''

NOTES

Minimum wheel base shown above with standard equipment, four speed transmission, standard size tires and fuel tanks.

If five speed transmission is used, minimum wheel base becomes 200''.

Special wheel base, load distribution, tire size and fuel tanks subject to factory approval.

Peterbilt Motors Company

10700 MacArthur Boulevard
Oakland, California

HEAVY DUTY TRUCKS   MacDONALD LOW - BODY TRUCKS   MacDONALD LIFT TRUCKS

MODEL 370

CAB— Cab manufactured by Peterbilt and completely new, using the time proved Peterbilt construction and designed for maximum driver comfort after an extensive survey of requirements and desires. Fully enclosed, deluxe all steel welded construction. Fire wall and toe boards are insulated, balance of cab is lined for reduction of heat transfer and noise. Two cowl ventilators, large sliding rear window and adjustable wind wings in the doors insure controlled ventilation. Doors are completely weather stripped and mounted on piano-type hinges. Cab dimensions 70" wide, 61 1/2" high, 59" long. Choice of de luxe bucket seats, or straight seat cushion and lazy back, all upholstered in genuine leather, using foam rubber cushions. Large tool box with cushion pad alongside driver's seat. Easily removable floor boards covered with heavy insulated rubber mat. Junction blocks for electrical and tubing connections facilitate removal of cab or engine. Flexible connections used on all lines between engine and chassis.

INSTRUMENTS— Heavy duty individually mounted instruments grouped in panel with non-glare indirect lighting and rheostat control. Instruments include speedometer, motor-mile recording tachometer, water temperature indicator, oil pressure gauge, air pressure gauge, electrical fuel gauges and ammeter. Instrument panel hinged to tilt out permitting easy access to switch controls and connections. Toggle switch controls for lights, electrical accesories and ignition. Automatic circuit breakers located in panel on fire wall inside of cab with wiring diagram showing all electrical circuits involved.

CONTROLS— Matched treadle pedals for foot brake and throttle controls. Hand brake and shifting levers in center of cab. Electric horn button in center of steering wheel. Air horn and arm signal controls in upper forward left hand corner of cab for easy access. Foot controlled high-low beam switch with beam indicator on dash. Hand trailer valve and front brake limit valve (when specified) accessibly mounted on dash.

COOLING SYSTEM— Deep tubular type core with 1,050 square inches frontal area. Assembled type radiator with top and bottom tanks and side plates bolted together with core to make a complete unit. No soldered joints. Tanks and side plates replaceable. Radiator supported independent of shell on two rubber mountings for freedom from cab and frame movement. Radiator shell mounted independent of core on two rubber mountings. three piece hood with wide center section bolted to shell and cowl permits cab, hood and radiator shell to move as a unit without any stresses on core. Shutter is mounted on radiator shell and is thermostatically controlled and air operated.

STEERING GEAR— Cam and lever type with ball bearings. Steering post set at proper angle for maximum driver comfort. 22-inch diameter steering wheel, dual steering ratio.

FRAME— Fish-bellied type, pressed chrome manganese, heat-treated steel channel 9/32" thick 3 1/2" flanges 10 3/8" at deepest section. Cast steel frame brackets, full double channel frame available for exceptionally heavy-duty operator.

FRONT BUMPER and TOW EYES— Heavy duty, deep sectional steel, securely fastened to front frame bracket, with recessed towing eyes.

FRONT AXLE— Manufactured by Timken, equipped with timken tapered roller bearings, Westinghouse air brakes, and 10 stud Budd hubs.

REAR AXLE— Manufactured by Timken, equipped with timken tapered roller bearings, Westinghouse air brakes, and 3/4 tapered liners. full floating axles, 10 stud Budd hubs and cast alloy brake drums. Adjustable radius rods are used to insure correct axle alignment at all times.

SPRINGS— Chrome manganese steel, front and rear. Front springs 48" x 3 1/2" insuring riding comfort and better handling.

MOTOR— Optional motors available diesel, butane or gasoline (See specification sheet.)

CLUTCH— Two-plate dry type with ball thrust release bearing.

TRANSMISSION— Unit power type transmission, four of five forward speeds, available in either steel or aluminum case.

COMPOUND— Three speed mounted amidships. Available in steel or aluminum case.

DRIVE SHAFT— Tubular with Spicer needle bearing universal joints.

BRAKES— Westinghouse air brakes on front and rear axles with front wheel brake limit valve available if desired. Molded, tapered linings, cast alloy drums, treadle pedal foot brake. Two air storage reservoirs of ample capacity. Tru-stop disc type parking brake mounted behind compound operating on drive line.

WHEELS— Budd ventilated disc type with wide base rims. Spare wheel supplied.

TIRES— Heavy duty type, of suitable size for both on and off highway operation; available in standard and premium types.

ELECTRICAL SYSTEM— Sealed beam head lights, combination stop and tail lights with reflector lens. Heavy duty generator with voltage regulator. Six (6), 12-24 volt systems. All batteries accessibly mounted in covered campartment on right hand running board.

FUEL SUPPLY— Two 50-gallon fuel tanks, mounted one each side of frame. Larger capacity tanks available at additional cost. Large filler openings, brass sump on bottom with drain cock. Electric fuel gauges. Two butane tanks, 100 gallons each, supplied on butane-powered trucks.

CHASSIS LUBRICATION— Alemite high pressure system.

ACCESSORIES— Standard accessories include cigar lighter and ash tray on dash, cab dome light, electric horn, large single tone air horn on roof of cab, adjustable rear view mirrors externally mounted on each side of cab, Dual air operated wind shield wipers, manually operated illuminated arm signal mounted on driver's side of cab, tool kit, 12-ton hydraulic jack, wheel wrench, Alemite lubricator, oil can and parts book.

Additional accessories available include spotlight, fog lights, heater, defroster fan, I.C.C. lights on cab, tachograph, sanders and radiator guard.

NOTE: For detailed specifications of component units see Specification sheet.

A Quality Truck to Meet Every HEAVY DUTY Requirement

Model 370 Body Builders Dimensions

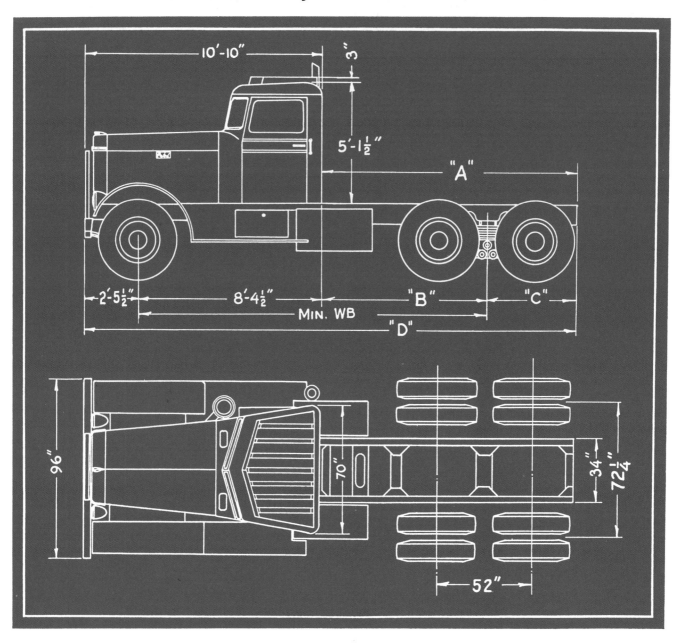

WHEEL BASE	A	B	C	D
198⅝"	12'-2⅛"	8'-2⅛"	4'-0"	23'-0⅛"
208"	15'-3"	8'-11½"	6'-3½"	26'-1"
227"	18'-3"	10'-6½"	8'-8½"	29'-1"
240"	20'-3"	11'-7½"	8'-7½"	31'-1"

NOTES

Minimum wheel base shown above with standard equipment, four speed transmission, standard size tires and fuel tanks.

If five speed transmission is used, minimum wheel base becomes 205⅜".

Special wheel base, load distribution, tire size and fuel tanks subject to factory approval.

Peterbilt Motors Company

10700 MacArthur Boulevard
Oakland, California

HEAVY DUTY TRUCKS   MacDONALD LOW - BODY TRUCKS   MacDONALD LIFT TRUCKS

 Peterbilt

MODEL 380

CAB— Cab manufactured by Peterbilt and completely new, using the time proved Peterbilt construction and designed for maximum driver comfort after an extensive survey of requirements and desires. Fully enclosed, deluxe all steel welded construction. Fire wall and toe boards are insulated, balance of cab is lined for reduction of heat transfer and noise. Two cowl ventilators, large sliding rear window and adjustable wind wings in the doors insure controlled ventilation. Doors are completely weather stripped and mounted on piano-type hinges. Cab dimensions 70" wide, 61 1/2" high, 59" long. Choice of de luxe bucket seats, or straight seat cushion and lazy back, all upholstered in genuine leather, using foam rubber cushions. Large tool box with cushion pad alongside driver's seat. Easily removable floor boards covered with heavy insulated rubber mat. Junction blocks for electrical and tubing connections facilitate removal of cab or engine. Flexible connections used on all lines between engine and chassis.

INSTRUMENTS— Heavy duty individually mounted instruments grouped in panel with non-glare indirect lighting and rheostat control. Instruments include speedometer, motor-mile recording tachometer, water temperature indicator, oil pressure gauge, air pressure gauge, electrical fuel gauges and ammeter. Instrument panel hinged to tilt out permitting easy access to switch controls and connections. Toggle switch controls for lights, electrical accessories and ignition. Automatic circuit breakers located in panel on fire wall inside of cab with wiring diagram showing all electrical circuits involved.

CONTROLS— Matched treadle pedals for foot brake and throttle controls. Hand brake and shifting levers in center of cab. Electric horn button in center of steering wheel. Air horn and arm signal controls in upper forward left hand corner of cab for easy access. Foot controlled high-low beam switch with beam indicator on dash. Hand trailer valve and front brake limit valve (when specified) accessibly mounted on dash.

COOLING SYSTEM— Deep tubular type core with 1,050 square inches frontal area. Assembled type radiator with top and bottom tanks and side plates bolted together with core to make a complete unit. No soldered joints. Tanks and side plates replaceable. Radiator supported independent of shell on two rubber mountings for freedom from cab and frame movement. Radiator shell mounted independent of core on two rubber mountings. three piece hood with wide center section bolted to shell and cowl permits cab, hood and radiator shell to move as a unit without any stresses on core. Shutter is mounted on radiator shell and is thermostatically controlled and air operated.

STEERING GEAR— Cam and lever type with ball bearings. Steering post set at proper angle for maximum driver comfort. 22-inch diameter steering wheel, dual steering ratio.

FRAME— Fish-bellied type, pressed chrome manganese, heat-treated steel channel 9/32" thick 3 1/2" flanges 10 3/8" at deepest section. Cast steel frame brackets, full double channel frame available for exceptionally heavy-duty operator.

FRONT BUMPER and TOW EYES— Heavy duty, deep sectional steel, securely fastened to front frame bracket, with recessed towing eyes.

FRONT AXLE— Manufactured by Timken, equipped with timken tapered roller bearings, Westinghouse air brakes, and 10 stud Budd hubs.

REAR AXLE— Manufactured by Timken, equipped with timken tapered roller bearings, Westinghouse air brakes, and 3/4 tapered liners. full floating axles, 10 stud Budd hubs and cast alloy brake drums. Adjustable radius rods are used to insure correct axle alignment at all times.

SPRINGS— Chrome manganese steel, front and rear. Front springs 48" x 3 1/2" insuring riding comfort and better handling.

MOTOR— Optional motors available diesel, butane or gasoline (See specification sheet.)

CLUTCH— Two-plate dry type with ball thrust release bearing.

TRANSMISSION— Unit power type transmission, four of five forward speeds, available in either steel or aluminum case.

COMPOUND— Three speed mounted amidships. Available in steel or aluminum case.

DRIVE SHAFT— Tubular with Spicer needle bearing universal joints.

BRAKES— Westinghouse air brakes on front and rear axles with front wheel brake limit valve available if desired. Molded, tapered linings, cast alloy drums, treadle pedal foot brake. Two air storage reservoirs of ample capacity. Tru-stop disc type parking brake mounted behind compound operating on drive line.

WHEELS— Budd ventilated disc type with wide base rims. Spare wheel supplied.

TIRES— Heavy duty type, of suitable size for both on and off highway operation; available in standard and premium types.

ELECTRICAL SYSTEM— Sealed beam head lights, combination stop and tail lights with reflector lens. Heavy duty generator with voltage regulator. Six (6), 12-24 volt systems. All batteries accessibly mounted in covered campartment on right hand running board.

FUEL SUPPLY— Two 50-gallon fuel tanks, mounted one each side of frame. Larger capacity tanks available at additional cost. Large filler openings, brass sump on bottom with drain cock. Electric fuel gauges. Two butane tanks, 100 gallons each, supplied on butane-powered trucks.

CHASSIS LUBRICATION— Alemite high pressure system.

ACCESSORIES— Standard accessories include cigar lighter and ash tray on dash, cab dome light, electric horn, large single tone air horn on roof of cab, adjustable rear view mirrors externally mounted on each side of cab, Dual air operated wind shield wipers, manually operated illuminated arm signal mounted on driver's side of cab, tool kit, 12-ton hydraulic jack, wheel wrench, Alemite lubricator, oil can and parts book.

Additional accessories available include spotlight, fog lights, heater, defroster fan, I.C.C. lights on cab, tachograph, sanders and radiator guard.

NOTE: For detailed specifications of component units see Specification sheet.

A Quality Truck to Meet Every HEAVY DUTY Requirement

Model 380 Body Builders Dimensions

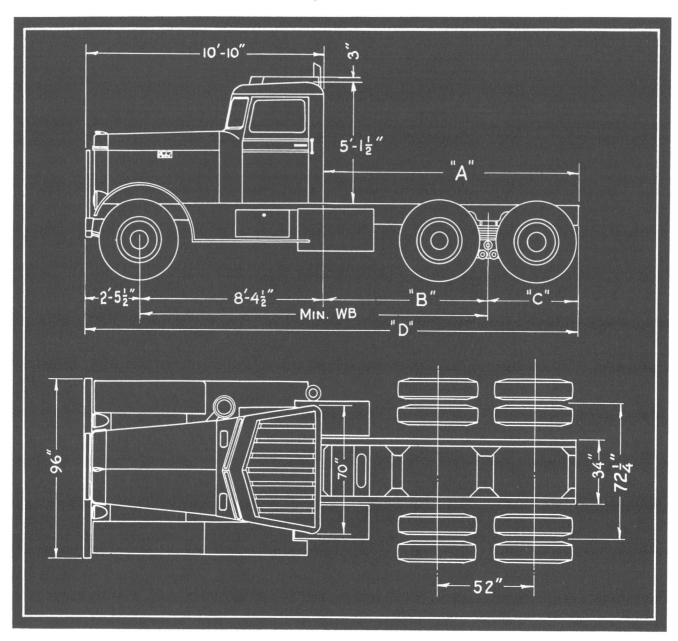

WHEEL BASE	A	B	C	D
194¼''	11'-9¾''	7'-9¾''	4'-0''	22'-7¾''
208''	15'-3''	8'-11½''	6'-3½''	26'-1''
227''	18'-3''	10'-6½''	8'-8½''	29'-1''
240''	20'-3''	11'-7½''	8'-7½''	31'-1''

NOTES

Minimum wheel base shown above with standard equipment, four speed transmission, standard size tires and fuel tanks.

If five speed transmission is used, minimum wheel base becomes 201''.

Special wheel base, load distribution, tire size, and fuel tanks subject to factory approval.

Peterbilt Motors Company

**10700 MacArthur Boulevard
Oakland, California**

HEAVY DUTY TRUCKS   MacDONALD LOW - BODY TRUCKS   MacDONALD LIFT TRUCKS

MODEL 390

CAB— Cab manufactured by Peterbilt and completely new, using the time proved Peterbilt construction and designed for maximum driver comfort after an extensive survey of requirements and desires. Fully enclosed, deluxe all steel welded construction. Fire wall and toe boards are insulated, balance of cab is lined for reduction of heat transfer and noise. Two cowl ventilators, large sliding rear window and adjustable wind wings in the doors insure controlled ventilation. Doors are completely weather stripped and mounted on piano-type hinges. Cab dimensions 70" wide, 61 1/2" high, 59" long. Choice of de luxe bucket seats, or straight seat cushion and lazy back, all upholstered in genuine leather, using foam rubber cushions. Large tool box with cushion pad alongside driver's seat. Easily removable floor boards covered with heavy insulated rubber mat. Junction blocks for electrical and tubing connections facilitate removal of cab or engine. Flexible connections used on all lines between engine and chassis.

INSTRUMENTS— Heavy duty individually mounted instruments grouped in panel with non-glare indirect lighting and rheostat control. Instruments include speedometer, motor-mile recording tachometer, water temperature indicator, oil pressure gauge, air pressure gauge, electrical fuel gauges and ammeter. Instrument panel hinged to tilt out permitting easy access to switch controls and connections. Toggle switch controls for lights, electrical accessories and ignition. Automatic circuit breakers located in panel on fire wall inside of cab with wiring diagram showing all electrical circuits involved.

CONTROLS— Matched treadle pedals for foot brake and throttle controls. Hand brake and shifting levers in center of cab. Electric horn button in center of steering wheel. Air horn and arm signal controls in upper forward left hand corner of cab for easy access. Foot controlled high-low beam switch with beam indicator on dash. Hand trailer valve and front brake limit valve (when specified) accessibly mounted on dash.

COOLING SYSTEM— Deep tubular type core with 1,050 square inches frontal area. Assembled type radiator with top and bottom tanks and side plates bolted together with core to make a complete unit. No soldered joints. Tanks and side plates replaceable. Radiator supported independent of shell on two rubber mountings for freedom from cab and frame movement. Radiator shell mounted independent of core on two rubber mountings. three piece hood with wide center section bolted to shell and cowl permits cab, hood and radiator shell to move as a unit without any stresses on core. Shutter is mounted on radiator shell and is thermostatically controlled and air operated.

STEERING GEAR— Cam and lever type with ball bearings. Steering post set at proper angle for maximum driver comfort. 22" diameter steering wheel, dual steering ratio, Hydraulic steering booster available.

FRAME— Fish-bellied type, pressed chrome manganese, heat-treated steel channel 9/32" thick 3 1/2" flanges 10 3/8" at deepest section. Cast steel frame brackets, full double channel frame available for exceptionally heavy-duty operator.

FRONT BUMPER and TOW EYES— Heavy duty, deep sectional steel, securely fastened to front frame bracket, with recessed towing eyes.

FRONT AXLE— Manufactured by Timken, equipped with timken tapered roller bearings, Westinghouse air brakes, and 10 stud Budd hubs.

REAR AXLE— Manufactured by Timken, equipped with timken tapered roller bearings, Westinghouse air brakes, and 3/4 tapered liners. full floating axles, 10 stud Budd hubs and cast alloy brake drums. Adjustable radius rods are used to insure correct axle alignment at all times.

SPRINGS— Chrome manganese steel, front and rear. Front springs 48" x 3 1/2" insuring riding comfort and better handling.

MOTOR— Optional motors available diesel, butane or gasoline (See specification sheet.)

CLUTCH— Two-plate dry type with ball thrust release bearing.

TRANSMISSION— Unit power type transmission, four of five forward speeds, available in either steel or aluminum case.

COMPOUND— Three speed mounted amidships. Available in steel or aluminum case.

DRIVE SHAFT— Tubular with Spicer needle bearing universal joints.

BRAKES— Westinghouse air brakes on front and rear axles with front wheel brake limit valve available if desired. Molded, tapered linings, cast alloy drums, treadle pedal foot brake. Two air storage reservoirs of ample capacity. Tru-stop disc type parking brake mounted behind compound operating on drive line.

WHEELS— Budd ventilated disc type with wide base rims. Spare wheel supplied.

TIRES— Heavy duty type, of suitable size for both on and off highway operation; available in standard and premium types.

ELECTRICAL SYSTEM— Sealed beam head lights, combination stop and tail lights with reflector lens. Heavy duty generator with voltage regulator. Six (6), 12-24 volt systems. All batteries accessibly mounted in covered campartment on right hand running board.

FUEL SUPPLY— Two 50-gallon fuel tanks, mounted one each side of frame. Larger capacity tanks available at additional cost. Large filler openings, brass sump on bottom with drain cock. Electric fuel gauges. Two butane tanks, 100 gallons each, supplied on butane-powered trucks.

CHASSIS LUBRICATION— Alemite high pressure system.

ACCESSORIES— Standard accessories include cigar lighter and ash tray on dash, cab dome light, electric horn, large single tone air horn on roof of cab, adjustable rear view mirrors externally mounted on each side of cab, Dual air operated wind shield wipers, manually operated illuminated arm signal mounted on driver's side of cab, tool kit, 12-ton hydraulic jack, wheel wrench, Alemite lubricator, oil can and parts book.

Additional accessories available include spotlight, fog lights, heater, defroster fan, I.C.C. lights on cab, tachograph, sanders and radiator guard.

NOTE: For detailed specifications of component units see Specification sheet.

A Quality Truck to Meet Every HEAVY DUTY Requirement

Model 390 Body Builders Dimensions

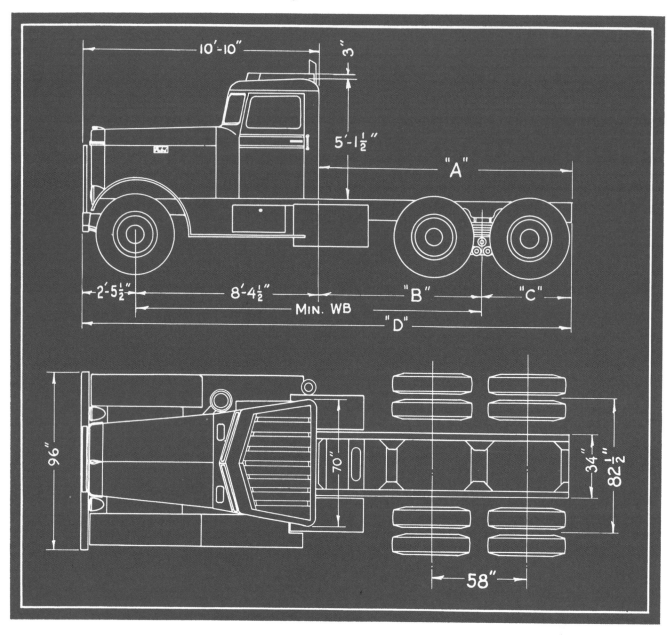

WHEEL BASE	A	B	C	D
197¼''	12'-8¾''	8'-0¾''	4'-8''	23'-6¾''
208''	15'-3''	8'-11½''	6'-3½''	26'-1''
227''	18'-3''	10'-6½''	8'-8½''	29'-1''
240''	20'-3''	11'-7½''	8'-7½''	31'-1''

NOTES

Minimum wheel base shown above with standard equipment, four speed transmission, standard size tires and fuel tanks.

If five speed transmission is used, minimum wheel base becomes 204''.

Special wheel base, load distribution, tire size and fuel tanks subject to factory approval.

Peterbilt Motors Company

10700 MacArthur Boulevard
Oakland, California

HEAVY DUTY TRUCKS   MacDONALD LOW - BODY TRUCKS   MacDONALD LIFT TRUCKS

Supreme In Its Field

IN THIS BOOKLET we have attempted to illustrate the applications of PETERBILT heavy duty trucks in transportation fields, serving various industries in which they have conclusively proved that they are **"supreme in their field."**

Herein are shown both conventional cab and cab-over-engine models, with and without sleeper cabs. We illustrate two and three axle tractor trucks, single and dual drives, trucks carrying their own bodies, pulling full trailers and bodies, tractors pulling semi-trailers, as well as double trailers.

No attempt is made to publicize either the operator of the equipment or the service he renders, and the selection of illustration is based solely on the type of equipment shown. It is not possible to illustrate in a small booklet all of the different types of applications in which PETERBILT TRUCKS have been successfully used, so we merely illustrate a few of the applications.

PETERBILT TRUCKS have, throughout the years, been eminently successful in many types of heavy duty applications, both on and off highway operations where loads are heavy and operating conditions are severe, such as logging, construction, mining, oil field development, cattle hauling, etc. PETERBILT lightweight models provide the most rugged construction, take full advantage of lightweight alloy metals of very high tensile strength, affording maximum payloads for highway operations.

PETERBILTS are famous for driver comfort, road ability, accessibility, and low maintenance costs in all fields of operations. If you are engaged in heavy hauling, and you do not find illustrated in this booklet a truck to meet your special requirements, please write direct to our factory and we will advise you of our nearest distributor, who will gladly assist you with your transportation problems. PETERBILTS are properly engineered, finest of expert craftsmanship is employed in construction to provide the most DEPENDABLE TRANSPORTATION.

Peterbilt MOTORS COMPANY
10700 MacARTHUR BOULEVARD
OAKLAND, CALIFORNIA

Freight. . . . .

Petroleum. . . .

Logging. . . . .

Lumber. . . . .

Excavating. . .

Livestock. . . .

Special. . . . .

Model 280 COE

Model 350 COE

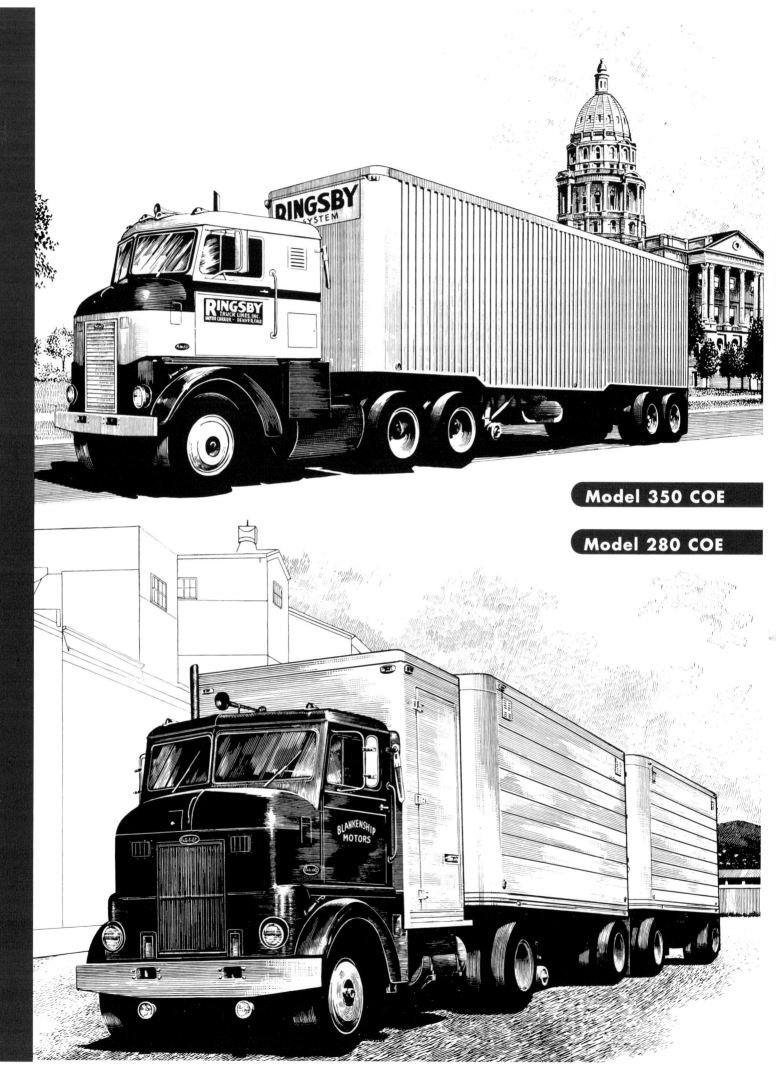

Model 350 COE

Model 280 COE

Model 351

Model 351

Model 280

Model 351

Model 350

Model 350

Model 350

Model 350

Model 380

Model 381

Model 350

Model 351

Model 281

Model 350

Model 351

Model 280 COE

Model 350

Model 381

Model 281

Model 281

Model 350 COE

Model 350 COE

Model 350 COE

Model 280 COE

Model 350 COE

Model 381

Model 360

Model 350

B3110
268-2

DELIVERY TRUCKS

FRAME

The frame and spring design of the MacDonald Low-Body Chassis incorporate patented features that permit the lowest possible ground to **body floor** height—thereby greatly reducing the physical effort of loading and delivering.

Low-Body design materially lowers the center of gravity of the truck load and provides a wide rigid base for the placement of the load between the wheels rather than over them. Lean and side-sway are therefore practically eliminated and the usual strains imposed on tires, wheels, bearings and hubs are greatly reduced—affecting an increase in the capacity and mileage; longer chassis and body life and lower operating costs.

The design and construction incorporated into the MacDonald Low-Body Chassis have been proved through many years of usage in hundreds of installations by large concerns. Definite savings in the labor cost of deliveries and truck operating expense have been experienced in these operations through Low-Body installations. Yes, low-body conversions really pay off.

Special rigid platform type extending the entire width of the body with six longitudinal members and cross members of deep section. This is the most modern automotive engineering practice in the truck field in that this Low-Body frame incorporates the important elements of the body (longitudinal and cross sills), making frame and body into one rigid integral unit.

All types of body structure (panel, rack, etc.) can be easily adapted to the simple rigid foundation. The prevention of swaying and twisting strain gives longer body life.

DRIVE AXLE

One piece cast alloy steel drop center housing with dual reduction type of drive. Secondary reduction in wheel hubs. Spiral bevel ring and pinion gear drive with 4 spider gears in differential carrier. Full floating type axle shafts.

Peterbilt acquired the MacDonald Low-Body Chassis in 1948.

MODEL 281

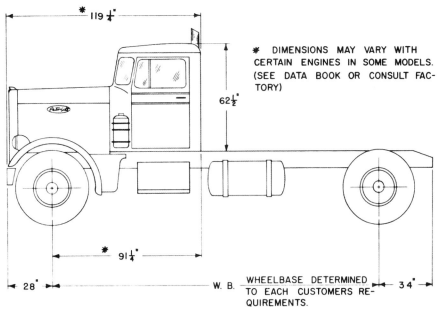

119¼"

62½"

91¼"

28"

34"

W. B.

✳ DIMENSIONS MAY VARY WITH
CERTAIN ENGINES IN SOME MODELS.
(SEE DATA BOOK OR CONSULT FAC-
TORY)

WHEELBASE DETERMINED
TO EACH CUSTOMERS RE-
QUIREMENTS.

 **PETERBILT MOTORS COMPANY**

38801 CHERRY STREET • NEWARK, CALIFORNIA 94560 • TELEPHONE (415) 797-3555

MODEL 281
STANDARD SPECIFICATIONS

Peterbilt

GVW 34,000 lbs.　　　**GCW 76,800 lbs.**

FRAME: A - 10½" x 3½" x ¾" (flange) x ½" (web) extruded aluminum alloy with aluminum crossmembers and gussets; std. chassis wt.: 10,150 lbs. (based on 9' - 11¼" loadspace).

M - 9" x 3½" x 7/32" or 10-3/8" x 3½" x ¼" heat-treated alloy steel with aluminum crossmembers and gussets; std. chassis wt.: 10,350 lbs. or 10,475 lbs. (based on 9'-11¼" loadspace).

ST - 9" x 3½" x 7/32" or 10-3/8" x 3½" x ¼" heat-treated alloy steel with steel crossmembers and gussets; std. chassis wt.: 10,850 lbs. or 10,975 lbs. (based on 9' - 11¼" loadspace).

Completely bolted frame construction; SAE Grade 5 heat-treated bolts and double length nuts throughout.

AXLES: Front: A & M - Rockwell-Standard FE-900-N with aluminum hubs; capacity: 11,000 lbs.; nominal track: 77".

ST - Same as A & M models except with iron hubs.

Rear: Rockwell-Standard R-170, hypoid single reduction with aluminum hubs; capacity: 23,000 lbs.; nominal track: 72"; ratios optional.

BRAKES: Service: Rear axle only, 16½" x 7" Timken P-Series; Centrifuse brake drums, 434 sq. in. effective lining area; trailer hand valve; tractor protection valve; Cummins 12 cu. ft. air compressor.

Parking: Overland Anchor-Lok air-operated spring brake with cab control.

CAB: A&M - Hand welded all aluminum construction; fully insulated with 1½" fiberglass; embossed aluminum cab lining; three point rubber mounting; extruded aluminum door frames; heavy-duty piano-type hinges; tinted safety glass throughout.

ST - Same as A & M models except all steel construction.

CLUTCH: Dana-Spicer 14" 2-plate; multiple lever; pull type with brake; 423 sq. in. area.

DRIVE LINES: Dana-Spicer 1700 series; needle-bearing yoke type.

ELECTRICAL SYSTEM: Delco-Remy Heavy-Duty 12-volt Long-Life Type 250 starter; 55 amp alternator; four Group HG-4A 160 amp. hr. batteries; automatic circuit breakers; hand-made wiring harnesses, heavy-duty insulation, wrapped with waterproof covering. All terminals numbered and routed through terminal blocks; double-faced front directional signals with 4-way emergency flasher switch; sealed beam headlights; combination stop and tail rear lights.

ENGINE: Cummins "Custom - Rated" diesel, model NHC-250 with lightweight components; 855 cu. in. displacement; horsepower: 250 @ 2,100 RPM; torque: 685 ft. lbs. @ 1,550 RPM; oil bath air cleaner; hi-mount fan; compression release; oil cooler; fuel filter; PT fuel system; full-flow lube oil filter; Luber-finer 750-C by-pass oil filter; corrosion resistor.

EXHAUST SYSTEM: Single 4" vertical system with muffler and guard; stainless steel exhaust flex; ceramic coated standpipe.

FENDERS: Crown Steel (rolled type).

FUEL TANK: One 50 gallon lt. wt. steel with heavy-duty mounting brackets; 4" diameter filler opening; tank mounted shut-off cock.

INSTRUMENTS: Tachometer, speedometer, water temperature, ammeter, fuel, oil pressure and air pressure gauges; low air pressure warning light; tilting dash panel; rheostat controlled lighting for all instruments.

RADIATOR: Tube and fin type core with 1,050 sq. in. frontal area; detachable bolt-assembled, aluminum alloy top and bottom tanks; fitted Cadillac "Ther-Mech" aluminum shutter with Peterbilt adjustment mechanism.

SEATS: Driver: Peterbilt-Bostrom deluxe "Thinline".

Passenger: Tool box with upholstered cushion.

STEERING: Ross Model TE-71 cam and lever type; steering ratio: 28 to 1; 22" diameter white steering wheel.

SUSPENSION: Front: Chrome vanadium steel split-progressive springs; spring width: 3½"; length: 48".

Rear: Peterbilt split-progressive spring with cast eye; spring width: 3½"; length: 54".

TRANSMISSION: Main: A - Dana-Spicer 8544-A; 4-speed; aluminum case and cover.

M&ST - Dana-Spicer 8542-A; 4-speed; iron case and cover.

Auxiliary: A - Dana-Spicer 8035-Q; 3-speed; aluminum case and cover.

M&ST - Dana-Spicer 8031-Q; 3-speed; iron case and cover.

TIRES: 10:00 x 20, 12-ply non-premium nylon highway tread (6 furnished).

WHEELS: 20" x 7.5 light weight, high tensile steel disc (6 furnished).

STD. ACCESSORIES: Dual motor, air operated, independently valved, variable speed, parking type windshield wipers; large adjustable 7" x 16" west coast type, stainless steel backed, rear view mirrors; single tone air horn; electric horn; front and rear mud flaps; flexible air piping throughout; insulated floor mats; tow pin; dual inside sun visors; cigar lighter; ash tray; left hand arm rest; red cab reflectors on tractor models; 12-ton jack; wheel wrench, and Operator's Manual.

ALL SPECIFICATIONS ARE SUBJECT TO CHANGE WITHOUT NOTICE

MODEL 351

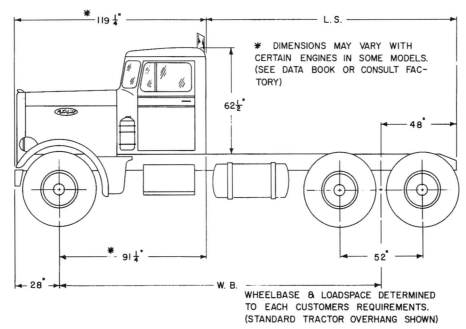

119¼"   L.S.

✱ DIMENSIONS MAY VARY WITH
CERTAIN ENGINES IN SOME MODELS.
(SEE DATA BOOK OR CONSULT FAC-
TORY)

62½"

48"

91¼"

52"

28"   W. B.

WHEELBASE & LOADSPACE DETERMINED
TO EACH CUSTOMERS REQUIREMENTS.
(STANDARD TRACTOR OVERHANG SHOWN)

 **PETERBILT MOTORS COMPANY**

38801 CHERRY STREET • NEWARK, CALIFORNIA 94560 • TELEPHONE (415) 797-3555

MODEL 351
STANDARD SPECIFICATIONS

GVW 49,000 lbs.   **GCW 76,800 lbs.**

FRAME: A - 10½" x 3½" x ¾" (flange) x ½" (web) extruded aluminum alloy with aluminum crossmembers and gussets; std. chassis wt.: 12,650 lbs. (based on 20'-3" loadspace).

M - 10-3/8" x 3½" x ¼" heat-treated alloy steel with aluminum crossmembers and gussets; std. chassis wt.: 13,150 lbs. (based on 20'-3" loadspace).

ST - 10-3/8" x 3½" x ¼" heat-treated alloy steel with steel crossmembers and gussets; std. chassis wt.: 13,775 lbs. (based on 20'-3" loadspace).

Completely bolted frame construction; SAE Grade 5 heat-treated bolts and double length nuts throughout.

AXLES: Front: A&M - Rockwell-Standard FE-900-N with aluminum hubs; capacity: 11,000 lbs.; nominal track: 77".

ST - Same as A&M models except with iron hubs.

Rear: A&M - Rockwell-Standard SQHD, hypoid single reduction tandem axle, with aluminum hubs; driver controlled interaxle differential; capacity: 38,000 lbs.; nominal track: 71-3/16"; ratios optional.

ST - Same as A&M models except with iron hubs.

BRAKES: Service: Rear axle only, 16½" x 7" Timken P-Series; Centrifuse brake drums, 868 sq. in. effective lining area; trailer hand valve; tractor protection valve; Cummins 12 cu. ft. air compressor.

Parking: Overland Anchor-Lok air-operated spring brake with cab control (one axle only).

CAB: A&M - Hand welded all aluminum construction; fully insulated with 1½" fiberglass; embossed aluminum cab lining; three point rubber mounting; extruded aluminum door frames; heavy-duty piano-type hinges; tinted safety glass throughout.

ST - Same as A & M models except all steel construction.

CLUTCH: Dana-Spicer 14" 2-plate; multiple lever; pull type with brake; 423 sq. in. area.

DRIVE LINES: Dana-Spicer 1700 series; needle-bearing yoke type.

ELECTRICAL SYSTEM: Delco-Remy Heavy-Duty 12-volt Long-Life Type 250 starter; 55 amp alternator; four Group HG-4A 160 amp. hr. batteries; automatic circuit breakers; hand-made wiring harnesses, heavy duty insulation, wrapped with waterproof covering; all terminals numbered and routed through terminal blocks; double faced front directional signals with 4-way emergency flasher switch; sealed beam headlights; combination stop and tail rear lights.

ENGINE: Cummins "Custom-Rated" diesel, model NHC-250 with lightweight components; 855 cu. in. displacement; horsepower: 250 @ 2,100 RPM; torque: 685 ft. lbs. @ 1,550 RPM; oil bath air cleaner; hi-mount fan; compression release; oil cooler; fuel filter; PT fuel system; full-flow lube oil filter; Luberfiner 750-C by-pass oil filter; corrosion resistor.

EXHAUST SYSTEM: Single 4" vertical system with muffler and guard; stainless steel exhaust flex; ceramic coated standpipe.

FENDERS: Crown steel (rolled type).

FUEL TANK: One 50 gallon lt. wt. steel with heavy-duty mounting brackets; 4" diameter filler opening; tank mounted shut-off cock.

INSTRUMENTS: Tachometer, speedometer, water temperature, ammeter, fuel, oil pressure and air pressure gauges; low air pressure warning light; tilting dash panel; rheostat controlled lighting for all instruments.

RADIATOR: Tube and fin type core with 1,050 sq. in. frontal area; detachable bolt-assembled, aluminum alloy top and bottom tanks; fitted Cadillac "Ther-Mech" aluminum shutter with Peterbilt adjustment mechanism.

SEATS: Driver: Peterbilt-Bostrom deluxe "Thinline".

Passenger: Tool box with upholstered cushion.

STEERING: Ross Model TE-71 cam and lever type; steering ratio: 28 to 1; 22" diameter white steering wheel.

SUSPENSION: Front: Chrome vanadium split-progressive steel springs; spring width: 3½"; length: 48".

Rear: Peterbilt-Hendrickson RSA-340; four rubber load cushions; aluminum saddles, torque rods and walking beams; completely rubber bushed; 52" axle centers; capacity: 34,000 lbs.

TRANSMISSION: Main: A - Dana-Spicer 8544-A; 4-speed; aluminum case and cover.

M&ST - Dana-Spicer 8542-A; 4-speed; iron case and cover.

Auxiliary: A - Dana-Spicer 8035-Q; 3-speed; aluminum case and cover.

M&ST - Dana-Spicer 8031-Q; 3-speed; iron case and cover.

TIRES: 10:00 x 20, 12-ply non-premium nylon highway tread (10 furnished).

WHEELS: 20" x 7.5 light weight, high tensile steel disc (10 furnished).

STD. ACCESSORIES: Dual motor, air operated, independently valved, variable speed, parking type windshield wipers; large adjustable 7" x 16" west coast type, stainless steel backed rear view mirrors; single tone air horn; electric horn; front and rear mud flaps; flexible air piping throughout; insulated floor mats; tow pin; dual inside sun visors; cigar lighter, ash tray, left hand arm rest; red cab reflectors on tractor models; 12-ton jack; wheel wrench, and Operator's Manual.

ALL SPECIFICATIONS ARE SUBJECT TO CHANGE WITHOUT NOTICE

Peterbilt

We offer in our new Panoramic Safe-T-Cab all of the modern, deluxe features and equipment that are possible to build into a cab-over-engine for heavy duty truck transportation.

This custom-built, well ventilated COE cab is furnished in two sizes, regular and sleeper. Note the sleeper compartment illustrated. In addition, a sleeper cab on top (not illustrated) is also available.

The broad panoramic curved (wrap-around) windshield gives the driver a Safe-T-View. The rugged cab construction results in driver protection and safety as well as providing a solid cab, free of rattles and noise. The cab is mounted on rubber.

The engine cover housing inside the cab is instantly removable and permits complete accessibility for minor or major repairs to the engine and its accessories. The cab is hinged for tilting, facilitating engine removal.

Peterbilt MOTORS COMPANY

10700 MacARTHUR BOULEVARD

OAKLAND, CALIFORNIA

The steering gear is located on the left side at the rear of the cab, so that service adjustments and repairs can be quickly and conveniently made. Also shown is the Luberfiner, which is quite accessible. At the extreme right, note the rubber mounted rear cab support.

This is the driver compartment, showing the comfortable, adjustable, driver's seat, the steering wheel and controls, including the clutch, brake, accelerator pedal, emergency brake lever, transmission shift control lever, the instrument panel and Tachograph.

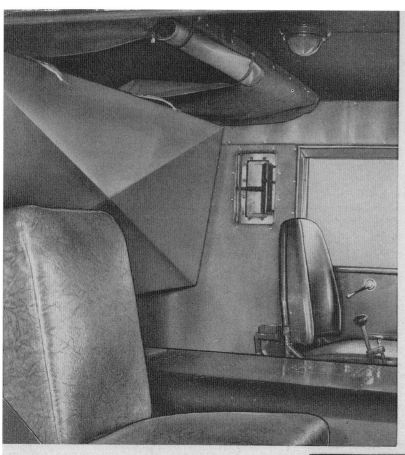

This is the sleeping compartment for use of the extra driver, showing the folding curtains, and the full, legal size, comfortable mattress furnished in all cabs. Here the auxiliary seat is folded forward to accommodate use of the sleeping compartment.

View showing the extra driver's seat and sleeping compartment which folds to the rear of the cab when not in use. Also shown is the insulated section of the engine hood and dome lights, as well as the ventilator of the sleeping compartment.

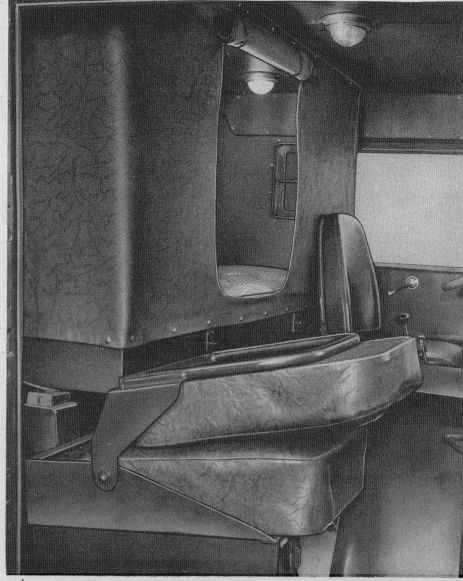

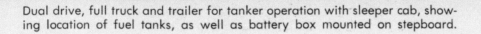

Two-axle tractor with double boxes, showing standard cab (without sleeper). Spare tire and battery are also shown.

Dual drive, full truck and trailer for tanker operation with sleeper cab, showing location of fuel tanks, as well as battery box mounted on stepboard.

Dual drive, full truck and trailer for livestock hauling, with standard cab (without sleeper) is shown, as well as door panel window for driver's convenience, adding additional vision necessary in some instances.

Dual drive tractor with large semi-trailer and dromedary box on tractor.

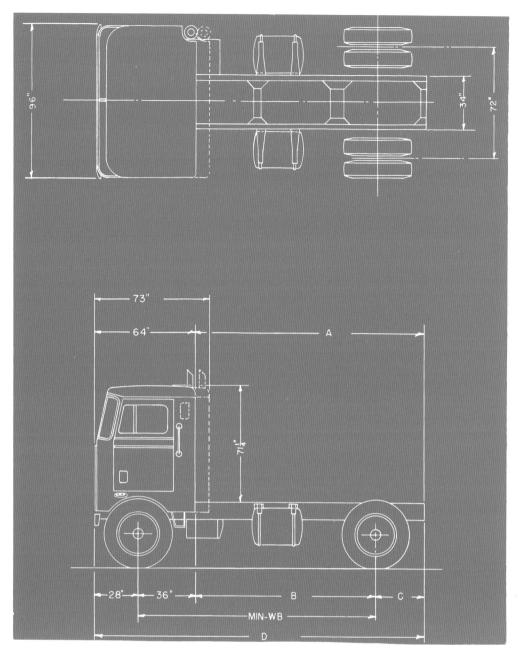

MODEL 281 — C.O.E.

MIN. WHEELBASE	A	B	C	D		SPECIALS
105 1/16″	8′-7 1/16″	5′-9 1/16″	2′-10″	13′-11 1/16″	4 Speed Trans. 2 Speed Axle	Parking brake on axle
110¾″	9′-0¾″	6′-2¾″	2′-10″	14′-4¾″	5 Speed Trans. 2 Speed Axle	Parking brake on axle
120 11/16″	9′-10 11/16″	7′-0 11/16″	2′-10″	15′-2 11/16″	10 Speed Trans.*	Parking brake on axle
121 15/16″	10′-1⅝″	7′-3⅝″	2′-10″	15′-5⅝″	10 Speed Trans.*	Drum type driveshaft Parking brake
143 11/16″	11′-9 11/16″	8′-11 11/16″	2′-10″	17′-1 11/16″	4 Speed Trans. 3 Speed Aux.	Parking brake on axle
146⅝″	12′-0⅝″	9′-2⅝″	2′-10″	17′-4⅝″	4 Speed Trans. 3 Speed Aux.	Drum or disc driveshaft parking brake
149⅜″	12′-3⅜″	9′-5⅜″	2′-10″	17′-7⅜″	5 Speed Trans. 3 Speed Aux.	Parking brake on axle
152 5/16″	12′-6 5/16″	9′-8 5/16″	2′-10″	17′-10 5/16″	5 Speed Trans. 3 Speed Aux.	Drum or disc driveshaft parking brake

* R-96 & R-960 only

Notes: Above minimum wheelbases are with standard rear axles. Different rear axle or additional tanks require special layout and are subject to factory approval.

Wheelbase must not be less than:

105 1/16″	to accommodate 1—50 gal. tank
116″	to accommodate 1—70 gal. tank
112½″	to accommodate 2—50 gal. tanks
116″	to accommodate 1—50 gal. tank & 1—70 gal. tank
124½″	to accommodate 2—70 gal. tanks

Because of drive shaft limitations it is not possible to make wheelbases between the minimum shown and less than 2½″ longer than the minimum, for a given transmission setup.

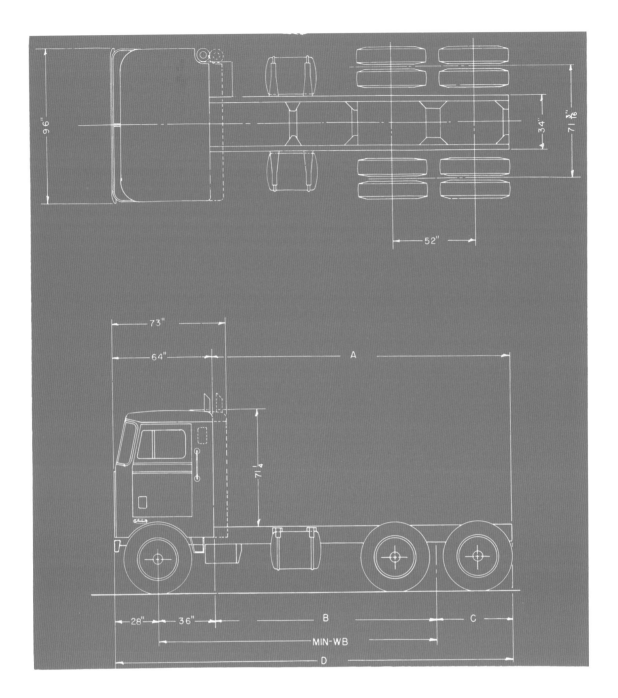

MODEL 351 — C.O.E.

MIN. WHEELBASE	A	B	C	D	SPECIALS	
141½"	12'-9½"	8'-9½"	4'-0"	18'-1½"	10 Speed Trans.*	Parking brake on axle
142¾"	12'-10¾"	8'-10¾"	4'-0"	18'-2¾"	10 Speed Trans.*	Drum type driveshaft Parking brake
164⅞"	14'-8⅞"	10'-8⅞"	4'-0"	20'-0⅞"	4 Speed Trans. 3 Speed Aux.	Parking brake on axle
167 13/16"	14-11 13/16"	10'-11 13/16"	4'-0"	20'-3 13/16"	4 Speed Trans. 3 Speed Aux.	Drum or disc type driveshaft parking brake
170 9/16"	15'-2 9/16"	11'-2 9/16"	4'-0"	20'-6 9/16"	5 Speed Trans. 3 Speed Aux.	Parking brake on axle 5 Speed Trans.
173½"	15'-5½"	11'-5½"	4'-0"	20'-9½"	5 Speed Trans. 3 Speed Aux.	Drum or disc type driveshaft parking brake

* R-96 & R-960 only

Notes: Above minimum wheelbases are with standard rear axles. Different rear axle or additional tanks require special layout and are subject to factory approval.

Wheelbase must not be less than:
147⅝" to accommodate 2—70 gal. tanks.
1—50 gal., 2—50 gal., 1—50 gal. & 1—70 gal., 1—70 gal. are possible on all minimum wheelbases shown.

Because of drive shaft limitations some wheelbases less than 2½" longer than minimum may not be possible.

Peterbilt

DON'T JUNK IT·DON'T FIX IT·REBUILD IT

with a (Peterbilt) REBUILD KIT

CUT YOUR NEW TRUCK COSTS

Frame crossmembers and fifth wheel are installed at factory. Custom-engineered to your requirements.

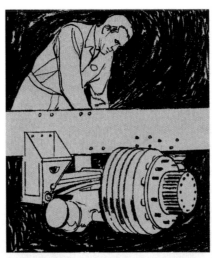

Rear axle and suspension are installed on the Peterbilt Rebuild Kit in the model of your choice.

Engine, transmission and axle are stripped from your old truck at Peterbilt distributor's facilities, or by you.

GOT A TIRED TRUCK? GOT A WRECK?

No matter what the model, no matter what the make, on-highway or off, if you have a heavy-duty truck engine, transmission and rear axle, you can install them in a brand-new Peterbilt Rebuild Chassis and...

RIGHT DOWN THE MIDDLE!

The Peterbilt Rebuild Kit is a complete cab and chassis unit. All new. All guaranteed. All ready to mount your engine and transmission and be registered as a current year Peterbilt for LESS THAN HALF THE COST!

ngine and transmission are installed
a single unit in new mounts provided.

Paint the cab and put your name on the door.

THEN...

Re-register what **was** a tired old truck to a current year model Peterbilt!

That's all there is to it. You can have the installation made at the complete, factory-approved facilities of your Peterbilt distributor or, if you're equipped, you can do the work in your own shop. Either way, you'll save HALF THE COST or MORE!

TAKE YOUR CHOICE OF MODELS

AIR-ASSISTED FULL-TILT ALUMINUM HOOD MODEL

A touch of an air valve makes the hood easy to tilt with one hand.

Combines the strength and convenience of a full-tilt hood with modular construction to keep repair costs low in case of accident. Exclusive Peterbilt features allow you to check and refill oil and water **without** lifting hood!

STANDARD CONVENTIONAL includes:

CAB

Insulated aluminum or steel cab with floor mat, tinted glass windows, fixed rear window, leather driver's seat, tool box with pad, right hand seat, chrome hood handles, painted hood latches, glove compartment.

Hinged wood grain inlay instrument panel includes tachometer, speedometer, water temperature gauge, ammeter, fuel, oil pressure and air pressure gauges, toggle switches, starter button, dimmer switch.

Accessories include dual windshield wipers, rear view mirrors, air horn, electrical horn, cigar lighter and ash tray, inside door locks, leather sun visors, driver's arm rest, left hand cab side grab handle.

All interiors painted Peterbilt Brown.

FRAME

Aluminum (10½" x 33') or steel (10⅜" x 32') with brackets assembled to back of cab. Includes installed aluminum bumper plus front and rear motor supports.

accessories include mud shield between bumper and fender and rubber fender blocks.

ENGINE

Tube and fin-type core radiator with 1,050 square inch frontal area. Installed with Cadillac shutters. Radiator hoses and connections.

Ceramic-coated exhaust stack, muffler, stainless steel flex tubing, piping from engine manifold, and muffler guard. (Exhaust items furnished loose.)

Brake, throttle and clutch pedals with linkage to engine and clutch. Ventilator screens. Air piping from engine to air cleaner.

SUSPENSION AND STEERING

Timken FE-900-N front axle with iron or aluminum hubs, including standard front springs, assembled.

Ross TE-71 steering gear, installed with wheel, horn button and drag link. Column assembly.

ELECTRICAL SYSTEM

Single headlights. Complete cab and chassis wiring harness. Stop, directional, instrument panel and cab dome lights. Battery cables and circuit breakers with wiring for five I.C.C. lights.

AIR SYSTEM

Two air tanks, treadle, safety, synchronizing and double check valves. Air governor, stoplight switch and air manifolds.

SHEET METAL

Hood, fenders, fender skirts, fuel tank step, fifty gallon steel fuel tank, battery box. (All assembled with required brackets.) Brackets for air cleaner and luberfiner.

YOUR CHOICE OF OPTIONAL EQUIPMENT

Aluminum or steel 9" frame rails (subject to engineering approval for job application).

Tractor taper, reverse taper, or square end of frame crossmember.

Standard frame will accommodate wheelbase up to approximately 300" for dual or single drive rear axles. (Maximum practical wheelbase is 255".)

Gunite spoke hubs in lieu of standard aluminum or steel hubs.

Trailer connections (assembled frame only) with locations for truck or tractor operation.

Built-in turbo cowling in hood panel for kits constructed around turbo charged engines.

All exterior surfaces prime finished—ready for final paint. Customized painting at factory is available.

Safety view window, right hand door.

FULL HYDRAULIC ASSIST TILTS YOUR PETERBILT CAB 90°—WITH EASE!

There's no strain lowering your Peterbilt C.O.E. cab. The easily operated hydraulic assist handles 100% of the work—and leaves **every** part of the engine and cooling system out in the open for quick and easy repairs and maintenance!

C.O.E. MODEL includes:

CAB

Insulated 63", 73", 80" or 86" aluminum cab installed on frame with all mounting brackets. Insulated motor cover, floor mat, right hand half seat. All cylinders, hydraulic valves and lines to tilt cab. Cab lock-down devices and main transmission shift lever. All cabs except 63" equipped with sleeper bunk, curtain, extra dome light, sleeper compartment, vent and baggage compartment. (Designate size of cab when ordering.) Safety view window, right hand door.

Hinged wood grain inlay instrument panel includes tachometer, speedometer, water temperature gauge, ammeter, fuel, oil pressure and air gauges. Toggle switches, starter button and dimmer switch.

Accessories include dual windshield wipers, rear view mirrors, air horn, electrical horn, cigar lighter and ash tray, inside door locks, leather sun visors, and driver's arm rest.

All interiors painted Peterbilt Brown.

FRAME

Steel frame (10⅜" x 32') or aluminum (10½" x 33') with brackets assembled to back of cab. Includes installed aluminum bumper plus front and rear motor supports.

Accessories include left and right grab handles, manifest pocket on engine cover, quilted blanket for engine cover, and engine oil gauge and tube.

ENGINE

Tube and fin-type core radiator with 1,050 square inch frontal area. Installed with Cadillac shutters. Radiator hoses and connections.

Ceramic-coated exhaust stack, muffler, stainless steel flex tubing, piping from engine manifold, and muffler guard. (Exhaust items furnished loose.)

Brake, throttle and clutch pedals with linkage to engine and clutch. Ventilator screens. Air piping from engine to air cleaner.

SUSPENSION AND STEERING

FE-900-N front axle with iron or aluminum hubs including standard front springs, assembled.

Gemmer 7J025 steering gear installed with 7JM75 column assembly. Double universal Spicer steering shaft, steering wheel and arm.

ELECTRICAL SYSTEM

Dual headlights. Complete cab and chassis wiring harness. Stop, directional, instrument panel and cab dome lights. Battery cables and circuit breakers with wiring for five I.C.C. lights.

SHEET METAL

Battery box and fifty gallon steel fuel tank assembled with brackets. Brackets for air cleaner and luberfiner.

AIR SYSTEM

Two air tanks, treadle, safety, synchronizing and double check valves. Air governor, stoplight switch and air manifolds.

YOUR CHOICE OF OPTIONAL EQUIPMENT

Aluminum or steel 9" frame rails (subject to engineering approval for job application).

Tractor taper, reverse taper, or square end of frame crossmember.

Standard frame will accommodate wheelbase up to approximately 300" for dual or single drive rear axles. (Maximum practical wheelbase is 255".)

Gunite spoke hubs in lieu of standard aluminum or steel hubs.

Trailer connections (assembled frame only) with locations for truck or tractor operation.

All exterior surfaces prime finished—ready for final paint. Customized painting at factory is available.

Access door for oil fill and dip stick located on pedestal of right hand companion seat.

Single or dual exhaust cut-outs.

THE PETERBUILT REBUILD KIT

Includes all the road-proven features available on the newest Peterbilt trucks with the classic design and extra-quality engineering that have made Peterbilt the acknowledged leader in the heavy-duty field.

Instead of getting "junkman's prices" for your old components—or the worry and higher maintenance costs of a "patch-up" repair job—you'll have a current-year model Peterbilt, ready to give you years of new-truck service, new-truck comfort, and money-saving new-truck efficiency!

BUT ONE WORD OF CAUTION: Make sure your engine, transmission, suspension and axle have a lot more miles left in them—because you're installing them in a Peterbilt—the Rebuild Kit that's built to last!

The Specifications are Yours—The Standards are Peterbilt's.

PETERBILT MOTORS COMPANY

General Offices and Plant—38801 Cherry St., Newark (Oakland Area), Calif. 94560   (415) 797-3555

Off-the-Highway
Heavy Duty Trucks
MODEL 381

PETERBILT
MODEL 381

In this booklet we illustrate and describe a few of the basic features of PETERBILT Model 381 heavy duty trucks which have been engineered and built specifically for off-highway applications.

It would be impossible in a booklet of this size to describe all of the very special heavy duty models for various off-highway applications. However, we have shown a few, and wish to point out in the following pages of this booklet the various basic standard features of this truck, and many optional units and accessories that can be engineered to the truck for any specific application in the various fields of operation in which the truck may be used.

This Model 381 is used in dump truck operation as a complete truck, or tractor truck with semi-trailer, for construction, mining, aggregate and any other application where a dump truck might be used. In oil field operations they are used for hauling drilling rigs, pipe line equipment, etc. They are popular in logging, lumber hauling and all types of operations where loads of large size and weight make it necessary for a very rugged truck to be used.

This model is constructed of all steel, which includes all sheetmetal work. Frames are of double construction, and sometimes triple, and material is of chrome manganese heat treated steel alloy of a very high tensile strength. All frame castings are of a nickel steel alloy.

Optional types and sizes of engines are used, including Diesel, gasoline and butane. Available also are torque converters, Hydrotarders, power steering, overwidth heavy duty axles to accommodate larger tires, extra large radiators to meet climatic conditions where severe heating problems might be encountered. Fuel tanks are well protected with heavy boiler plate shields, Diamonette tread plate fenders, radiator and lamp guards and many other protecting devices are supplied. Aeroquip flexible air, oil and fuel lines are used extensively throughout the truck.

Cabs, radiators and many other essential parts are mounted in rubber, for protection against breakage and failures in the heavy service and severe usage these trucks are subjected to.

Peterbilt MOTORS COMPANY
10700 MacARTHUR BOULEVARD
OAKLAND, CALIFORNIA

The front view shows the general heavy construction, the heavy duty bumper, heavy radiator guard mounted in rubber which protects the radiator core from external injury, the shielded headlights and the heavy Diamonette tread plate fenders. Cast steel bronze bushed spring eyes are shown on front end of front springs.

This illustration shows the heavy double frame construction with its rigid crossmembers, heavy duty axles and a "stinger" type rear end of frame. A full depth, full length crossmember may be had in place of the "stinger." The cab is supported on three rubber mountings and exhaust pipe and muffler are well shielded with heavy mesh metal protector shield.

1

This illustration shows the construction of the "walk-on" type of heavy duty fenders, facilitating easy access for engine maintenance. Wheelbases of various lengths are optional. The "pop out" windshield glass is set in rubber to resist shock, afford a tight seal and to provide an additional safety feature. All accessories such as side view mirrors, turn signals and oil filter are securely mounted.

This tractor truck shows our extra wide "tropic radiator" which is supplied on trucks for operation under conditions of extreme heat. The heavy duty radiator core, as well as the radiator protector guard are mounted in rubber and relieved of the strains of severe operating conditions. The battery box is between the steel steps under the running board. Oil bath air cleaner is accessible for servicing.

2

This model tractor truck is designed for operation in muddy sugar cane fields. The front axle has been set back to afford a shorter turning radius and is equipped with power steering. It is also equipped with an Allison torque converter. Rear axles are of suitable width to allow the mounting of 16:00x21 single tires, which give this unit greater flotation.

This is another unit used in sugar cane hauling and is equipped with three driving axles, power steering and Allison torque converter. This unit has a long wheelbase, and our own special PETERBILT power transfer case is used between the dual rear driving axles and the front drive axle.

This view shows a standard off-highway logger with double frame, equipped with a Timken SFDD-4600 rear axle, two fuel tanks protected with heavy plate shields, as well as wood platform on top of cab, and large oil bath air cleaner.

This 3 axle tractor incorporates a triple frame, a Shuler 18,000 lb. front axle with Budd Steel Wheels; 13 3/16" bolt circles; a Timken SFDD-4600 rear axle; Hydrotarder Brake and power steering.

This 3-axle tractor incorporates a triple frame; a Shuler 18,000# front axle with Budd Steel Wheels; 13 3/16" bolt circles; a Timken SFDD-4600 Rear Axle; Hydrotarder Brake and Power Steering. It pulls a semi-trailer with a 20 cu. yd. Rock Body.

This heavy duty dump truck has a triple frame; a Shuler 18,000# Front Axle with Budd Steel Wheels, 13 3/16" bolt circles; a Timken SFDD-4600 Rear Axle with 87⅞" wide track; Allison Torque Converter and Power Steering. It carries a 16 cu.yd. Rock Body.

This view shows the special oil tank, oil filter and flexible lines used in connection with Allison torque converter and Allison 3 speed transmission. Under the running board is an air starter reservoir, used when air starting of engine is required because of unusual operating conditions.

6

This view shows crossmember mounting support for Allison torque converter and transmission, as well as flexible hydraulic lines used in connection with this equipment. This combination permits shifting of the transmission under full torque, and provides a hydraulic brake to eliminate use of service brakes, except for making a complete stop.

7

This view shows the front drive steering axle and Vickers Hydraulic Power Steering Booster, linkage, and Aeroquipt hydraulic lines. The fuel tank is shown in the upper right hand portion of the picture.

8

This view shows the heavy duty front drive steering axle, showing spring mountings, steering knuckles, pump and hydraulic lines used in connection with power steering. Front drive axles are particularly desirable in muddy sugar cane fields and other soft terrain encountered in off-highway operations.

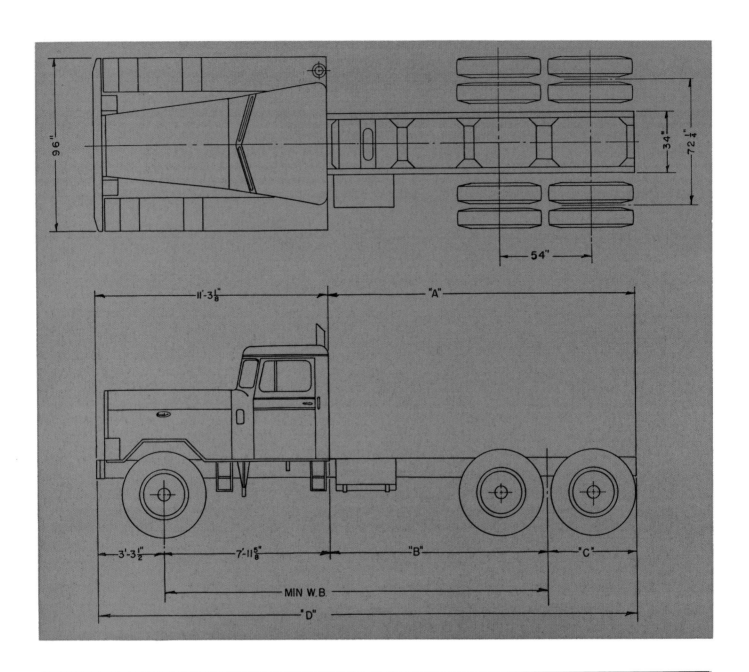

MIN. WHEELBASE	A	B	C	D	TRANSMISSIONS
182¾"	11'-5⅛"	7'-3⅛"	4'-2"	22'-8¼"	4 Speed Trans.—3 Speed Aux.
188⅜"	11'-10¾"	7'-8¾"	4'-2"	23'-1⅞"	5 Speed Trans.—3 Speed Aux.
201⅝"	13'-0"	8'-10"	4'-2"	24'-3⅛"	10B1120 Trans.—3 Speed Aux.

NOTES:
Wheelbases to be not less than shown to accommodate the following fuel tank combinations:

1-100 Gallon Tank 187" W.B.
1- 50 Gallon Tank 176⅛" W.B.
1- 60 Gallon Tank 176⅛" W.B.
1- 70 Gallon Tank 176⅛" W.B.
2- 50 Gallon Tanks 188" W.B.
2- 60 Gallon Tanks 202" W.B.
2- 70 Gallon Tanks 209" W.B.

NOTE: These W.B. & Tank Capacity figures are for trucks without power steering. Power steering will necessitate more wheelbase for each tank setup. Above minimum wheelbases are with SFDD 4600 rear axle. SFD 4600 rear axle requires 6⅝" less wheelbase in each case. Other transmissions, different rear axles, additional fuel tanks, 1800 series drivelines, power steering, different engines and extra wide axle spacing for oversize tires require special layout and are subject to factory approval.

Model
451/356
and the **IPB/QR** Manuals

Sam Brown worked in Parts Sales. his career began in 1952 and spanned 37 years. Before the advent of illustrations in parts books, he would take pictures of the various models to more readily identify components. So, when a customer called requesting a particular part, Sam could look at the pictures and confer with the customer to identify the proper part. This eventually led to the IPB or Illustrated Parts Books, circa 1963.

Incidentally, Bert Johnson was known to maintain illustrations and parts lists in his desk for quick reference. This led to the QR or Quick Reference Manual.

The model 451 and 356 were built for Ringsby in Denver., Colorado. these trucks were unusual in that they had a flat or pancake engine located below the frame rails, and the sleeper on top of the cab. Later on, these trucks and similar trucks that were built by Kenworth were brought back to the factory, cabs and engines removed, then fitted with a conventional engine and a special 76 inch sleeper/cab similar to the model 351COE sleeper/cab.

Peterbilt model 451

Model 451/356
Continued

451 C.O. E. – October 1956   Ringsby Freight Lines
Sam Brown Photos

Model
451/356
Continued

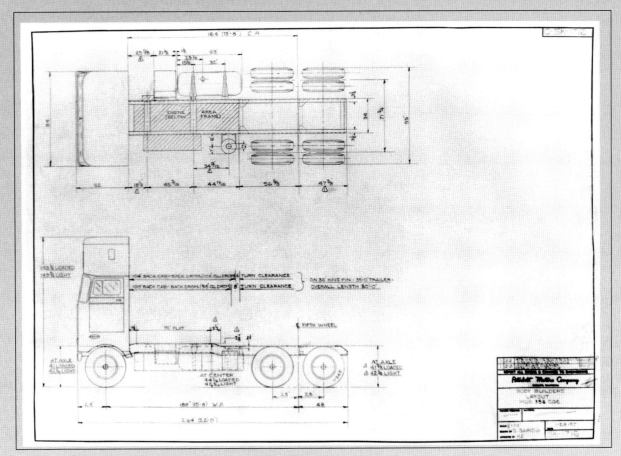

Peterbilt model 356

451 C.O. E. – October 1956   Ringsby Freight Lines
Sam Brown Photos

451 C.O. E. – October 1956   Ringsby Freight Lines
Sam Brown Photos

Model
451/356

Continued

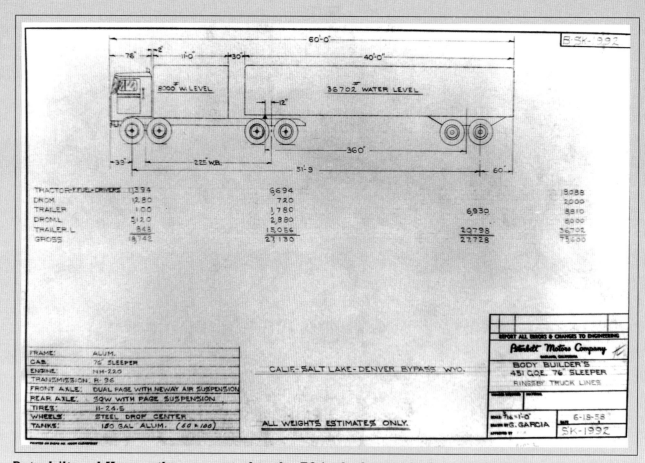

Peterbilt and Kenworth — converted to the 76 inch sleeper/cab.

MODEL 282

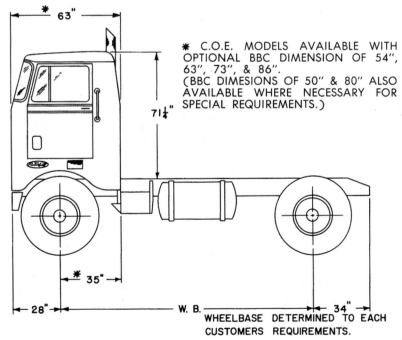

63"

71¼"

✳ 35"

28"

34"

W. B.

WHEELBASE DETERMINED TO EACH
CUSTOMERS REQUIREMENTS.

✳ C.O.E. MODELS AVAILABLE WITH
OPTIONAL BBC DIMENSION OF 54",
63", 73", & 86".
(BBC DIMESIONS OF 50" & 80" ALSO
AVAILABLE WHERE NECESSARY FOR
SPECIAL REQUIREMENTS.)

MODEL 282
STANDARD SPECIFICATIONS

GVW 34,000 lbs.   **GCW 76,800 lbs.**

FRAME: A - 10½" x 3½" x ¾" (flange) x ½" (web) extruded aluminum alloy with aluminum crossmembers and gussets; std. chassis wt.: 10,350 lbs. (based on 10'-7" loadspace).

M - 9" x 3½" x 7/32" or 10-3/8" x 3½" x ¼" heat treated alloy steel with aluminum crossmembers and gussets; std. chassis wt.: 10,350 lbs. or 10,470 lbs. (based on 10'-7" loadspace).

ST - 9" x 3½" x 7/32" or 10-3/8" x 3½" x ¼" heat-treated alloy steel with steel crossmembers and gussets; std. chassis wt.: 10,500 lbs. or 10,620 lbs. (based on 10'-7" loadspace).

Completely bolted frame construction; SAE Grade 5 heat-treated bolts and double length nuts throughout.

AXLES: Front: A&M - Rockwell-Standard FE-900-N with aluminum hubs; capacity: 11,000 lbs.; nominal track: 77".

ST - Same as A&M models except with iron hubs.

Rear: Rockwell-Standard R-170, hypoid single reduction with aluminum hubs; capacity: 23,000 lbs.; nominal track: 72"; ratios optional.

BRAKES: Service: Rear axle only, 16½" x 7" Timken P-Series; Centrifuse brake drums, 434 sq. in. effective lining area; trailer hand valve; tractor protection valve; Cummins 12 cu. ft. air compressor.

Parking: Overland Anchor-Lok air-operated spring brake with cab control.

CAB: 63" 90° tilt cab; hand welded all aluminum construction; fully insulated with 1½" fiberglass; embossed aluminum cab lining; independent hydraulic system controls cab tilting; positive dual locking cab hold-down devices; extruded aluminum door frames; heavy-duty piano-type hinges; safety view window mounted in right hand door; tinted safety glass throughout.

CLUTCH: Dana-Spicer 14" 2-plate; multiple lever; pull type with brake; 423 sq. in. area.

DRIVE LINES: Dana-Spicer 1700 Series; needle bearing; yoke type.

ELECTRICAL SYSTEM: Delco-Remy Heavy-Duty 12-volt Long-Life Type 250 starter; 55 amp alternator; four Group HG-4A 160 amp. hr. batteries; automatic circuit breakers; hand-made wiring harnesses, heavy-duty insulation, wrapped with waterproof covering; all terminals numbered and routed through terminal blocks; double faced front directional signals with 4-way emergency flasher switch; dual sealed beam headlights; combination stop and tail rear lights.

ENGINE: Cummins "Custom-Rated" diesel, model NHC-250 with lightweight components; 855 cu. in. displacement; horsepower: 250 @ 2,100 RPM; torque: 685 ft. lbs. @ 1,550 RPM; oil bath air cleaner; hi-mount fan; compression release; oil cooler; fuel filter; PT fuel system; full-flow lube oil filter; Luberfiner 750-C by-pass oil filter; corrosion resistor.

EXHAUST SYSTEM: Single 4" vertical system with muffler and guard; stainless steel exhaust flex; ceramic coated standpipe.

FUEL TANK: One 50 gallon lt. wt. steel with heavy-duty mounting brackets; 4" diameter filler opening; tank mounted shut-off cock.

INSTRUMENTS: Tachometer, speedometer, water temperature, ammeter, fuel, oil pressure and air pressure gauges; low air pressure warning light; tilting dash panel; rheostat controlled lighting for all instruments.

RADIATOR: Tube and fin type core with 1,050 sq. in. frontal area; detachable bolt-assembled, aluminum top and bottom tanks; fitted Cadillac "Ther-Mech" aluminum shutter with Peterbilt adjustment mechanism.

SEAT: Driver: Peterbilt-Bostrom Deluxe "Thinline".

Passenger: Peterbilt half-seat with lower storage compartment.

STEERING: Gemmer Model 500, cam and lever type; steering ratio: 28.4 to 1; 22" diameter white steering wheel.

SUSPENSION: Front: Chrome vanadium split-progressive steel springs; spring width: 3½"; length: 48".

Rear: Peterbilt split progressive spring with cast eye; spring width: 3½", length: 54".

TRANSMISSION: Fuller RTO-915; 15-speed with overdrive; iron case and cover.

TIRES: 10:00 x 20, 12-ply, non-premium nylon highway tread (6 furnished).

WHEELS: 20" x 7.5 Hi-Tensile lightweight steel (6 furnished).

STD. ACCESSORIES: Dual motor, air operated, independently valved, variable speed, parking type windshield wipers; large adjustable 7" x 16" west coast type, stainless steel backed rear view mirrors; single tone air horn; electric horn; rear mud flaps; flexible air piping throughout; insulated floor mats; tow pin; dual inside sun visors; cigar lighter, ash tray; right and left side arm rest; red cab reflectors on tractor models; 12-ton jack; wheel wrench, and Operator's Manual.

ALL SPECIFICATIONS ARE SUBJECT TO CHANGE WITHOUT NOTICE

MODEL 352

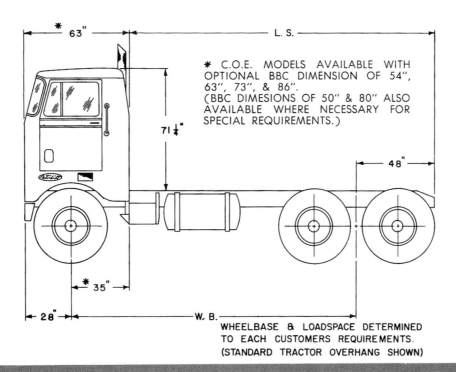

63"

L. S.

* C.O.E. MODELS AVAILABLE WITH OPTIONAL BBC DIMENSION OF 54", 63", 73", & 86". (BBC DIMESIONS OF 50" & 80" ALSO AVAILABLE WHERE NECESSARY FOR SPECIAL REQUIREMENTS.)

71¼"

48"

* 35"

28"

W. B.

WHEELBASE & LOADSPACE DETERMINED TO EACH CUSTOMERS REQUIREMENTS. (STANDARD TRACTOR OVERHANG SHOWN)

PETERBILT MOTORS COMPANY

38801 CHERRY STREET • NEWARK, CALIFORNIA 94560 • TELEPHONE (415) 797-3555

MODEL 352
STANDARD SPECIFICATIONS

GVW 49,000 lbs.   **GCW 76,800 lbs.**

FRAME: A - 10½" x 3½" x ¾" (flange) x ½" (web) extruded aluminum alloy with aluminum crossmembers and gussets; std. chassis wt.: 12,550 lbs. (based on 14' - 9" loadspace), or 12,850 lbs. (based on 21' - 3" loadspace).

M - 9" x 3½" x 7/32" or 10-3/8" x 3½" x ¼" heat-treated alloy steel with aluminum crossmembers and gussets; std. chassis wt.: 12,550 lbs. (based on 14' - 9" loadspace) or 12,975 lbs. (based on 21' - 3" loadspace), respectively with 9" or 10-3/8" frame rails.

ST - 9" x 3½" x 7/32" or 10-3/8" x 3½" x ¼" heat-treated alloy steel with steel crossmembers and gussets; std. chassis wt.: 12,900 lbs. (based on 14' - 9" loadspace) or 13,350 lbs. (based on 21' - 3" loadspace), respectively with 9" or 10-3/8" frame rails.

Completely bolted frame construction; SAE Grade 5 heat-treated bolts and double length nuts throughout.

AXLES: Front: A&M - Rockwell-Standard FE-900-N with aluminum hubs; capacity: 11,000 lbs.; nominal track: 77".

ST - Same as A&M models except with iron hubs.

Rear: A&M - Rockwell-Standard SQHD, hypoid single reduction tandem axle, with aluminum hubs; driver controlled interaxle differential; capacity: 38,000 lbs.; nominal track: 71-3/16"; ratios optional.

ST - Same as A&M models except with iron hubs.

BRAKES: Service: Rear axle only, 16½" x 7" Timken P-Series; Centrifuse brake drums, 868 sq. in. effective lining area; trailer hand valve; tractor protection valve; Cummins 12 cu. ft. air compressor.

Parking: Overland Anchor-Lok air-operated spring brake with cab control (one axle only).

CAB: 63" 90° tilt cab; hand welded all aluminum construction; fully insulated with 1½" fiberglass; embossed aluminum cab lining; independent hydraulic system controls cab tilting; positive dual locking, cab hold-down devices; extruded aluminum door frames; heavy-duty piano-type hinges; safety view window mounted in right hand door; tinted safety glass throughout.

CLUTCH: Dana-Spicer 14" 2-plate; multiple lever; pull type with brake; 423 sq. in. area.

DRIVE LINES: Dana-Spicer 1700 series; needle-bearing yoke type.

ELECTRICAL SYSTEM: Delco-Remy Heavy-Duty 12-volt Long-Life Type 250 starter; 55 amp alternator; four Group HG-4A 160 amp. hr. batteries; automatic circuit breakers; hand-made wiring harnesses, heavy-duty insulation, wrapped with waterproof covering; all terminals numbered and routed through terminal block; double faced front directional signals with 4-way emergency flasher switch; dual sealed beam headlights; combination stop and tail rear lights.

ENGINE: Cummins "Custom - Rated" diesel, model NHC-250 with lightweight components; 855 cu. in. displacement; horsepower: 250 @ 2,100 RPM; torque: 685 ft. lbs. @ 1,550 RPM; oil bath air cleaner; hi-mount fan; compression release; oil cooler; fuel filter; PT fuel system; full-flow lube oil filter; Luberfiner 750-C by-pass oil filter; corrosion resistor.

EXHAUST SYSTEM: Single 4" vertical system with muffler and guard; stainless steel exhaust flex; ceramic coated standpipe.

FUEL TANK: One 50 gallon lt. wt. steel with heavy-duty mounting brackets; 4" diameter filler opening; tank mounted shut-off cock.

INSTRUMENTS: Tachometer, speedometer, water temperature, ammeter, fuel, oil pressure and air pressure gauges; low air pressure warning light; tilting dash panel; rheostat controlled lighting for all instruments.

RADIATOR: Tube and fin type core with 1,050 sq. in. frontal area; detachable bolt-assembled, aluminum top and bottom tanks; fitted Cadillac "Ther-Mech" aluminum shutter with Peterbilt adjustment mechanism.

SEAT: Driver: Peterbilt-Bostrom deluxe "Thinline".

Passenger: Peterbilt half-seat with lower storage compartment.

STEERING: Gemmer Model 500, cam and lever type; steering ratio: 28.4 to 1; 22" diameter white steering wheel.

SUSPENSION: Front: Chrome vanadium split-progressive steel springs; spring width: 3½"; length: 48".

Rear: Peterbilt-Hendrickson RSA-340; four rubber load cushions; aluminum saddles; torque rods and walking beams; completely rubber bushed; 52" axle centers; capacity: 34,000 lbs.

TRANSMISSION: Fuller RTO-915; 15-speed with overdrive; iron case and cover.

TIRES: 10:00 x 20, 12-ply non-premium nylon, highway tread (10 furnished).

WHEELS: 20" x 7.5 light weight, high tensile steel disc (10 furnished).

STD. ACCESSORIES: Dual motor, air operated, independently valved, variable speed, parking type windshield wipers; large adjustable 7" x 16" west coast type, stainless steel backed rear view mirrors; single tone air horn; electric horn, rear mud flaps; flexible air piping throughout; insulated floor mats; tow pin; dual inside sun visors; cigar lighter, ash tray; right and left side arm rest; red cab reflectors on tractor models; 12-ton jack; wheel wrench, and Operator's Manual.

ALL SPECIFICATIONS ARE SUBJECT TO CHANGE WITHOUT NOTICE

Peterbilt

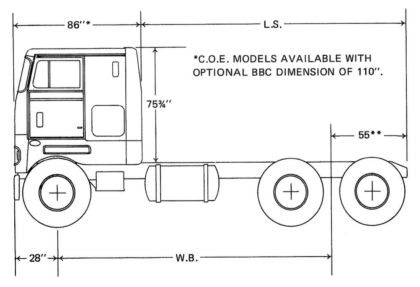

86''*   L.S.

*C.O.E. MODELS AVAILABLE WITH
OPTIONAL BBC DIMENSION OF 110''.

75¾''

55**

28''   W.B.

*The above illustration may include optional equipment and
accessories and may not include all standard equipment.*

WHEELBASE & LOADSPACE DETERMINED TO EACH
CUSTOMER'S REQUIREMENTS.** STANDARD TRACTOR
OVERHANG DEPENDS UPON SUSPENSION — CONSULT
ENGINEERING DATA BOOK.

PETERBILT MOTORS COMPANY
A DIVISION OF PACCAR
GENERAL OFFICES: 38801 CHERRY STREET   •   NEWARK, CALIFORNIA 94560
TENNESSEE PLANT: 430 MYATT DRIVE   •   MADISON, TENNESSEE 37115

3-1-76

STANDARD SPECIFICATIONS

FRAME: Completely bolted construction; SAE Grade heat-treated bolts, lock nuts and hardened washers.

Model 352-A: 10½″ × 3½″ × ¾″ (flange) × ½″ (web) extruded aluminum alloy with aluminum crossmembers and gussets.

Model 352-M: 10⅜″ × 3½″ × ¼″ or 9″ × 3½″ × 7/32″ heat-treated alloy steel with aluminum crossmembers and gussets.

Model 352-S: 10⅜″ × 3½″ × ¼″ or 9″ × 3½″ × 7/32″ heat-treated alloy steel with steel crossmembers and gussets.

Wheelbase and loadspace to Customer's requirements.

AXLES: Front: Rockwell-Standard, tractor: FF-931-TW; full trucks: FF-931-P; with aluminum hubs; oil seals; capacity: 12,000 lbs.; nominal track: 78⅜″.

Rear: Rockwell-Standard SQHP hypoid single reduction tandem axle; aluminum hubs; oil seals, outboard mounted drums, driver controlled inter-axle differential with dash indicator light; capacity 38,000 lbs.; nominal track: 71-3/16″, ratios optional.

BRAKES: Service: Front axle:—tractors: 15″ × 4″, flat cam type; 250 sq. in. effective lining with automatic limit valve.

—full trucks: 16½″ × 5″, "S" cam type; 312 sq. in. effective lining with automatic limit valve.

Rear axle: 16½″ × 7″; "S" Cam Type; 868 sq. in. effective lining area; trailer hand valve; tractor protection valve; B-W 12 CFM air compressor. Dual air system.

Parking: Air-operated spring brake with cab control (one axle only).

Anti-skid system: All axles.

STEERING: Gemmer Model 500, worm and roller type; steering ratio: 32.5 to 1:22″ diameter white steering wheel.

SUSPENSION: Front: Chrome vanadium split-progressive steel springs; spring width: 3½″; length: 48″.

Rear: Peterbilt tandem four spring, six point frame attachment; Longitudinal torque arms to center frame bracket; 52″ axle centers; capacity: 34,000 lbs.

ENGINE: Detroit diesel, model 8V-92TA with lightweight components; 736 cu. in. displacement: horsepower: 430 SAE @ 2,100 RPM; torque: 1200 ft. lbs. @ 1400 RPM; dry air cleaner; oil cooler; fuel filter; full flow lube oil filter; pulley driven alternator; ventless (rapid warm up) thermostat.

EXHAUST SYSTEM: Dual 4″ vertical system with muffler, muffler guard, stainless steel exhaust flex tubing, stainless steel clamps, ceramic coated standpipe and automatic cab tilt release and reseal connection.

RADIATOR: Tube and fin type core with high capacity 1512 sq. in. frontal area; detachable bolt-assembled, aluminum alloy top and bottom tanks. Chrome stainless steel bugscreen.

ELECTRICAL SYSTEM: Delco-Remy Heavy-Duty 12-volt Long-Life Type 250 starter; 85 amp alternator; four Group 4, batteries, 800 cold cranking amps @ 0°F; automatic circuit breakers; hand-made wiring harnesses, heavy-duty insulation wrapped with braided covering. All terminals numbered and routed through terminal blocks; mounted inside the cab; double-faced front directional signals; sealed beam headlights; combination stop and tail lights; automatically actuated back-up light and turn signals with 4-way emergency flasher switch. Applicable marker lights and reflectors. Key ignition.

TRANSMISSION: Fuller RTO-12513, 13 speed with iron case and cover.

CLUTCH: Dana-Spicer 15½″ self adjusting, angle spring 2 plate, multiple lever; pull type with brake; 484 sq. in. area.

DRIVE LINES: Dana-Spicer 1810 Series; needle bearing; yoke type, with glide coated splines.

TIRES: 10:00 × 22, 12-ply nylon tread. (10 furnished).

WHEELS: 22 × 7.5 Disc, Hi-tensile lightweight steel. (10 furnished).

FUEL TANK: One 50-gallon, 23″ diameter aluminum with aluminum mounting brackets; 3″ diameter filler opening; tank mounted shut-off cock.

CAB: 86″ 90° tilt cab, all aluminum construction; fully insulated with embossed aluminum cab lining; independent hydraulic system controls cab tilting; positive dual locking cab hold-down devices; extruded aluminum door frames; heavy-duty piano-type hinges; tinted safety glass throughout.

HEATER: 48,000 B.T.U. Fresh air heater with integral windshield defroster and central controls.

SEAT: Driver: Peterbilt-Bostrom Deluxe "Thinline" with black naugahyde upholstery and seat belt.

Passenger: Bucket type with lower storage compartment, naugahyde upholstered cushion and seat belt.

INSTRUMENTS: Tachometer, speedometer, water temperature, ammeter, fuel, oil pressure and air pressure gauges; low air pressure warning light; tilting dash panel; rheostat controlled lighting for all instruments.

STD. ACCESSORIES: Dual motor, air operated windshield wipers, adjustable 7″ × 16″ rear view mirrors with stainless steel heads and brackets, windshield washers, single tone air horn; electric horn; front and rear mud flaps; flexible air piping throughout; insulated floor mats; tow pin; full classic interior; dual inside sun visors; cigar lighter; ash tray; L & R arm rest; easy entry system L & R; wheel wrench and Operator's Manual.

*Model designation varies with cab size, i.e., 352 H with 86″ cab would be 352 86 H.

ALL SPECIFICATIONS ARE SUBJECT TO CHANGE WITHOUT NOTICE

MODEL 341, MIXER CHASSIS

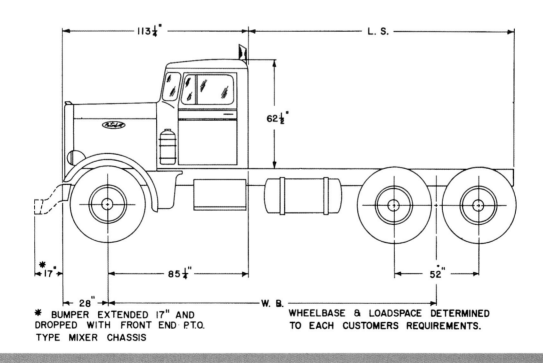

113¼"   L. S.

62½"

17"

85¼"

52"

28"

W. B.

* BUMPER EXTENDED 17" AND
DROPPED WITH FRONT END P.T.O.
TYPE MIXER CHASSIS

WHEELBASE & LOADSPACE DETERMINED
TO EACH CUSTOMERS REQUIREMENTS.

 **PETERBILT MOTORS COMPANY**

38801 CHERRY STREET   •   NEWARK, CALIFORNIA 94560   •   TELEPHONE (415) 797-3555

MODEL 341, MIXER CHASSIS
STANDARD SPECIFICATIONS

GVW 56,000 lbs.

FRAME: 10½" x 3½" x ¾" (flange) x ½" (web) heavy-duty extruded aluminum alloy (2014-T6) with aluminum inserts, cross-members and gussets.

Flywheel P.T.O.: Std. chassis wt.: Front: 6,290 lbs.; Rear: 6,110 lbs. Total: 12,400 lbs.

Front Engine P.T.O.: Std. chassis wt.: Front: 6,170 lbs.; Rear: 6,070 lbs. Total: 12,240 lbs.

AXLES: Front: Rockwell-Standard FL-901-N with iron hubs; capacity: 18,000 lbs.; nominal track: 77½".

Rear: Rockwell-Standard SQHD, hypoid single reduction tandem axle with aluminum hubs; driver controlled interaxle differential; capacity: 38,000 lbs.; nominal track: 71 3/16"; ratios optional.

BRAKES: Service: Rear axle only, 16½" x 7" Timken P-Series; Centrifuse brake drums, 868 sq. in. effective lining area; Bendix-Westinghouse 12 cu. ft. air compressor.

Parking: Overland Anchor-Lok air-operated spring brake with cab control (one axle only).

CAB: Hand welded all aluminum construction; fully insulated with 1½" fiberglass; embossed aluminum cab lining; three point rubber mounting; extruded aluminum door frames; heavy-duty piano-type hinges; tinted safety glass throughout.

CLUTCH: Lipe-Rollway 13" 2-plate; multiple lever; pull type.

DRIVE LINES: Dana-Spicer 1700 Series; needle bearing yoke type.

ELECTRICAL SYSTEM: Delco-Remy Heavy-Duty 12-volt Long-Life Type 250 starter; 55 amp alternator; two Group HG-4A 160 amp. hr. batteries; automatic circuit breakers; hand-made wiring harnesses, heavy-duty insulation, wrapped with waterproof covering; all terminals numbered and routed through terminal blocks; double-faced front directional signals with 4-way emergency flasher switch; sealed beam headlights; combination stop and tail rear lights.

ENGINE: Detroit Diesel, model 6V-53N; 318 cu. in. displacement; horsepower: 195 @ 2,600 RPM; torque: 446 ft. lbs. @ 1,500 RPM; oil bath air cleaner; oil cooler; fuel filter; fuel strainer; full-flow lube oil filter.

EXHAUST SYSTEM: Single 4" vertical system with muffler and guard; stainless steel exhaust flex; ceramic coated standpipe.

FENDERS: Crown aluminum (rolled type).

FUEL TANK: One 50 gallon lt. wt. aluminum with heavy-duty mounting brackets; 4" diameter filler opening; tank mounted shut-off cock.

INSTRUMENTS: Tachometer, speedometer, water temperature, ammeter, fuel, oil pressure and air pressure gauges; low air pressure warning light; tilting dash panel; rheostat controlled lighting for all instruments.

RADIATOR: Tube and fin type core with 1,050 sq. in. frontal area; detachable bolt-assembled, aluminum alloy top and bottom tanks; fitted Cadillac "Ther-Mech" aluminum shutter with Peterbilt adjustment mechanism.

SEATS: Driver: Peterbilt-Bostrom deluxe "Thinline".

STEERING: Gemmer Model 500, cam and lever type; Garrison hydraulic steering booster; steering ratio: 28.4 to 1; 22" diameter white steering wheel.

SUSPENSION: Front: Chrome vanadium steel split progressive springs; spring width: 3½"; length: 48".

Rear: Peterbilt-Hendrickson RSA-340; four rubber load cushions; aluminum saddles; torque rods and walking beams; completely rubber bushed; 52" axle centers; capacity: 34,000 lbs.

TRANSMISSION: Main: Fuller 5-CW-65AT; 5-speed; iron case and cover.

Auxiliary: Dana-Spicer 7041; 4-speed; iron case and cover.

TIRES: 10:00 x 20, 12-ply non-premium nylon highway tread (10 furnished).

WHEELS: 20" x 7.5 light weight, high tensile steel disc (10 furnished).

STD. ACCESSORIES: Dual motor, air operated, independently valved, variable speed, parking type windshield wipers; large adjustable 7" x 16" west coast type, stainless steel backed rear view mirrors; single tone air horn; front and rear mud flaps; flexible air piping throughout; electric horn; insulated floor mats; tow pin; rear tow eye; dual inside sun visors; cigar lighter; ash tray; left hand arm rest; 12-ton jack; wheel wrench, and Operator's Manual.

ALL SPECIFICATIONS ARE SUBJECT TO CHANGE WITHOUT NOTICE

MODEL 341, DUMP CHASSIS

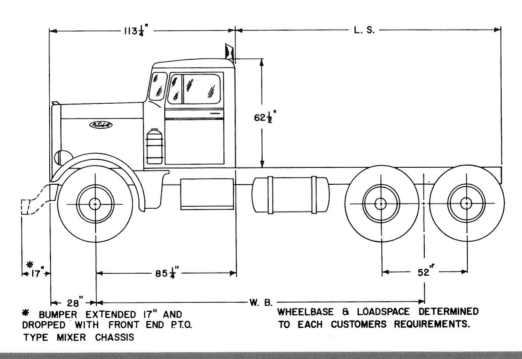

* BUMPER EXTENDED 17" AND
DROPPED WITH FRONT END P.T.O.
TYPE MIXER CHASSIS

WHEELBASE & LOADSPACE DETERMINED
TO EACH CUSTOMERS REQUIREMENTS.

 **PETERBILT MOTORS COMPANY**

38801 CHERRY STREET • NEWARK, CALIFORNIA 94560 • TELEPHONE (415) 797-3555

MODEL 341, DUMP CHASSIS
STANDARD SPECIFICATIONS

GVW 56,000 lbs.

FRAME: 10½" x 3½" x ¾" (flange) x ½" (web) heavy-duty extruded aluminum alloy (2014-T6) with aluminum inserts, cross-members and gussets; std. chassis wt.: Front: 6,090 lbs.; Rear: 6,130 lbs.; Total 12,220 lbs.; (the above chassis weights are based on a 235" wheelbase and 16' - 7¾" loadspace)

Completely bolted frame construction; SAE Grade 5 heat-treated bolts and double length nuts throughout.

AXLES: Front: Rockwell-Standard FL-901-N with iron hubs; capacity: 18,000 lbs.; nominal track 77½".

Rear: Rockwell-Standard SQHD, hypoid single reduction tandem axle with aluminum hubs; driver controlled interaxle differential; capacity: 38,000 lbs.; nominal track: 71 3/16"; ratios optional.

BRAKES: Service: Rear axle only, 16½" x 7" Timken P-Series; Centrifuse brake drums, 868 sq. in. effective lining area; Bendix-Westinghouse 12 cu. ft. air compressor.

Parking: Overland Anchor-Lok air-operated spring brake with cab control (one axle only).

CAB: Hand welded all aluminum construction; fully insulated with 1½" fiberglass; embossed aluminum cab lining; three point rubber mounting; extruded aluminum door frames; heavy-duty piano-type hinges; tinted safety glass throughout.

CLUTCH: Lipe-Rollway 13" 2-plate; multiple lever; pull type.

DRIVE LINES: Dana-Spicer 1700 Series; needle bearing yoke type.

ELECTRICAL SYSTEM: Delco-Remy Heavy-Duty 12-volt Long-Life Type 250 starter; 55 amp alternator; two Group HG-4A 160 amp. hr. batteries; automatic circuit breakers; hand-made wiring harnesses, heavy-duty insulation, wrapped with waterproof covering; all terminals numbered and routed through terminal blocks; double-faced front directional signals with 4-way emergency flasher switch; sealed beam headlights; combination stop and tail rear lights.

ENGINE: Detroit Diesel, model 6V-53N; 318 cu. in. displacement; horsepower: 195 @ 2,600 RPM; torque: 446 ft. lbs. @ 1,500 RPM; oil bath air cleaner; oil cooler; fuel filter; fuel strainer; full-flow lube oil filter.

EXHAUST SYSTEM: Single 4" vertical system with muffler and guard; stainless steel exhaust flex; ceramic coated standpipe.

FENDERS: Crown aluminum (rolled type).

FUEL TANK: One 50 gallon lt. wt. aluminum with heavy-duty mounting brackets; 4" diameter filler opening; tank mounted shut-off cock.

INSTRUMENTS: Tachometer, speedometer, water temperature, ammeter, fuel, oil pressure and air pressure gauges; low air pressure warning light; tilting dash panel; rheostat controlled lighting for all instruments.

RADIATOR: Tube and fin type core with 1,050 sq. in. frontal area; detachable bolt-assembled, aluminum alloy top and bottom tanks; fitted Cadillac "Ther-Mech" aluminum shutter with Peterbilt adjustment mechanism.

SEATS: Driver: Peterbilt-Bostrom deluxe "Thinline".

STEERING: Gemmer Model 500, cam and lever type; Garrison hydraulic steering booster; steering ratio: 28.4 to 1; 22" diameter white steering wheel.

SUSPENSION: Front: Chrome vanadium steel split progressive springs; spring width: 3½"; length: 48".

Rear: Peterbilt-Hendrickson RSA-380 with 340 beam end bushings and heavy-duty brackets; four rubber load cushions; aluminum saddles, torque rods and walking beams; completely rubber bushed; 52" axle centers; capacity: 38,000 lbs.

TRANSMISSION: Main: Fuller 5-CW-65AT; 5-speed; iron case and cover.

Auxiliary: Dana-Spicer 7041; 4-speed; iron case and cover.

TIRES: 10:00 x 20, 12-ply non-premium nylon highway tread (10 furnished).

WHEELS: 20" x 7.5 light weight, high tensile steel disc (10 furnished).

STD. ACCESSORIES: Dual motor, air operated, independently valved, variable speed, parking type windshield wipers; large adjustable 7" x 16" west coast type, stainless steel backed rear view mirrors; single tone air horn; front and rear mud flaps; flexible air piping throughout; electric horn; insulated floor mats; tow pin; rear tow eye; dual inside sun visors; cigar lighter; ash tray; left hand arm rest; 12-ton jack; wheel wrench, and Operator's Manual.

ALL SPECIFICATIONS ARE SUBJECT TO CHANGE WITHOUT NOTICE

Left and Below: Model 287 Interior and Chassis.

Top and Middle:
Model 371;
Bottom:
343, Chassis only.

STABILAIRE

SUSPENSION

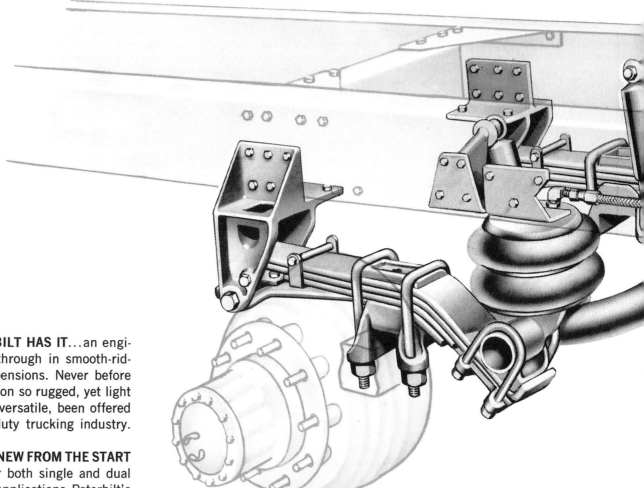

ONLY PETERBILT HAS IT...an engineering breakthrough in smooth-riding truck suspensions. Never before has a suspension so rugged, yet light in weight and versatile, been offered to the heavy-duty trucking industry.

ENGINEERED NEW FROM THE START —Available for both single and dual drive highway applications, Peterbilt's Stabilaire suspension assures a firm, smooth and level ride. Stabilaire's exclusive combination of heavy-duty torque-absorbing springs and high shock-dissipating air load cushions brings new smoothness, new ruggedness and new operating economy to you.

STABILAIRE ACTUALLY ADJUSTS TO THE ROAD—Lightly loaded, fully loaded or with no load at all; driver, chassis, and cargo enjoy the same smooth level ride.

Two independent leveling valves, one on each side of the suspension, automatically control the height of the chassis by regulating the air pressure within the load cushions, to maintain a constant relationship between the axle and frame.

Adjustment of spring rate of the cushions by matching air pressure to load, provides smooth riding qualities fully or lightly laden.

A delayed action feature in the air leveling valves prevents over correction of air pressure so that air is not wasted by minor road irregularities. The same delay feature also prevents an over correction of the load cushions on curves or when on winding roads.

On dual drive applications, a balance line between the front and rear axle load cushions distributes vehicle weight equally on each axle assuring increased tire, axle and brake lining life.

PROLONGS VEHICLE LIFE—Heavy-duty shock absorbers soak up axle rebound and help control driving and braking forces. Trailing arm-type leaf springs with shim adjustment and rubber bushed pins act as radius rods to insure positive axle alignment and resist side sway.

The 4-point suspension mounting on dual drive applications distributes frame loading over a wide area, eliminating high stress points.

LOW MAINTENANCE—Stabilaire's smooth level ride reduces wear and tear on other truck and trailer components, thereby lowering over-all maintenance costs.

TABILAIRE

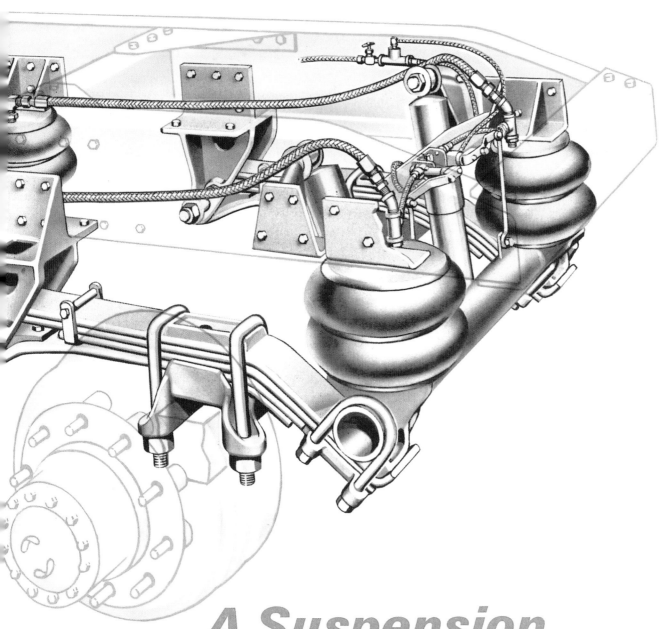

A Suspension
to Smooth the Road
With Any Load!

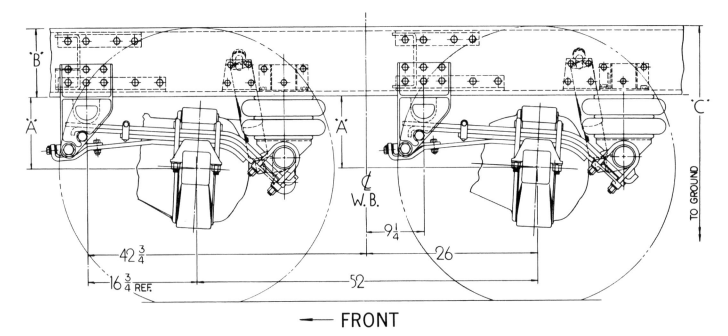

— FRONT

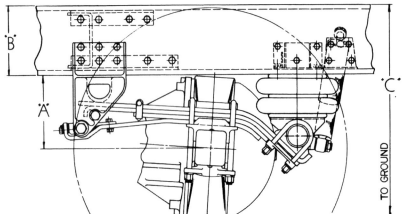

— FRONT

SQHD TANDEM AXLES			
TIRE SIZE	DIM *A	DIM B	DIM *C
11 X 22.5 & 10.00 X 20	10¾	9	40⅜
		10½	41⅞
11 X 24.5 & 10.00 X 22	10¾	9	41⅛
		10½	42⅝
11.00 X 22	10¾	9	41⅜
		10½	42⅞

* ADD ¼" FOR R-170 SINGLE AXLE

	Single Drive	Dual Drive
WEIGHT:	470#	895#
SUSPENSION RATING:	18,000#	34,000#

FEATURES

- Lightweight
- Smooth level ride
- Longer vehicle life
- Excellent stability
- Positive load equalization
- Constant frame height
- Longer tire mileage
- Minimum maintenance

PETERBILT MOTORS COMPANY

General Offices and Plant · 38801 Cherry Street, Newark (Oakland area), California · Area Code 415 · Phone 797-3555

MODEL 383, OFF-HIGHWAY

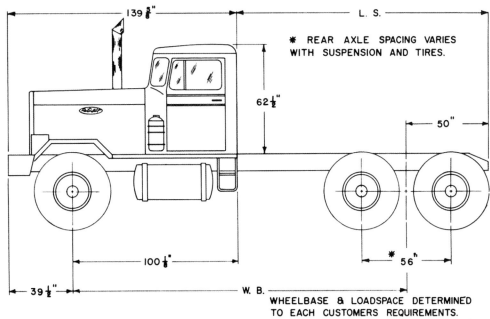

139⅜"

L. S.

✳ REAR AXLE SPACING VARIES
WITH SUSPENSION AND TIRES.

62½"

50"

100⅛"

✳ 56"

39½"

W. B.

WHEELBASE & LOADSPACE DETERMINED
TO EACH CUSTOMERS REQUIREMENTS.
(STANDARD TRACTOR OVERHANG SHOWN)

PETERBILT MOTORS COMPANY

38801 CHERRY STREET • NEWARK, CALIFORNIA 94560 • TELEPHONE (415) 797-3555

MODEL 383, OFF-HIGHWAY
STANDARD SPECIFICATIONS

GVW 83,000 lbs.   GCW 150,000 lbs.

FRAME: 10-5/8" x 3-5/8" x 3/8" heat-treated alloy steel with steel cross-members and gussets; std. chassis wt.: 18,950 lbs. (based on 22' - 5" loadspace).

Completely bolted frame construction; SAE Grade 5 heat-treated bolts and double length nuts throughout.

AXLES: Front: Rockwell-Standard FL-901-N with iron hubs; capacity: 18,000 lbs.; nominal track: 77½".

Rear: Rockwell-Standard SFDD-4640; double reduction tandem axle with iron hubs; driver controlled interaxle differential; capacity: 65,000 lbs.; nominal track: 74⅛"; ratios optional.

BRAKES: Service: Rear axle only, 16½" x 7" Timken P-Series; Centrifuse brake drums, 868 sq. in. effective lining area; trailer hand valve; tractor protection valve; Cummins 12 cu. ft. air compressor.

Parking: Overland Anchor-Lok air-operated spring brake with cab control (one axle only).

CAB: Hand welded all steel construction; fully insulated with 1½" fiberglass; embossed aluminum cab lining; three point rubber mounting; extruded aluminum door frames; heavy-duty piano-type hinges; tinted safety glass throughout.

CLUTCH: Dana-Spicer 14" 2-plate; multiple lever; pull type with brake; 423 sq. in. area.

DRIVE LINES: Dana-Spicer 1700 series; needle-bearing yoke type.

ELECTRICAL SYSTEM: Delco-Remy Heavy-Duty 12-volt Long-Life Type 250 starter; 55 amp alternator; four Group HG-4A 160 amp. hr. batteries; automatic circuit breakers; hand-made wiring harnesses, heavy-duty insulation, wrapped with waterproof covering; all terminals numbered and routed through terminal blocks; double-faced front directional signals with 4-way emergency flasher switch; sealed beam headlights; combination stop and tail rear lights.

ENGINE: Cummins "Custom - Rated" diesel, model NHC-250; 855 cu. in. displacement; horsepower: 250 @ 2,100 RPM; torque: 685 ft. lbs. @ 1,550 RPM; oil bath air cleaner; hi-mount fan; compression release; oil cooler; fuel filter; PT fuel system; full-flow lube oil filter; Luberfiner 750-C by-pass oil filter corrosion resistor.

EXHAUST SYSTEM: Single 4" vertical system with muffler and heavy-duty guard; stainless steel exhaust flex; ceramic coated standpipe.

FENDERS: Flat; heavy-duty walk on; steel.

FUEL TANK: One 50 gallon lt. wt. steel with heavy-duty mounting brackets; 4" diameter filler opening; tank mounted shut-off cock.

INSTRUMENTS: Tachometer, speedometer, water temperature, ammeter, fuel, oil pressure and air pressure gauges; low air pressure warning light; tilting dash panel; rheostat controlled lighting for all instruments.

RADIATOR: Tube and fin type core with 1,050 sq. in. frontal area; detachable bolt-assembled, aluminum alloy top and bottom tanks; fitted Cadillac "Ther-Mech" aluminum shutter with Peterbilt adjustment mechanism; heavy-duty integral radiator guard.

SEATS: Driver: Peterbilt-Bostrom deluxe "Thinline".

Passenger: Tool box with upholstered cushion.

STEERING: Ross Model TE-71 cam and lever type; steering ratio: 28 to 1; 22" diameter white steering wheel.

SUSPENSION: Front: Chrome vanadium split-progressive steel springs; spring width: 3½"; length: 48".

Rear: Rockwell-Standard 4600 Series, Off-Highway A/C Group; 56" axle centers; 5" spring width; rubber bushed torque rod ends; nylon trunnion bushing; capacity: 65,000 lbs.

TRANSMISSION: Main: Dana-Spicer 8542-A; 4-speed; iron case and cover.

Auxiliary: Dana-Spicer 8031-Q; 3-speed; iron case and cover.

TIRES: 10:00 x 20, 12-ply non-premium nylon highway tread (10 furnished).

WHEELS: 20" x 7.5 light weight, high tensile steel disc (10 furnished).

STD. ACCESSORIES: Dual motor, air operated, independently valved, variable speed, parking type windshield wipers; large adjustable 7" x 16" west coast type, stainless steel backed rear view mirrors; heavy-duty front bumper; single tone air horn; electric horn; front and rear mud flaps; heavy-duty cab side grab handles; flexible air piping throughout; insulated floor mats; directional and headlight guards; tow pin; dual inside sun visors; cigar lighter; ash tray; left hand arm rest; red cab reflectors on tractor models; 12-ton jack; wheel wrench, and Operator's Manual.

ALL SPECIFICATIONS ARE SUBJECT TO CHANGE WITHOUT NOTICE

MODEL 358

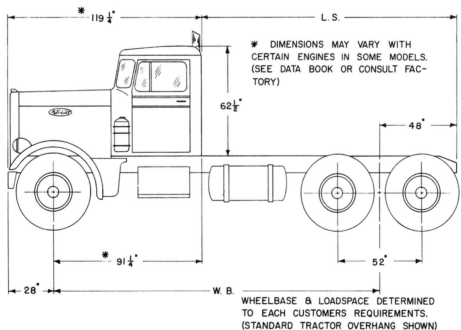

119 ¼"   L. S.

* DIMENSIONS MAY VARY WITH
CERTAIN ENGINES IN SOME MODELS.
(SEE DATA BOOK OR CONSULT FAC-
TORY)

62 ½"

48"

91 ¼"

52"

28"   W. B.

WHEELBASE & LOADSPACE DETERMINED
TO EACH CUSTOMERS REQUIREMENTS.
(STANDARD TRACTOR OVERHANG SHOWN)

PETERBILT MOTORS COMPANY

38801 CHERRY STREET • NEWARK, CALIFORNIA 94560 • TELEPHONE (415) 797-3555

GVW 49,000 lbs.   GCW 76,800 lbs.

FRAME: A - 10½" x 3½" x ¾" (flange) x ½" (web) extruded aluminum alloy with aluminum crossmembers and gussets; std. chassis wt.: 12,650 lbs. (based on 20' - 3" loadspace).

M - 10-3/8" x 3½" x ¼" heat-treated alloy steel with aluminum crossmembers and gussets; std. chassis wt.: 13,150 lbs. (based on 20' - 3" loadspace).

ST - 10-3/8" x 3½" x ¼" heat-treated alloy steel with steel crossmembers and gussets; std. chassis wt.: 13,775 lbs. (based on 20' - 3" loadspace).

Completely bolted frame construction; SAE Grade 5 heat-treated bolts and double length nuts throughout.

TILT HOOD: Multi-piece all metal, air-assisted tilt hood with convenient outside check and fill for oil and coolant.

AXLES: Front: A&M - Rockwell-Standard FE-900-N with aluminum hubs; capacity: 11,000 lbs.; nominal track: 77".

ST - Same as A&M models except with iron hubs.

Rear: A&M - Rockwell-Standard SQHD, hypoid single reduction tandem axle, with aluminum hubs; driver controlled interaxle differential; capacity: 38,000 lbs.; nominal track: 71-3/16"; ratios optional.

BRAKES: Service: Rear axle only, 16½" x 7" Timken P-Series; Centrifuse brake drums, 868 sq. in. effective lining area; trailer hand valve; tractor protection valve; Cummins 12 cu. ft. air compressor.

Parking: Overland Anchor-Lok air-operated spring brake with cab control (one axle only).

CAB: A&M - Hand welded all aluminum construction; fully insulated with 1½" fiberglass; embossed aluminum cab lining; three point rubber mounting; extruded aluminum door frames; heavy-duty piano-type hinges; tinted safety glass throughout.

ST - Same as A & M models except all steel construction.

CLUTCH: Dana-Spicer 14" 2-plate; multiple lever; pull type with brake; 423 sq. in. area.

DRIVE LINES: Dana-Spicer 1700 series; needle-bearing yoke type.

ELECTRICAL SYSTEM: Delco-Remy Heavy-Duty 12-volt Long-Life Type 250 starter; 55 amp alternator; four Group HG-4A 160 amp. hr. batteries; automatic circuit breakers; hand-made wiring harnesses, heavy duty insulation, wrapped with waterproof covering; all terminals numbered and routed through terminal blocks; double faced front directional signals with 4-way emergency flasher switch; sealed beam headlights; combination stop and tail rear lights.

ENGINE: Cummins "Custom-Rated" diesel, model NHC-250 with lightweight components; 855 cu. in. displacement; horsepower: 250 @ 2,100 RPM; torque: 685 ft. lbs. @ 1,550 RPM; oil bath air cleaner; hi-mount fan; compression release; oil cooler; fuel filter; PT fuel system; full-flow lube oil filter; Luberfiner 750-C by-pass oil filter; corrosion resistor.

EXHAUST SYSTEM: Single 4" vertical system with muffler and guard; stainless steel exhaust flex; ceramic coated standpipe.

FENDERS: Crown steel (rolled type).

FUEL TANK: One 50 gallon lt. wt. steel with heavy-duty mounting brackets; 4" diameter filler opening; tank mounted shut-off cock.

INSTRUMENTS: Tachometer, speedometer, water temperature, ammeter, fuel, oil pressure and air pressure gauges; low air pressure warning light; tilting dash panel; rheostat controlled lighting for all instruments.

RADIATOR: Tube and fin type core with 1,050 sq. in. frontal area; detachable bolt-assembled, aluminum alloy top and bottom tanks; fitted Cadillac "Ther-Mech" aluminum shutter with Peterbilt adjustment mechanism.

SEATS: Driver: Peterbilt-Bostrom deluxe "Thinline".

Passenger: Tool box with upholstered cushion.

STEERING: Ross Model TE-71 cam and lever type; steering ratio: 28 to 1; 22" diameter white steering wheel.

SUSPENSION: Front: Chrome vanadium split-progressive steel springs; spring width: 3½"; length: 48".

Rear: Peterbilt-Hendrickson RSA-340; four rubber load cushions; aluminum saddles, torque rods and walking beams; completely rubber bushed; 52" axle centers; capacity: 34,000 lbs.

TRANSMISSION: Main: A - Dana-Spicer 8544-A; 4-speed; aluminum case and cover.

M&ST - Dana-Spicer 8542-A; 4-speed; iron case and cover.

Auxiliary: A - Dana-Spicer 8035-Q; 3-speed; aluminum case and cover.

M&ST - Dana-Spicer 8031-Q; 3-speed; iron case and cover.

TIRES: 10:00 x 20, 12-ply non-premium nylon highway tread (10 furnished).

WHEELS: 20" x 7.5 light weight, high tensile steel disc (10 furnished).

STD. ACCESSORIES: Dual motor, air operated, independently valved, variable speed, parking type windshield wipers; large adjustable 7" x 16" west coast type, stainless steel backed rear view mirrors; single tone air horn; electric horn; front and rear mud flaps; flexible air piping throughout; insulated floor mats; tow pin; dual inside sun visors; cigar lighter, ash tray, left hand arm rest; red cab reflectors on tractor models; 12-ton jack; wheel wrench, and Operator's Manual.

ALL SPECIFICATIONS ARE SUBJECT TO CHANGE WITHOUT NOTICE

MODEL 288

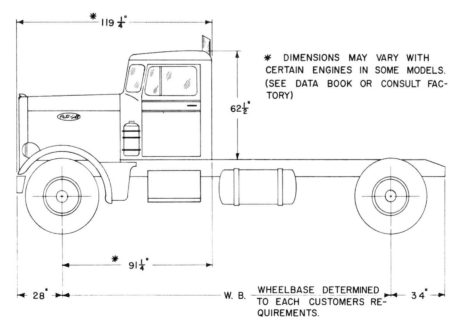

* 119¼"

62½"

* DIMENSIONS MAY VARY WITH
CERTAIN ENGINES IN SOME MODELS.
(SEE DATA BOOK OR CONSULT FAC-
TORY)

* 91¼"

28"   W. B.   WHEELBASE DETERMINED
TO EACH CUSTOMERS RE-
QUIREMENTS.   34"

PETERBILT MOTORS COMPANY

38801 CHERRY STREET • NEWARK, CALIFORNIA 94560 • TELEPHONE (415) 797-3555

MODEL 288
STANDARD SPECIFICATIONS

GVW 34,000 lbs.   **GCW 76,800 lbs.**

FRAME: A - 10½" x 3½" x ¾" (flange) x ½" (web) extruded aluminum alloy with aluminum crossmembers and gussets; std. chassis wt.: 10,150 lbs. (based on 9' - 11¼" loadspace).

M - 9" x 3½" x 7/32" or 10-3/8" x 3½" x ¼" heat-treated alloy steel with aluminum crossmembers and gussets; std. chassis wt.: 10,350 lbs. or 10,475 lbs. (based on 9' - 11¼" loadspace).

ST - 9" x 3½" x 7/32" or 10-3/8" x 3½" x ¼" heat-treated alloy steel with steel crossmembers and gussets; std. chassis wt.: 10,850 lbs. or 10,975 lbs. (based on 9' - 11¼" loadspace).

Completely bolted frame construction; SAE Grade 5 heat-treated bolts and double length nuts throughout.

TILT HOOD: Multi-piece all metal, air-assisted tilt hood with convenient outside check and fill for oil and coolant.

AXLES: Front: A&M - Rockwell-Standard FE-900-N with aluminum hubs; capacity: 11,000 lbs.; nominal track: 77".

ST - Same as A&M models except with iron hubs.

Rear: Rockwell-Standard R-170, hypoid single reduction with aluminum hubs; capacity: 23,000 lbs.; nominal track: 72"; ratios optional.

BRAKES: Service: Rear axle only, 16½" x 7" Timken P-Series; Centrifuse brake drums, 434 sq. in. effective lining area; trailer hand valve; tractor protection valve; Cummins 12 cu. ft. air compressor.

Parking: Overland Anchor-Lok air-operated spring brake with cab control.

CAB: A&M - Hand welded all aluminum construction; fully insulated with 1½" fiberglass; embossed aluminum cab lining; three point rubber mounting; extruded aluminum door frames; heavy-duty piano-type hinges; tinted safety glass throughout.

ST - Same as A & M models except all steel construction.

CLUTCH: Dana-Spicer 14" 2-plate; multiple lever; pull type with brake; 423 sq. in. area.

DRIVE LINES: Dana-Spicer 1700 series; needle-bearing yoke type.

ELECTRICAL SYSTEM: Delco-Remy Heavy-Duty 12-volt Long-Life Type 250 starter; 55 amp alternator; four group HG-4A 160 amp. hr. batteries; automatic circuit breakers; hand-made wiring harnesses, heavy-duty insulation, wrapped with waterproof covering. All terminals numbered and routed through terminal blocks; double-faced front directional signals with 4-way emergency flasher switch; sealed beam headlights; combination stop and tail rear lights.

ENGINE: Cummins "Custom - Rated" diesel, model NHC-250 with lightweight components; 855 cu. in. displacement; horsepower: 250 @ 2,100 RPM; torque: 685 ft. lbs. @ 1,550 RPM; oil bath air cleaner; hi-mount fan; compression release; oil cooler; fuel filter; PT fuel system; full-flow lube oil filter; Luberfiner 750-C by-pass oil filter; corrosion resistor.

EXHAUST SYSTEM: Single 4" vertical system with muffler and guard; stainless steel exhaust flex; ceramic coated standpipe.

FENDERS: Crown Steel (rolled type).

FUEL TANK: One 50 gallon lt. wt. steel with heavy-duty mounting brackets; 4" diameter filler opening; tank mounted shut-off cock.

INSTRUMENTS: Tachometer, speedometer, water temperature, ammeter, fuel, oil pressure and air pressure gauges; low air pressure warning light; tilting dash panel; rheostat controlled lighting for all instruments.

RADIATOR: Tube and fin type core with 1,050 sq. in. frontal area; detachable bolt-assembled, aluminum alloy top and bottom tanks; fitted Cadillac "Ther-Mech" aluminum shutter with Peterbilt adjustment mechanism.

SEATS: Driver: Peterbilt-Bostrom deluxe "Thinline".

Passenger: Tool box with upholstered cushion.

STEERING: Ross Model TE-71 cam and lever type; steering ratio: 28 to 1; 22" diameter white steering wheel.

SUSPENSION: Front: Chrome vanadium steel split-progressive springs; spring width: 3½"; length: 48".

Rear: Peterbilt split-progressive spring with cast eye; spring width: 3½"; length: 54".

TRANSMISSION: Main: A - Dana-Spicer 8544-A; 4-speed; aluminum case and cover.

M&ST - Dana-Spicer 8542-A; 4-speed; iron case and cover.

Auxiliary: A - Dana-Spicer 8035-Q; 3-speed; aluminum case and cover.

M&ST - Dana-Spicer 8031-Q; 3-speed; iron case and cover.

TIRES: 10:00 x 20, 12-ply non-premium nylon highway tread (6 furnished).

WHEELS: 20" x 7.5 light weight, high tensile steel disc (6 furnished).

STD. ACCESSORIES: Dual motor, air operated, independently valved, variable speed, parking type windshield wipers; large adjustable 7" x 16" west coast type, stainless steel backed, rear view mirrors; single tone air horn; electric horn; front and rear mud flaps; flexible air piping throughout; insulated floor mats; tow pin; dual inside sun visors; cigar lighter; ash tray; left hand arm rest; red cab reflectors on tractor models; 12-ton jack; wheel wrench, and Operator's Manual.

ALL SPECIFICATIONS ARE SUBJECT TO CHANGE WITHOUT NOTICE

MODEL 348

MIXER

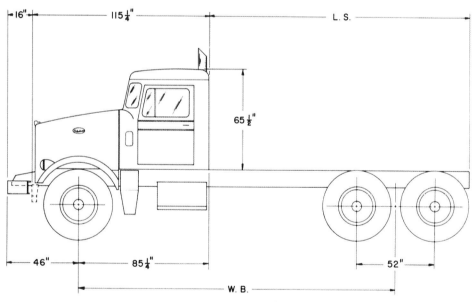

WHEELBASE & LOADSPACE DETERMINED
TO EACH CUSTOMERS REQUIREMENTS.

PETERBILT MOTORS COMPANY

GENERAL OFFICES: 38801 CHERRY STREET • NEWARK, CALIFORNIA 94560 • TELEPHONE (415) 797-3555
TENNESSEE PLANT: 430 MYATT DRIVE • MADISON, TENNESSEE 37115 • TELEPHONE (615) 865-8910

3-1-71

MIXER

GVW 56,000

FRAME: Completely bolted frame construction; SAE Grade 5 heat-treated bolts and double length nuts.

10½" x 3½" x ¾" (flange) x ½" (web) heavy duty extruded aluminum alloy (2014-T6) rails. 9" heavy duty aluminum alloy frame inserts centered at forward mixer supports for standard type mixer OR steel angle tie strip from under cab to end of frame for mounting higher load capacity, dolley-type mixers.

Aluminum crossmembers and gussets. Wheelbase and loadspace to customer's requirments.

AXLES: Front: Rockwell-Standard FL-901-N with iron hubs; capacity: 18,000 lbs.; nominal track 77½".

Rear: Rockwell-Standard SQHD hypoid single reduction tandem axle, aluminum hubs; oil seals, outboard mounted drums, driver controlled inter-axle differential with dash indicator light; capacity 38,000 lbs.; nominal track: 71-3/16", ratios optional.

BRAKES: Service: Rear axles only, 16½" x 7"; "S" Cam Type; Centrifuse drums, 868 sq. in. effective lining area; Bendix-Westinghouse 12 cu. ft. air compressor.

Parking: Air-operated spring brake with cab control. (one axle only).

CAB: Aluminum construction; fully insulated with 1½" fiberglass; embossed aluminum cab lining; three point rubber mounting; extruded aluminum door frames; heavy-duty piano type hinges; tinted safety glass throughout.

CLUTCH: Lipe-Rollway 13" 2-plate; multiple lever; pull type.

DRIVE LINES: Dana-Spicer 1700 Series; needle bearing; yoke type.

ELECTRICAL SYSTEM: Delco-Remy Heavy-Duty 12 volt Long-Life type 250 starter; 55 amp alternator; two Group 4, 165 amp. hr. batteries; automatic circuit breakers; hand-made wiring harnesses, heavy-duty insulation, wrapped with waterproof covering; all terminals numbered and routed through terminal blocks; double-faced front directional signals with 4-way emergency flasher switch; sealed beam headlights; 2 rear combination 4 way directional, stop, and tail lights; automatically actuated back-up light. Applicable marker lights and reflectors.

ENGINE: Detroit Diesel, model 6V-53N; 318 cu. in. displacement; horsepower: 195 @ 2,600 RPM; torque: 446 ft. lbs. @ 1,500 RPM; oil bath air cleaner; oil cooler; fuel filter; fuel strainer; full-flow lube oil filter.

EXHAUST SYSTEM: Single 4" vertical system with muffler, muffler guard, stainless steel exhaust flex tubing, stainless steel clamps, and ceramic coated standpipe.

FUEL TANK: One 30 gallon, 20' diameter lt. wt. aluminum with aluminum mounting brackets; 4" diameter filler opening; tank mounted shut-off cock.

INSTRUMENTS: Tachometer, speedometer, water temperature, ammeter, fuel, oil pressure and air pressure gauges; low air pressure warning light; tilting dash panel; rheostat controlled lighting for all instruments.

RADIATOR: Tube and fin type core with 840 sq. in. frontal area; detachable bolt-assembled, aluminum alloy top and bottom tanks; fitted Cadillac "Ther-Mech" aluminum shutter with Peterbilt adjustment mechanism; anti-freeze.

HOOD: Fiberglass, full 90° spring assisted tilt hood; crown aluminum rolled fenders; chrome bug screen.

SEATS: Driver: Peterbilt-Bostrom Deluxe "Thinline" with black naugahyde upholstery.

STEERING: Gemmer Model 500, cam and lever type outboard mounted; Steering ratio: 28.4 to 1; 22" diameter white steering wheel; Garrison hydraulic steering booster.

SUSPENSION: Front: Chrome vanadium steel split progressive springs; spring width: 3½"; length: 48".

Rear: Peterbilt-Hendrickson RSA-340; four rubber load cushions; aluminum saddles, torque rods and walking beams; completely rubber bushed; 52" axle centers; capacity: 34,000 lbs.

TRANSMISSION: Main: Fuller 5-CW-65; 5-speed; iron case and cover.
Auxiliary: Dana-Spicer 7041; 4-speed; iron case and cover.

TIRES: 10:00 x 20, 12-ply nylon highway tread. (10 furnished).

WHEELS: 20 x 7.5 Disc, Hi-tensile lightweight steel. (10 furnished).

STD. ACCESSORIES: Dual motor, air operated windshield wipers, adjustable 7" x 16" rear view mirrors with stainless steel heads and brackets, windshield washers, single tone air horn; electric horn; defroster fan; front and rear mud flaps; flexible air piping throughout; insulated floor mats; tow pin; tow eye E.O.F.; dual inside visors; cigar lighter; ash tray, L & R arm rests; L. H. Grab Handle; wheel wrench; and Operator's Manual.

Peterbilt Model

348

6x6
BASIC
SPECIFICATIONS

Peterbilt

MODEL 348 6x6 BASIC SPECIFICATIONS

FRAME

Heat-treated, 110,000 P.S.I. yield, alloy steel with SAE grade 8 flanged heat treated bolts, and flanged nuts

10⅝" frame depth with 3⅝" flange width and ⅜" web thickness, up to 324", with steel crossmembers and gussets

Square end of frame
Peterbilt rear mudflaps with straight hangers
Front wheel mudflaps

FRONT AXLE

FABCO SDA-12* 12,000 lb. capacity

12,000 lb. capacity chrome vanadium split-progressive twelve leaf steel springs

TRW HFB-70 integral power steering gear

Iron hubs, 11¼" bolt circle and ¾" studs
Cast brake drums

REAR AXLE

Rockwell SQHD hypoid single reduction tandem axle; 38,000 lb. capacity

Forged aluminum hubs, 11¼" bolt circle and ¾" studs
Cast brake drums

Eaton 16½" x 7" "S" cam service brakes

Anchorlok 30" parking brake on one axle
Manual slack adjusters

REAR SUSPENSION

Hendrickson RSA-380 rubber load cushion suspension; 52" aluminum walking beams, 50/50 load distribution, rubber center bearings, 60-durometer orange load cushions, 17¼" saddle height, 52" axle spacing, 38,000 lb. capacity
Heavy-duty frame brackets

ENGINE

Caterpillar 3306
638 cu. in. displacement
250 BHP (S.A.E.) at 2200 RPM
690 lb. feet maximum torque at 1400 RPM
Water-cooled with 180° ventless thermostat
Six cylinder turbocharged
26" diameter high-mount fan
Oil cooler

Horton automatic fan clutch with override switch

Spicer 14" 2-plate non-asbestos, rigid disc, angle spring clutch

ENGINE ELECTRICAL

Leece-Neville 90 amp (belt drive) 12 volt alternator with integral regulator

12 volt starter
Glow plug cold weather starting aid with heat/start switch
Key ignition

Four Peterbilt 6-volt, Group 4 low-maintenance batteries rated at 800 cold cranking amps each

COOLING SYSTEM

Standard core radiator with 1444 in² frontal area
Steel sidemembers
Removable aluminum top tank
Removable steel bottom tank
Peterbilt "Air sweep"
Full fan shroud
Dynacraft "B" ("Kevlar" aramid fiber) radiator hoses
Shutterless cooling
Permanent type anti-freeze effective to 20°F below 0°
Polished Aluminum radiator shell and stainless steel grille

TRANSMISSION

Fuller "Roadranger" RTO-11608; twin countershaft; 10 speed (with 2 low gear ratios) overdrive, iron case and cover, 1100 lb.-ft. nominal torque capacity

Main transmission rear support

Transfer case Dana model 738**

TIRES

Front: 11x24.5 14-PR steel radial
(2 furnished)

Rear: 11x24.5 14-PR steel radial
(8 furnished)

WHEELS

Front: 24x8.25 disc, high tensile
lightweight steel (2 furnished)

Rear: 24x8.25 disc, high tensile
lightweight steel (8 furnished)

CAB & HOOD

Aluminum cab with all aluminum construction, fully insulated with foam four-point rubber mounting; extruded aluminum door frames; heavy-duty piano-type hinges; tinted safety glass throughout; dual air-operated windshield wipers and washers; interior lining beige; tilt-out instrument panel; coat hooks

113" B.B.C. fiberglass non-sloped hood with SBFA and 90° spring assisted tilt; fiberglass fenders

Options available:

*FABCO SDA-16 series
FABCO SDA-18 series
Rockwell FDS 1800
**FABCO TC80 series
FABCO TC110 series
FABCO TC140 series

A DIVISION OF **PACCAR**

Headquarters
Peterbilt Motors Company
38801 Cherry Street
Newark, California 94560
Tel: 415-796-2011

Peterbilt Motors Company
430 Myatt Drive
Madison, Tennessee 37115
Tel: 615-865-8910

Peterbilt Motors Company
3200 Airport Road
Denton, Texas 76201
Tel: 817-566-7100

MODEL 359-A WIDE FRONT

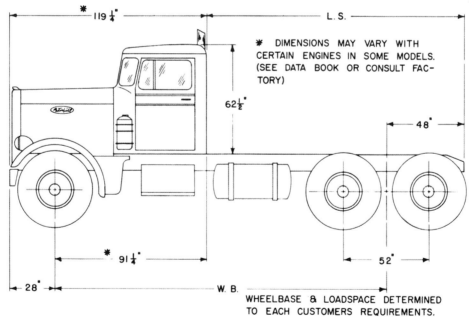

* DIMENSIONS MAY VARY WITH
CERTAIN ENGINES IN SOME MODELS.
(SEE DATA BOOK OR CONSULT FAC-
TORY)

WHEELBASE & LOADSPACE DETERMINED
TO EACH CUSTOMERS REQUIREMENTS.
(STANDARD TRACTOR OVERHANG SHOWN)

PETERBILT MOTORS COMPANY

38801 CHERRY STREET • NEWARK, CALIFORNIA 94560 • TELEPHONE (415) 797-3555

MODEL 359-A WIDE FRONT
STANDARD SPECIFICATIONS

GVW 49,000 lbs.   **GCW 76,800 lbs.**

FRAME: 10½'' x 3½'' x ¾'' (Flange) x ½'' (Web) extruded aluminum alloy with aluminum cross-members and gussets; std. chassis wt.: 12,635 lbs. (based on 20' - 3'' loadspace)

Completely bolted frame construction; SAE Grade 5 heat-treated bolts and double length nuts throughout.

AXLES: Front: Rockwell-Standard FE-900-N with aluminum hubs; capacity: 11,000 lbs.; nominal track: 77''.

Rear: Rockwell-Standard SQHD, hypoid single reduction tandem axle, with aluminum hubs; driver controlled interaxle differential; capacity: 38,000 lbs.; nominal track: 71 3/16''; ratios optional.

BRAKES: Service: Rear axle only, 16½'' x 7'' Timken P-Series; Centrifuse brake drums, 868 sq. in. effective lining area; trailer hand valve; tractor protection valve; Cummins 12 cu. ft. air compressor.

Parking: Overland Anchor-Lok air-operated spring brake with cab control (one axle only).

CAB: Hand welded all aluminum construction; fully insulated with 1½'' fiberglass; embossed aluminum cab lining; three point rubber mounting; extruded aluminum door frames; heavy-duty piano-type hinges; tinted safety glass throughout.

CLUTCH: Dana-Spicer 14'' 2-plate; multiple lever; pull type with brake; 423 sq. in. area.

DRIVE LINES: Dana-Spicer 1700 series; needle-bearing yoke type.

ELECTRICAL SYSTEM: Delco-Remy Heavy-Duty 12-volt Long-Life Type 250 starter; 55 amp alternator; four Group HG-4A 160 amp. hr. batteries; automatic circuit breakers; hand-made wiring harnesses, heavy duty insulation, wrapped with waterproof covering; all terminals numbered and routed through terminal blocks; double faced front directional signals with 4-way emergency flasher switch; sealed beam headlights; combination stop and tail rear lights.

ENGINE: Cummins "Custom-Rated" diesel, model NHC-250 with lightweight components; 855 cu. in. displacement; horsepower: 250 @ 2,100 RPM; torque: 685 ft. lbs. @ 1,550 RPM; oil bath air cleaner; hi-mount fan; compression release; oil cooler; fuel filter; PT fuel system; full-flow lube oil filter; Luberfiner 750-C by-pass oil filter; corrosion resistor.

EXHAUST SYSTEM: Single 4'' vertical system with muffler and guard; stainless steel exhaust flex; ceramic coated standpipe.

FUEL TANK: One 50 gallon lt. wt. steel with heavy-duty mounting brackets; 4'' diameter filler opening; tank mounted shut-off cock.

INSTRUMENTS: Tachometer, speedometer, water temperature, ammeter, fuel, oil pressure and air pressure gauges; low air pressure warning light; tilting dash panel; rheostat controlled lighting for all instruments.

RADIATOR: 3 inch thick core, 7 ripple fins per square inch, 244 tubes with 1444 square inch-frontal area; detachable bolt-assembled, aluminum alloy top and bottom tanks; Cadillac split-vane shutters with center control "flex mount" full length elastic hinge.

SEATS: Driver: Peterbilt-Bostrom deluxe "Thinline" with genuine leather covering.

Passenger: Tool box with upholstered cushion.

STEERING: Ross Model TE-71 cam and lever type; steering ratio: 28 to 1; 22'' diameter white steering wheel.

SUSPENSION: Front: Chrome vanadium split-progressive steel springs; spring width: 3½''; length 48''.

Rear: Peterbilt-Hendrickson RSA-340; four rubber load cushions; aluminum saddles, torque rods and walking beams; completely rubber bushed; 52'' axle centers; capacity: 34,000 lbs.

TRANSMISSION: Main: Dana-Spicer 8544-A; 4-speed; aluminum case and cover.

Auxiliary: Dana-Spicer 8035-Q; 3-speed; aluminum case and cover.

TIRES: 10:00 x 20, 12-ply non-premium nylon highway tread (10 furnished)

WHEELS: 20'' x 7.5V Budd 84770-3 Hi-tensile lightweight steel (10 furnished).

STD. ACCESSORIES: Multi-piece all metal, air-assisted tilt hood with convenient outside check and fill for oil and coolant; dual motor, air operated, independently valved, variable speed, parking type windshield wipers, large adjustable 7'' x 16'' west coast type, stainless steel backed rear view mirrors; single tone air horn; electronic horn; front and rear mud flaps; flexible air piping throughout; insulated floor mats; swing-out tow yokes recessed in bumper; dual inside sun visors; ash tray; cigar lighter; left hand arm rest; red cab reflectors on tractor models; 12-ton jack; wheel wrench and Operator's Manual.

ALL SPECIFICATIONS ARE SUBJECT TO CHANGE WITHOUT NOTICE

MODEL 289

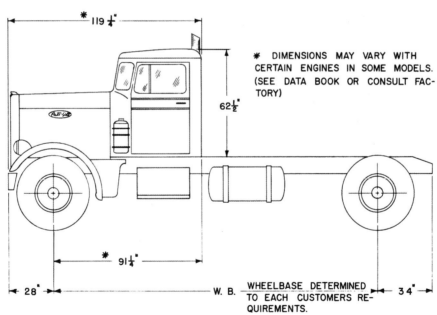

119¼"

62½"

* DIMENSIONS MAY VARY WITH
CERTAIN ENGINES IN SOME MODELS.
(SEE DATA BOOK OR CONSULT FAC-
TORY)

91¼"

28"

W. B. WHEELBASE DETERMINED
TO EACH CUSTOMERS RE-
QUIREMENTS.

34"

PETERBILT MOTORS COMPANY

38801 CHERRY STREET • NEWARK, CALIFORNIA 94560 • TELEPHONE (415) 797-3555

MODEL 289
STANDARD SPECIFICATIONS

GVW 34,000 lbs.   **GCW 76,800 lbs.**

FRAME: A - 10½" x 3½" x ¾" (flange) x ½" (web) extruded aluminum alloy with aluminum crossmembers and gussets; std. chassis wt.: 10,220 lbs. (based on 9' - 11¼" loadspace).

M - 9" x 3½" x 7/32" or 10-3/8" x 3½" x ¼" heat-treated alloy steel with aluminum crossmembers and gussets; std. chassis wt.: 10,420 lbs. or 10,545 lbs. (based on 9' - 11¼" loadspace).

ST - 9" x 3½" x 7/32" or 10-3/8" x 3½" x ¼" heat-treated alloy steel with steel crossmembers and gussets; std. chassis wt.: 10,920 lbs. or 11,045 lbs. (based on 9' - 11¼" loadspace).

Completely bolted frame construction; SAE Grade 5 heat-treated bolts and double length nuts throughout.

TILT HOOD: Multi-piece all metal, air-assisted tilt hood with convenient outside check and fill for oil and coolant.

AXLES: Front: A&M - Rockwell-Standard FE-900-N with aluminum hubs; capacity: 11,000 lbs.; nominal track: 77".

ST - Same as A&M models except with iron hubs.

Rear: Rockwell-Standard R-170 hypoid single reduction with aluminum hubs; capacity: 23,000 lbs.; nominal track: 72"; ratios optional.

BRAKES: Service: Rear axle only, 16½" x 7" Timken P-Series; Centrifuse brake drums, 434 sq. in. effective lining area; trailer hand valve; tractor protection valve; Cummins 12 cu. ft. air compressor.

Parking: Overland Anchor-Lok air-operated spring brake with cab control.

CAB: A&M - Hand welded all aluminum construction; fully insulated with 1½" fiberglass; embossed aluminum cab lining; three point rubber mounting; extruded aluminum door frames; heavy-duty piano-type hinges; tinted safety glass throughout.

ST - Same as A & M models except all steel construction.

CLUTCH: Dana-Spicer 14" 2-plate; multiple lever; pull type with brake; 423 sq. in. area.

DRIVE LINES: Dana-Spicer 1700 series; needle-bearing yoke type.

ELECTRICAL SYSTEM: Delco-Remy Heavy-Duty 12-volt Long-Life Type 250 starter; 55 amp alternator; four Group HG-4A 160 amp. hr. batteries; automatic circuit breakers; hand-made wiring harnesses, heavy-duty insulation, wrapped with waterproof covering; all terminals numbered and routed through terminal blocks; double faced front directional signals with 4-way emergency flasher switch; sealed beam headlights; combination stop and tail rear lights.

ENGINE: Cummins "Custom - Rated" diesel, model NHC-250 with lightweight components; 855 cu. in. displacement; horsepower: 250 @ 2,100 RPM; torque: 685 ft. lbs. @ 1,550 RPM; oil bath air cleaner; hi-mount fan; compression release; oil cooler; fuel filter; PT fuel system; full-flow lube oil filter; Luberfiner 750-C by-pass oil filter; corrosion resistor.

EXHAUST SYSTEM: Single 4" vertical system with muffler and guard; stainless steel exhaust flex; ceramic coated standpipe.

FENDERS: Crown steel (rolled type).

FUEL TANK: One 50 gallon lt. wt. steel with heavy-duty mounting brackets; 4" diameter filler opening; tank mounted shut-off cock.

INSTRUMENTS: Tachometer, speedometer, water temperature, ammeter, fuel, oil pressure and air pressure gauges; low air pressure warning light; tilting dash panel; rheostat controlled lighting for all instruments.

RADIATOR: 3 inch thick core, 7 ripple fins per square inch, 244 tubes with 1,444 square inch frontal area; detachable bolt-assembled, aluminum alloy top and bottom tanks; Cadillac split-vane shutters with center control "flex mount" full length elastic hinge.

SEATS: Driver: Peterbilt-Bostrom deluxe "Thinline".

Passenger: Tool box with upholstered cushion.

STEERING: Ross Model TE-71 cam and lever type; steering ratio 28 to 1; 22" diameter white steering wheel.

SUSPENSION: Front: Chrome vanadium steel split-progressive springs; spring width: 3½"; length: 48".

Rear: Peterbilt split-progressive spring with cast eye; spring width: 3½"; length: 54".

TRANSMISSION: Main: A - Dana-Spicer 8544-A; 4-speed; aluminum case and cover.

M&ST - Dana-Spicer 8542-A; 4-speed; iron case and cover.

Auxiliary: A - Dana-Spicer 8035-Q; 3-speed; aluminum case and cover.

M&ST - Dana-Spicer 8031-Q; 3-speed; iron case and cover.

TIRES: 10:00 x 20, 12-ply non-premium nylon highway tread (6 furnished).

WHEELS: 20" x 7.5 light weight, high tensile steel disc (6 furnished).

STD. ACCESSORIES: Dual motor, air operated, independently valved, variable speed, parking type windshield wipers; large adjustable 7" x 16" west coast type, stainless steel backed rear view mirrors; single tone air horn; electronic horn; front and rear mud flaps; flexible air piping throughout; insulated floor mats; swing-out tow yokes recessed in bumper; dual inside sun visors; ash tray; cigar lighter; left-hand arm rest; red cab reflectors on tractor models; 12-ton jack; wheel wrench and Operator's Manual.

ALL SPECIFICATIONS ARE SUBJECT TO CHANGE WITHOUT NOTICE

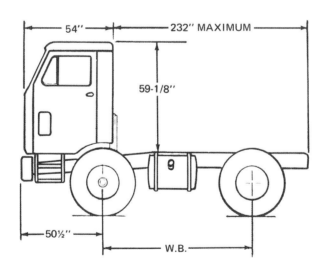

WHEELBASE DETERMINED TO EACH CUSTOMERS
REQUIREMENTS.
(STANDARD TRACTOR OVERHANG SHOWN)

PETERBILT MOTORS COMPANY

GENERAL OFFICES: 38801 CHERRY STREET • NEWARK, CALIFORNIA 94560 • TELEPHONE (415) 797-3555
TENNESSEE PLANT: 430 MYATT DRIVE • MADISON, TENNESSEE 37115 • TELEPHONE (615) 865-8910

3-1-71

STANDARD SPECIFICATIONS

GVW 31,000 lbs.   **GCW 55,000 lbs.**

FRAME: Completely bolted construction; SAE Grade 5 heat-treated bolts and double length nuts throughout.

MODEL CB-200: 9″ x 3½″ x ¼″ heat treated alloy steel with steel crossmembers.

Wheelbase and loadspace to Customer's requirements.

AXLES: Front: Rockwell-Standard FD-903 RSA; capacity: 9,000 lbs.; nominal tract: 79-7/8″, oil seals.

Rear: Eaton 18121 Spiral Bevel, with steel housing; capacity: 22,000 lbs; nominal track: 71¼″; ratios optional. Oil Seals.

BRAKES: Service: Front Axle: Stopmaster 15″ x 3½″ with cast drums; Rear Axle: Stopmaster 15″ x 7″ with centrifuse drums.

Parking: Air operated Super Failsafe spring brake with cab control.

CAB: 54″ tilt cab. Steel structure with fiberglass and steel panels; double wall floor; insulated; spring-counterbalanced cab tilting; positive locking cab hold down; Steel doors with wing ventilator windows; piano type hinges; safety view window in right hand door; safety glass throughout.

CLUTCH: Lipe Rollway 13″ 2 Plate; hydraulic actuated.

DRIVE LINES: Dana-Spicer 1700 Series; needle bearing; yoke type.

ELECTRICAL SYSTEM: Delco-Remy Heavy-Duty 12-volt Long-Life Type 250 starter; 55 amp alternator; four Group 4, 160 amp. hr. batteries; (with optional Detroit Diesel 6V53 engine, two Group 4, 160 amp. hr. batteries standard); automatic circuit breakers; heavy duty wiring; double-faced front directional signals with 4-way emergency flasher switch; single sealed beam headlights; combination stop and tail rear lights; automatically actuated back-up light. 5 cab marker lights and applicable Federal Safety Standard marker lights and reflectors.

ENGINE: Cummins V8 210 diesel, 504 cu. in. displacement; horsepower: 210 @ 3300 rpm; dry type air cleaner; full flow lube oil filter; fuel filter; 13.2 CFM air compressor.

EXHAUST SYSTEM: Horizontal system with muffler.

FUEL TANK: One 40 gallon, lightweight steel, 23″ tank.

INSTRUMENTS: Tachometer, speedometer, water temperature, ammeter, fuel level gauge, oil pressure and air pressure gauges; low air pressure warning light.

RADIATOR: Tube and fin type core with 720 sq. in. frontal area; fitted automatic shutters and shroud.

SEATS: Driver: Peterbilt-Bostrom Deluxe "Thinline" with black upholstery.

Passenger: Peterbilt deluxe passenger seat with black upholstery.

STEERING: Gemmer model 7J with deluxe 20″ diameter black steering wheel.

SUSPENSION: Front: 53″ x 4″ springs, six leaves, 9,000 capacity with rubber auxiliary springs.

Rear: Peterbilt split progressive with cast eye; 54″ x 3½″ springs.

TRANSMISSION: Fuller 5 CW 65 AT; 5 speed iron case and cover.

TIRES: 9:00 x 20, 10 ply rating, highway tread. (6 furnished)

WHEELS: 20″ spoke wheels; rims: 20 x 7.0 (6 furnished).

STD. ACCESSORIES: Dual motor, air operated windshield wipers; windshield washers; flexible air piping throughout; electric horn; left side arm rest; 4 grab handles; heater and defroster; two-way ventilators; inside sun visor; adjustable rear view mirrors; cigar lighter and ash tray.

Model 300

The Peterbilt Heavy Duty Compact. Ruggedly built — designed to solve suburban hauling problems. A short turning radius, easy entry-tilting cab, excellent engine accessibility, heavy duty bolted frame and a long list of options separate this model from the also rans. From the people who build'em for the guys who drive'em.

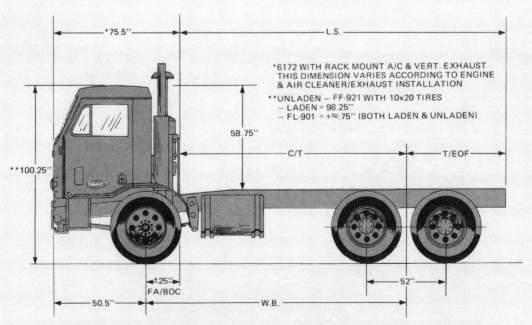

*6172 WITH RACK MOUNT A/C & VERT. EXHAUST
THIS DIMENSION VARIES ACCORDING TO ENGINE
& AIR CLEANER/EXHAUST INSTALLATION

**UNLADEN — FF-921 WITH 10x20 TIRES
— LADEN = 98.25''
— FL-901 = +≈.75'' (BOTH LADEN & UNLADEN)

The above photograph may include optional equipment and accessories and may not include all standard equipment.

MODEL 300

FRAME: 10-1/8" x 3-1/4" x 5/16" heat treated steel rails (110,000 P.S.I.). Completely bolted construction; S.A.E. Grade 5 heat treated bolts and nuts throughout. Extruded aluminum bumper (steel opt.). Wheelbase and loadspace to customer's specifications. *Optional frames: 11-1/4" x 3-3/4" x 3/8" and 11-1/4" x 3-3/4" x 3/8" with full inner liner.*

ENGINE: Detroit Diesel 6172; 426 cu. in. displacement; 218 HP @ 2,100 RPM (S.A.E.); nominal horsepower 238 @ 2,100 RPM; 649 ft. lbs. of torque @ 1,400 RPM; dry air cleaner (rack mounted); 4" vertical exhaust with muffler. B.W. 12 C.F.M. compressor; A.C. fuel and lube filters. *Optional Engines: Caterpillar 1673-C (3306), Detroit Diesel 6V53H, and Cummins V-555 (E).*

RADIATOR: 860 sq. in. frontal area radiator with detachable bolt-assembled top and bolt tanks; Kysor radiator shutters.

ELECTRICAL: Delco-Remy heavy duty 12 volt starter; Delco-Remy **65 amp alternator; four six volt batteries;** automatic circuit breakers; heavy duty wiring; double faced front directional signals with 4-way emergency flasher; dual headlights; combination stop and tail lights; automatically actuated backup lights; key ignition; and applicable Federal Safety Standard marker lights and reflectors.

TRANSMISSION: Fuller RT-910; 10 speed with iron case and cover. *Optional Transmissions: RT-610, RT-613, RTO-9513, RT-915, Allison MT-650 Automatic, and Cummins Sundstrand Responder Automatic.*

CLUTCH & DRIVE LINE: Dana Spicer angle spring 14" 2-plate; hydraulic actuated. Dana Spicer 1710 series drive lines; needle-bearing yoke type, with glide coated splines. *Optional: Midship bearing.*

FRONT AXLE: Rockwell Standard **FF-921TW,** 12,000 lb. capacity; 78-3/8" track, aluminum hubs; oil seals; 12,000 lb. rated springs (54" x 4") with rubber auxiliary springs; 50.5" set back axle setting. *Optional Axle: FL-901 18,000 lbs. capacity with 18,000 lb. rated springs.*

FRONT BRAKES: 16-1/4" x 7"; "S" cam type (TW); cast drums; 112 sq. in. effective lining with limit valve. *Option Brakes: Rockwell Standard wedge brakes.*

STEERING: Gemmer gear with 20" black steering wheel. *Option: Garrison or Sheppard power steering.*

REAR AXLE: Rockwell Standard **SQHD** hypoid single reduction tandem axle, aluminum hubs; oil seals; outboard mounted drums; driver controlled inter-axle differential; 38,000 lb. capacity; 71-3/16" nominal track, ratios optional. *Optional Axles: SSHD, 38 series, D-380, D-400.*

REAR BRAKES: Service — 16-1/2" x 7" "S" cam type; cast drums; 868 sq. in. effective lining area; **automatic third air tank.** *Optional Brakes: Rockwell Standard wedge brakes.* Parking Brakes — air operated spring brake with cab control (one axle only).

REAR SUSPENSION: Hendrickson **RT-340** spring suspension, 34,000 lb. capacity. *Optional Suspensions: Peterbilt 4-spring and Air Leaf; Hendrickson RT, RTA, RS, RSA suspensions.*

TIRES: 10:00 x 20, 12 ply nylon highway tread (10 furnished). *Wide variety of optional sizes and treads.*

WHEELS: 20 x 7.5 steel disc wheels (10 furnished). *Wide variety of wheel sizes in both steel and aluminum, also spoke hubs and rims.*

CAB: 54" tilt cab with steel supporting structure, fiberglass roof, fiberglass/aluminum side panels and laminated fiberglass cab floor. Fiberglass rear cab quarter fenders. Hydraulic cab lift (50°). Hydraulic cab latch with positive lockdown warning light. Steel doors with wing ventilator windows; piano hinges; 2-way door vent in left hand door, safety view window in right hand door. Recessed door handles, individual door locks. Safety glass throughout with tinted windshield. Dual air variable speed windshield wipers with windshield washers. **Interior:** Totally insulated throughout. Padded vinyl back of cab (black) and roof (off white). Fresh air heater (35,000 B.T.U.'s) with integral defroster. Deluxe adjustable vinyl driver's seat and vinyl cushion rider's seat (both black) with seat belts and retractors. *Options: 50,000 BTU heater, air conditioning, padded doors and engine blanket, Bostrom thinline; torsion bar; and AirViking driver's seats; 40" x 20" rear window.*

INSTRUMENTATION: Speedometer (0-80mph); tachometer (0 to 3500 RPM); air pressure, oil pressure, water temperature, ammeter, and fuel gauges. Low air pressure warning light. Cigarette lighter. Above installed in R.C.C.C. panel with rheostat controlled lighting for all instruments. *Options: full line of optional gauges, tachographs, etc.*

FUEL TANK: One **50 gallon** 24-1/2" diameter aluminum fuel tank. *Options: fuel tanks up to 105 gallons capacity.*

STANDARD ACCESSORIES: Single electric air horn, grab handles both sides of cab, adjustable 7" x 16" rear view mirrors, two ashtrays, single sun visor, insulated floor mats, aluminum battery box with fiberglass cover, wheel wrench and cab tilt handle.

PETERBILT MOTORS COMPANY
GENERAL OFFICES: 38801 CHERRY STREET • NEWARK, CALIFORNIA 94560
ALL SPECIFICATIONS ARE SUBJECT TO CHANGE WITHOUT NOTICE

10-15-73

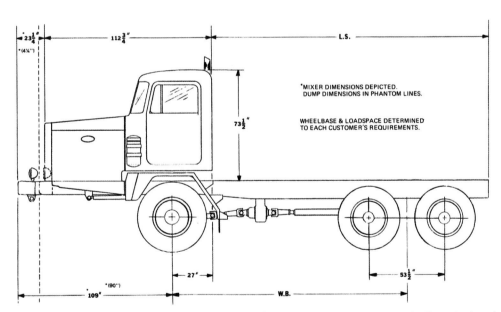

*MIXER DIMENSIONS DEPICTED.
DUMP DIMENSIONS IN PHANTOM LINES.

WHEELBASE & LOADSPACE DETERMINED
TO EACH CUSTOMER'S REQUIREMENTS.

The above illustration may include optional equipment and accessories and may not include all standard equipment.

PETERBILT MOTORS COMPANY

GENERAL OFFICES: 38801 CHERRY STREET • NEWARK, CALIFORNIA 94560
TENNESSEE PLANT: 430 MYATT DRIVE • MADISON, TENNESSEE 37115

4-15-73

STANDARD SPECIFICATIONS

DUMP & MIXER CHASSIS*

FRAME: Completely bolted frame construction; SAE Grade 5 heat-treated bolts and elastic stopnuts.

Steel fishbelly rail, 110,000 P.S.I. yield. 9 3/8″ x 3½″ x 3/8″ (forward section) to 12 3/8″ x 3½″ x 3/8″ (B.O.C. to E.O.F.). Steel or aluminum crossmembers and gussets. Wheelbase and loadspace to customer's requirements.

AXLE: Front: Rockwell Standard FDS-1800 driving axle with iron hubs; 21,000 lb. capacity carrier; nominal track 77½″; Cantilever axle setting.

Rear: Rockwell-Standard SQHD hypoid single reduction tandem axle, aluminum hubs; oil seals, outboard mounted drums, driver controlled inter-axle differential with dash indicator light; capacity 38,000 lbs; nominal track: 71-3/16″, ratios optional.

BRAKES: Service: Front axle: Rockwell-Standard Stopmaster wedge brakes, 4″ x 17¼″; 268 sq. in. effective lining area.

Rear axles: 16½″ x 7″; "S" Cam Type; Centrifuse drums, 868 sq. in. effective lining area; Cummins 12 CFM air compressor. Automatic third air tank.

Parking: Air operated spring brake with cab control (one axle only).

CAB: Aluminum construction; fully insulated; cycolac-aluminum cab lining; three point rubber mounting; extruded aluminum door frames; heavy-duty piano type hinges; tinted safety glass throughout.

CLUTCH: Dana-Spicer 14″ angle spring 2 plate, multiple lever, pull type with brake; 423 sq. in. area.

TRANSMISSION: Fuller RT-613; 13 speed; iron case and cover.

TRANSFER CASE: Dana-Spicer TC-738, single speed, with driver control. Ratio 1 to 1. Front axle declutch.

DRIVE LINES: Dana-Spicer 1710 series throughout; needle bearing; yoke type; with glide coated splines.

ELECTRICAL SYSTEM: Delco-Remy Heavy-Duty 12 volt Long-Life type 250 starter; 65 amp alternator (V-555); four Group 4, 165 amp. hr. batteries; automatic circuit breakers; hand-made wiring harnesses, heavy-duty insulation, wrapped with waterproof covering; all terminals numbered and routed through terminal blocks; double-faced front directional signals with 4-way emergency flasher switch; sealed beam headlights; 2 rear combination 4 way directional, stop, and tail lights; automatically actuated back-up light. Applicable marker lights and reflectors.

ENGINE: Cummins Diesel, Model V-555; 555 cubic inches displacement; horsepower: 216 @ 3300 (SAE); nominal horsepower 225, 387 ft. lbs. @ 1,900 RPM; dry air cleaner; full flow lube oil filter; water conditioner; Peterbilt by-pass oil filter.

EXHAUST SYSTEM: Single 4″ vertical system with muffler, muffler guard, stainless steel exhaust flex tubing, stainless steel clamps, and ceramic coated standpipe.

FUEL TANK: One 50-gallon, 23″ diameter aluminum with aluminum mounting brackets; 4″ diameter filler opening; tank mounted shut-off cock.

RADIATOR: Tube and fin type core with 840 sq. in. frontal area; detachable bolt-assembled, aluminum alloy top and bottom tanks; fitted Evans "Ther-Mech" aluminum shutter with Peterbilt adjustment mechanism; anti-freeze.

SEAT: Driver: Peterbilt-Bostrom Deluxe "Thinline" with naugahyde upholstery with seat belt.

STEERING: Gemmer Model 500, cam and lever type outboard mounted; Steering ratio: 28.4 to 1; 22″ diameter white steering wheel; Vickers dual ram steering boosters with Vicker direct drive pump.

SUSPENSION: Front: Chrome vanadium steel split progressive springs; spring width: 4″; length 52″.

Rear: Peterbilt-Hendrickson RSA-380 with 3 beam end bushings and heavy-duty brackets; four rubber load cushions; aluminum saddles, torque rods and walking beams; completely rubber bushed; 52″ axle centers; capacity: 38,000 lbs.

HOOD: Aluminum butterfly type hood with detachable side panels and metal latches.

FENDERS: Flat steel fenders mounted under cab with cab access steps (both sides).

INSTRUMENTS: Tachometer, speedometer, water temperature, ammeter, fuel, oil pressure and air pressure gauges; low air pressure warning light; tilting dash panel; rheostat controlled lighting for all instruments. Key ignition.

HEATER: 40,000 B.T.U. Fresh air heater with integral windshield defroster and central controls.

TIRES: Front: 16.5 x 22.5, 16 ply flotation type tires (2 furnished).

Rear: 10:00 x 22, 12 ply nylon highway tread (8 furnished).

WHEELS: Front: 22.5 x 14″ steel Disc (2 furnished).

Rear: 22 x 7.5 Disc, hi tensile lightweight steel. (8 furnished).

STD. ACCESSORIES: Dual motor, air operated windshield wipers, adjustable 7″ x 16″ rear view mirrors with stainless steel heads and brackets, windshield washers, single tone air horn; electric horn; defroster fan; front and rear mud flaps; flexible air piping throughout; insulated floor mats; tow pin; tow eye E.O.F.; dual inside visors; cigar lighter; ash tray, L & R arm rests; L.H. Heavy duty grab handle; wheel wrench; and Operator's Manual.

*Mixer — Extended bumper with P.T.O. provision & engine adapter. **Dump** — Heavy duty bumper - no P.T.O. provision. B.B.C. 117″, see side view on reverse side.

ALL SPECIFICATIONS ARE SUBJECT TO CHANGE WITHOUT NOTICE

353 17B

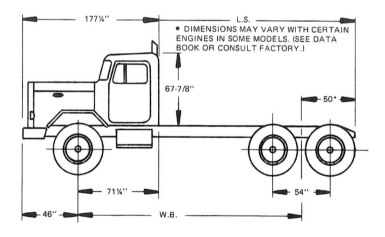

177¼"   L.S.

• DIMENSIONS MAY VARY WITH CERTAIN
ENGINES IN SOME MODELS. (SEE DATA
BOOK OR CONSULT FACTORY.)

67-7/8"

50*

71¼"   54"

46"   W.B.

*The above illustration may include optional equipment and
accessories and may not include all standard equipment.*

WHEELBASE & LOADSPACE DETERMINED TO EACH
CUSTOMER'S REQUIREMENTS. *STANDARD TRACTOR
OVERHANG DEPENDS UPON SUSPENSION — CONSULT
ENGINEERING DATA BOOK.

PETERBILT MOTORS COMPANY
A DIVISION OF **PACCAR**
GENERAL OFFICES: 38801 CHERRY STREET • NEWARK, CALIFORNIA 94560
TENNESSEE PLANT: 430 MYATT DRIVE • MADISON, TENNESSEE 37115

3-1-76

STANDARD SPECIFICATIONS

FRAME: Completely bolted construction; SAE Grade 5 heat-treated bolts, lock nuts and hardened washers.

10⅝" x 3⅝" heat-treated alloy steel with steel crossmembers and gussets.

Wheelbase and loadspace to Customer's requirements.

AXLES: Front: Rockwell-Standard FL-931-RDA with aluminum hubs; capacity: 18,000 lbs.; nominal track: 77½". Setback.

Rear: Peterbilt-Timken PBDD-55; double reduction tandem axle with iron hubs; driver controlled inter-axle differential with dash indicator light; capacity: 55,000 lbs.; nominal track: 74-1/8"; ratios optional.

BRAKES: Service: Front axle: Rockwell-Standard Stopmaster wedge brakes; 15" x 6"; 375 sq. in. effective lining area with automatic limit valve.

Rear axle: 16½" x 7"; "S" Cam Type; 868 sq. in. effective lining area; trailer hand valve; tractor protection valve; Cummins 13.2 CFM air compressor. Dual air system.

Parking: Air-operated spring brake with cab control (one axle only).

STEERING: Gemmer Model 500, worm and roller type; steering ratio: 32.5 to 1; 22" diameter white steering wheel.

SUSPENSION: Front: Chrome vanadium split-progressive steel springs; spring width: 3½"; length: 48".

Rear: Rockwell-Standard SUD Off-Highway A/C Group; 54" axle centers; 5" spring width; rubber bushed torque rod ends; nylon trunnion bushing; capacity: 55,000 lbs.

ENGINE: Cummins diesel, model NTC-350 with lightweight components; 855 cu. in. displacement; horsepower: 350 SAE @ 2,100 RPM; torque: 1006 ft. lbs. @ 1,500 RPM; dry air cleaner; hi-mount fan; compression release; oil cooler; fuel filter; PT fuel system; full-flow lube oil filter; Peterbilt by-pass oil filter; corrosion resistor; crankdriven alternator. Ventless (rapid warmup) thermostat.

EXHAUST SYSTEM: Single 5" vertical system with muffler, heavy-duty guard, stainless steel exhaust flex and clamps, and ceramic coated standpipe.

RADIATOR: Tube and fin type core with 1444 sq. in. frontal area; detachable bolt-assembled, aluminum alloy top and bottom tanks. Steel side members; engine mounted tie rods; steel radiator shell.

TRANSMISSION: Fuller RTO 9513; 13-speed with overdrive; iron case and cover.

CLUTCH: Dana-Spicer 14" self-adjusting angle spring 2 plate, multiple lever; pull type with brake; 423 sq. in. area.

DRIVE LINES: Dana-Spicer 1710 Series; needle bearing; yoke type, with glide coated splines.

ELECTRICAL SYSTEM: Delco-Remy Heavy-Duty 12-volt Long-Life Type 250 starter; 85 amp alternator; four Group 4 batteries, 800 cold cranking amps @ 0°F; automatic circuit breakers; hand-made wiring harnesses, heavy-duty insulation wrapped with braided covering. All terminals numbered and routed through terminal blocks; double-faced front directional signals; sealed beam headlights; combination stop and tail lights; automatically actuated back-up light and turn signals with 4-way emergency flasher switch. Applicable marker lights and reflectors. Key ignition.

TIRES: 10:00 x 22, 12-ply nylon tread. (10 furnished).

WHEELS: 22 x 7.5 Disc, Hi-tensile lightweight steel. (10 furnished).

FUEL TANK: One 50-gallon steel, 23" diameter; with heavy-duty mounting brackets; 3" diameter filler opening; tank mounted shut-off cock.

CAB: Severe Service; fully insulated; cycolac-aluminum cab lining; three point rubber mounting; extruded aluminum door frames; heavy-duty piano-type hinges; tinted safety glass throughout.

HOOD: Aluminum butterfly type hood with hinged aluminum side panels; heavy-duty flat steel fenders with "safety walk" anti-skid surfacing.

HEATER: 40,000 B.T.U. Fresh air heater with integral windshield defroster and central controls.

SEATS: Driver: Peterbilt-Bostrom Deluxe "Thinline" with black naugahyde upholstery and seat belt.

Passenger: Bucket type with lower storage compartment, naugahyde upholstered cushion and seat belt.

INSTRUMENTS: Tachometer, speedometer, water temperature, ammeter, fuel, oil pressure and air pressure gauges; low air pressure warning light; tilting dash panel; rheostat controlled lighting for all instruments.

STD. ACCESSORIES: Dual motor, air operated windshield wipers, adjustable 7" x 16" rear view mirrors with stainless steel heads and brackets, windshield washers, electric horn; defroster fan; front and rear mud flaps, heavy-duty cab side grab handles; flexible air piping throughout; insulated floor mats; directional light guards; tow pin; dual inside sun visors; cigar lighter; ash tray; L & R arm rests; wheel wrench; and Operator's Manual.

ALL SPECIFICATIONS ARE SUBJECT TO CHANGE WITHOUT NOTICE

Peterbilt Model 353

TANDEM FRONT AXLE BASIC SPECIFICATIONS

MODEL 353 TANDEM FRONT AXLE BASIC SPECIFICATIONS

FRAME

Heat-treated, 110,000 P.S.I. Yield, alloy steel with SAE Grade 8 flanged heat-treated bolts, and flanged nuts

10⅝" frame depth with 3⅝" flange width and ⅜" web thickness, up to 324", with steel crossmembers and gussets

Steel front cab support cross-tie
Steel rear cab crossmember

Tractor-tapered end of frame

Peterbilt rear mudflaps with straight hangers
Front wheel mudflaps

FRONT AXLE

Dual Rockwell FF931P*, 12,000 lb. capacity, 16½" x 5" "S" cam brakes*

24,000 lb. tandem equalizer type suspension

Dual integral power steering gears, 22" diameter steering wheel

Forged aluminum hubs, 11¼" bolt circle and 1⅛" studs

24,000 lb. total capacity

REAR AXLE

Eaton DS440-P single reduction tandem axle; 44,000 lb. capacity

Forged aluminum hubs, 11¼" bolt circle and 1⅛" studs cast brake drums

Eaton 16½" x 7" "S" cam service brakes

Manual slack adjusters

REAR SUSPENSION

Hendrickson RS-440 rubber load cushion suspension; 52" alloy steel walking beams, 50/50 load distribution, bronze center bearings, 60-durometer blue load conditions, heavy-duty cushion kit, 14" saddle height, 52" axle spacing, 44,000 lb. capacity
Heavy-duty frame brackets

ENGINE

Cummins NTC350 Big Cam II
855 cu. in. displacement
350 BHP (S.A.E.) at 2100 RPM
1120 lb. feet maximum torque at 1400 RPM
Water-cooled with 180° ventless thermostat
Six cylinder turbocharged
32" diameter high-mount fan
Oil Cooler
PTG fuel system
Horton automatic fan clutch with override switch

ENGINE ELECTRICAL

Leece-Neville 90 amp (crankshaft/belt drive) 12 volt alternator with integral regulator

12 volt starter

Peterbilt ether injection system
Push button start switch
Key ignition

Four Peterbilt 6-volt, Group 4 low-maintenance batteries rated at 800 cold cranking amps each

COOLING SYSTEM

High-capacity core radiator with 1444 in² front area

Steel radiator sidemembers
Removable aluminum top tank
Removable aluminum bottom tank

Heavy-duty radiator crosstube

Cowl mounted radiator tie rods
Peterbilt "Air Sweep"
10-lb. pressure relief cap
Full fan shroud
Dynacraft "B" ("Kevlar" aramid fiber) radiator hoses
Shutterless cooling
Permanent-type anti-freeze effective to 20° F below
Steel radiator shell (painted) and stainless steel grill

TRANSMISSION

Fuller "Roadranger" RTO-14613; twin countershaft, 13 speed with overdrive, iron case and cover, 14000 lb.-ft. nominal torque capacity

Main transmission rear support

1710 series with needle bearing and glidecote spline

CLUTCH

Spicer 14" 2-plate super duty, non-asbestos rigid disc, angle spring clutch

Manually-adjustable clutch with greasable bearing

TIRES

10.0" x 22", 12 PR, 100 level, nylon highway tread (12 furnished)

22" x 7.5" disc, high tensile lightweight steel (12 furnished)

CAB & HOOD

Severe service cab; all aluminum construction with steel back panels, roof panels, and windshield mask; fully insulated with foam and; three point rubber mounting; extruded aluminum door frame; heavy-duty piano-type hinges; tinted safety glass throughout; dual air operated windshield wipers and washers; interior lining beige; tilt-out instrument panel; coat hooks

126" B.B.C. steel slide-in sides type hood; flat steel fenders with "safety walk" surface

Options available:

*Dual Rockwell FL93IRDA
w/36,000 16 lb. suspension

A DIVISION OF **PACCAR**

Headquarters
Peterbilt Motors Company
38801 Cherry Street
Newark, California 94560
Tel: 415-796-2011

Peterbilt Motors Company
430 Myatt Drive
Madison, Tennessee 37115
Tel: 615-865-8910

Peterbilt Motors Company
3200 Airport Road
Denton, Texas 76201
Tel: 817-566-7100

PMC-2689 1-82 10M

Peterbilt Model

359

STANDARD SPECIFICATIONS

MODEL 359 STANDARD SPECIFICATIONS

The above illustration may include optional equipment and accessories; it may not include all standard equipment.

FRAME

Heat-treated, 110,000 P.S.I. yield, alloy steel with SAE Grade 8 flanged heat treated bolts, and flanged nuts

10.375" frame depth with 3.5" flange width and .25" web thickness with steel crossmembers and gussets

Tractor-tapered end of frame

Peterbilt rear mudflaps with straight hangers

Front wheel mudflaps

FRONT AXLE

Rockwell FF941; 12,000 lb. capacity 15"x 4" cam brakes

12,000 lb. capacity chrome vanadium rolled-eye eight leaf steel springs

NSK, recirculating ball type manual steering gear; 22" diameter steering wheel

Forged aluminum hubs, 11.25" bolt circle and 1.125" studs

Centrifuse brake drums

Oil seals

REAR AXLE

Rockwell SQ100 single reduction tandem axle; 38,000 lb. capacity

Forged aluminum hubs, 11.25" bolt circle and 1.125" studs

Centrifuse brake drums

Eaton 16.5"x 7" "S" cam service brakes

30" parking brake on one axle

Manual slack adjusters

Oil seals

Inter-axle differential lock-out with dash mounted warning light

REAR SUSPENSION

Peterbilt tandem four spring suspension; six point frame attachment, longitudinal torque arms to center frame bracket, center equalizer beam for 50/50 load distribution, 52" axle spacing, 34,000 lb. capacity

MODEL 359 STANDARD SPECIFICATIONS

ENGINE
Cummins FNTC300 Big Cam IV (LFC)

855 cu. in. displacement

300 BHP (SAE) at 1800 RPM

1000 lb. feet maximum torque at 1300 RPM

Water-cooled with 180° ventless thermostat

Six cylinder-turbocharged after cooled

High-mount fan · Oil cooler · PTG fuel system

ENGINE ELECTRICAL
Leece-Neville 90 amp (crankshaft/belt driven) 12 volt alternator with integral regulator

12 volt starter

Peterbilt Ether injection system

Push button start switch · Key ignition

Three Peterbilt 12 volt, maintenance-free batteries rated at 1875 cold cranking amps

FAN CLUTCH
Horton automatic fan clutch with override switch

AIR COMPRESSOR
Cummins 13.2 CFM air compressor

Stainless steel/teflon discharge line

FILTERS
Integral spin-on full flow oil filter

F/G engine mounted bypass oil filter

Spin-on fuel filter · Peterbilt spin-on water filter

COOLING SYSTEM
Standard core radiator with 1270 sq. in. frontal area

Aluminum sidemembers

Removable aluminum top tank

Removable aluminum bottom tank

Peterbilt "Air Sweep"

10 lb. pressure relief cap

Full fan shroud

Dynacraft "B" ("Kevlar" aramid fiber) radiator hoses

Shutterless cooling

Permanent-type anti-freeze effective to 20° below zero

Polished outer radiator shell and stainless steel grill

AIR CLEANER
Donaldson EBA15-0117 dry-type air cleaner cowl mounted with vacuator

Air restriction indicator in cab

Stainless steel clamps at all air intake connections

EXHAUST
Single 5" vertical exhaust system with 10" muffler, stainless steel flex tubing and clamps

Chrome steel standpipe with 45° cut-off

Aluminum full round muffler guard

TRANSMISSION
Fuller "Roadranger" RT11609A; twin-countershaft, 9 speed, iron case and cover, 1150 lb.-ft. nominal torque capacity

DRIVELINES
1710 type

CLUTCH
Spicer 14" 2-plate non-asbestos dampened disc, angle spring clutch

Torque-limiting clutch brake

Manually-adjustable clutch with greasable bearing

AIR SYSTEM
Peterbilt dual air system

Rubber chassis hose

Trailer hand valve located on steering column

Tractor protection valve

Trailer charge valve

TIRES
24.5," 14-ply, low profile radial tread (10 furnished)

WHEELS
24.5"x 8.25"disc, high tensile lightweight steel (10 furnished)

FUEL TANK
One 60-gallon 23" diameter aluminum tank under cab on right-hand side (unpainted)

Aircraft style fuel cap

Heavy-duty aluminum fuel tank brackets and straps

Grip-strut fuel tank step

MODEL 359 STANDARD SPECIFICATIONS

BATTERY BOX
Aluminum battery box with grip-strut step under cab on left-hand side

BUMPER
Tapered aluminum with dual recessed tow eyes and one tow pin

ELECTRICAL SYSTEM
"Pop-out" style manual-reset circuit breakers; cross-linked polyethelene insulated wiring harnesses with braided covering; all circuits numbered, color-coded, and routed through "hard shell" connectors in weather-proof enclosure; automatically actuated back-up light; four-way emergency flasher switch

CAB & HOOD
Aluminum cab fully insulated with foam; three-point rubber mounting; extruded aluminum door frames; heavy-duty piano-type hinges; tinted safety glass throughout; dual air-operated windshield wipers and washers; tilt-out instrument panel; coat hooks

119.25″ BBC aluminum hood with 90° spring assisted tilt; steel fenders. Severe service hood mounting.

SEATS
Driver: Peterbilt/UltraRide™ air-suspension seat (low back w/ seatbelt)

Passenger: Peterbilt/UltraRide™ non-suspension seat (low back w/seatbelt)

Vinyl upholstery

CAB FEATURES
Vinyl headliner inserts

Rubber floor mats

Padded doors with carpet inserts

6″ stainless steel grab handle on left side

19.5″x 36″ fixed rear window

Vent window locks

Fresh air heater, 40,000 BTU, with integral windshield defroster, and central controls

Dual padded interior sunvisors

Dual 7″x 16″ adjustable, stainless steel rear view mirrors

Electric horn

Single Grover 1024 air horn with chrome finish

Cigar lighter and ashtray

INSTRUMENTS
Speedometer, 0-80 MPH with odometer (electric)

Tachometer, 0-3000 RPM (electric)

Engine oil pressure gauge

Water temperature gauge

Fuel level gauge · Ammeter

Dual air pressure gauge

Low air pressure warning light

Rheostat controlled lighting for all instruments

High beam indicator

LIGHTS
Single round headlights (halogen)

Double faced front directional signals located on fenders

Five ICC-type marker lights

Single dome light in cab

Combination stop, turn, and tail lights

PAINT
DuPont Thermosetting Acrylic Enamel (TAE) paint

One solid color or two solid colors applied separately on cab, chassis, or wheels

MISCELLANEOUS
Operator's Manual

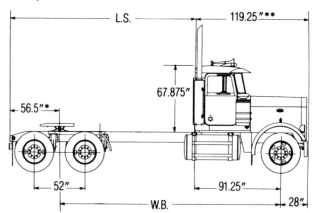

WHEEL BASE & LOAD SPACE DETERMINED TO EACH CUSTOMER'S REQUIREMENTS
*STANDARD TRACTOR OVERHANG DEPENDS UPON SUSPENSION — CONSULT ENGINEERING DATA BOOK
**AVAILABLE WITH OPTIONAL BBC DIMENSIONS OF 113.25″ AND 127.25″

MODEL 359
OPTIONAL COMPONENTS
AND EQUIPMENT

ENGINES

Caterpillar	3306 Series	245-300 HP
	3406 Series	285-425 HP
Cummins	NTC Series	240-475 HP
	L10 Series	240-300 HP
Detroit Diesel	6V92 Series	290-350 HP
	8V92 Series	350-475 HP

TRANSMISSIONS

Allison
Fuller
Spicer

Virtually all popular main and auxiliary transmissions are available to match engine torque and vehicle application

FRONT AXLES

Rockwell/Eaton   12,000-20,000 lb. capacity

REAR AXLES

Rockwell	Single drive 23,000 lb. capacity
Eaton	Single drive 23,000-26,000 and 35,000 lb. series
Rockwell	Tandem drive 38,000-50,000 lb. capacity
Eaton	Tandem drive 38,000-48,000 lb. capacity

SUSPENSIONS

Peterbilt	Single drive:	Air Trac 20,000 lb. capacity Leaf Spring 23,000-35,000 lb. capacity
	Tandem:	Air Trac 38,000 lb. capacity Air Leaf 38,000 lb. capacity
Hendrickson	Tandem:	U. RT. RS Series 34,000-50,000 lb. capacity
Reyco:	Tandem:	101, 102 Series 34,000-44,000 lb. capacity

FUEL TANKS

23" steel; 23", 26", and 29" aluminum in various gallonages

FRAME

Aluminum or steel channel with aluminum or steel crossmembers

MISCELLANEOUS

A wide choice of interiors, instruments, mirrors, seats, air equipment, electrical equipment, severe service options, radios and CB installation packages. Choose from a variety of factory designed paint schemes or design your own (customer specifies colors). Paint available in either Dupont TAE or Imron.

BBC

Available in 113", 119", and 127" BBC with a 28" axle setting. 113" with a 42" set-back front axle. and 119" with a 48" set-back front axle. (Note: Not all engines are available with all BBC's.)

SLEEPER BOX

36" Crawl-thru and 36" and 63" Walk-thru sleeper boxes

It's easy, even fashionable these days to blame the country's industrial manufacturers for most of the environmental pollution that we all encounter every day.

It's much more difficult to take the time to find out what manufacturers are doing to alleviate pollution: the research they're conducting, the tests they're carrying out and the investment of money, time and brains they're allocating in solving the problem.

Take the turbine-powered truck for example. There's been talk for years about it, but now, instead of talk, diligent and consistent efforts are being applied to perfect and produce it.

Today, in fact, the trucking industry appears to be nearing the threshold of an expansive program for the use of the turbine engine. Because it is quieter and emits less pollutant exhaust than other engines, the turbine should help reduce the problem of air and noise pollution on our highways and in our cities. That's only one step in the right direction, of course, but it's the very best kind of step for the trucking industry to be taking. It should also be noted that progress is being made in the design of present and second generation diesel engines to overcome the problems of pollution.

Those of us at Peterbilt Motors are completely behind the testing of the turbine engines, and are hopeful of the final outcome. Already we have installed turbine engines in two of our trucks and are cooperating in joint programs with turbine manufacturers and trucking companies to test them, to evaluate the results, and to make necessary design changes which will benefit both the trucking industry and the general public alike.

As members of the American Trucking Association Foundation, we support similar efforts by other manufacturers.

W. I. Waterhouse

W. I. Waterhouse
General Marketing Manager
Peterbilt Motors Company

MEMBER
ATA
FOUNDATION **INC.**
AMERICAN TRUCKING INDUSTRY

Peterbilt

The ad on the opposite page will appear in the October 9 issue of Newsweek, reaching more than 13,600,000 responsible and responsive American adults.

An idea whose time has come?

The idea has been around for two decades. It's the turbine engine, potentially a tremendous asset in the fight against air and noise pollution. Boats and planes have been tapping its power for years. But it hasn't been so easy to build turbine-powered trucks.

Now it is. And almost every truck manufacturer is testing several different engines to see if they make the grade technically and ecologically.

First impressions are good. The turbine is about 15 percent quieter than present truck diesel engines,

and cuts emissions well below the Federal Clean Air Act standards and the even tougher 1975 California state limits. It needs no tune-ups, because there is no timing, carburetor or fuel injection system to adjust.

As there's no way to enjoy the good life in America without both trucking and a healthy environment, it's encouraging to see so many turbine test vehicles on the road today. You can spot them by their fat, smokeless dual stacks and that futuristic low whine from the engine. It's also encouraging to

see the progress being made in the area of noise and air pollution with present and second generation diesel engines.

It will probably be years before the turbine becomes a permanent addition to the country's highways. By then we'll know for sure whether the turbine is one answer to cleaner air.

We all want cleaner air. Truck drivers, manufacturers, and the whole trucking industry like to breathe clean air just as much as you do.

 AMERICAN TRUCKING INDUSTRY

Peterbilt test vehicle, powered by a gas turbine engine.

Peterbilt Model
387

STANDARD SPECIFICATIONS

MODEL 387 STANDARD SPECIFICATIONS

The above illustration may include optional equipment and accessories and may not include all standard equipment.

FRAME

Heat-treated, 110,000 P.S.I. Yield, alloy steel with SAE Grade 8 flanged heat-treated bolts, and flanged nuts

10-5/8" frame depth with 3-5/8" flange width and 3/8" web thickness, 325" to 384", with steel crossmembers and gussets

Full ¼" inner liner

Steel front spring forward bracket

Severe service front cab mount bracket

Steel front cab support crosstie
Steel rear cab crossmember

Square end of frame
Front wheel mudflaps

FRONT AXLE

Rockwell FL931N, 20,000 lb. capacity

24,000 lb. capacity chrome vanadium non-progressive (02-01111) ten leaf steel springs with torque rods

Hydraulic power steering with Sheppard 592 integral gear 22" diameter steering wheel

Iron hubs, 13-3/16" bolt circle and 1-5/16" studs

Stemco oil seals with "Grit Guard" deflector ring

REAR AXLE

Rockwell SFD-4640 planetary double reduction tandem axle; 65,000 lb. capacity

Iron hubs, 13-3/16" bolt circle and 1-5/16" studs
Cast brake drums

Rockwell 18" x 7" "S" cam service brakes

Dust shields

Rear brake camshaft reinforcement

Anchorlok 36" parking brake on one axle

Grease seals

REAR SUSPENSION

Rockwell 6-Rod spring suspension; rubber bushed torque rod ends, bronze trunnion bushing, 15.16" pedestal height, 5" spring width, 58" axle spacing, 65,000 lb. capacity

ENGINE

Cummins NTC350 Big Cam II
855 cu. in. displacement
350 BHP (S.A.E.) at 2100 RPM
1120 lb. feet maximum torque at 1400 RPM
Water-cooled with 180° ventless thermostat

MODEL 387 STANDARD SPECIFICATIONS

Six cylinder turbocharged
32'' diameter high-mount fan
Oil cooler
PTG fuel system

Iron flywheel housing

Oil pan guard

Hand throttle

ENGINE ELECTRICAL

Leece-Neville 85 amp (crankshaft/belt driven) 12 volt alternator with integral regulator

12 volt starter

Peterbilt ether injection system
Push button start switch
Key ignition

Four Peterbilt 6-volt, Group 4 low-maintenance batteries rated at 800 cold cranking amps each.

FAN CLUTCH

None Furnished

AIR COMPRESSOR

Cummins 13.2 CFM air compressor

FILTERS

Integral spin-on full flow oil filter

Peterbilt (painted) remote mounted bypass oil filter

Spin-on fuel filter

Peterbilt spin-on water filter

COOLING SYSTEM

High-capacity core radiator with 1444 in² frontal area

Steel radiator sidemembers
Removable aluminum top tank

Removable steel bottom tank

Heavy-duty radiator crosstube

Cowl mounted radiator tie rods
Peterbilt ''Air Sweep''
10-lb. pressure relief cap
Full fan shroud
Dynacraft ''B'' (''Kevlar'' aramid fiber) radiator hoses
Shutterless cooling
Permanent-type anti-freeze effective to 20°F below
Steel radiator shell (painted) and stainless steel grill

AIR CLEANER

Donaldson EBA15-0058 dry-type air cleaner with vacuator
Air restriction indicator
Molded rubber sleeves and elbows with stainless steel clamps at all connections

EXHAUST

Single 5'' vertical exhaust system with 10'' muffler, stainless steel flex tubing and clamps
Ceramic coated standpipe with 45° cut-off

Heavy-duty stainless steel full round muffler guard

TRANSMISSION

Fuller ''Roadranger'' RT-12515; twin countershaft, 15 speed with iron case and cover, 1250 lb.-ft. nominal torque capacity

Main transmission rear support

DRIVELINES

1810 series with needle bearing and glidecote spline

CLUTCH

Spicer 14'' 2-plate super duty, rigid disc, angle spring clutch

Manually-adjustable clutch with greasable bearing

AIR SYSTEM

Peterbilt dual air system
Dynacraft 3069 rubber chassis hose
Tractor protection valve
Trailer charge valve

TIRES

12.00'' x 24'', 16 ply, all traction tread
(10 furnished)

WHEELS

24'' x 9.0'' disc, h.d. steel (10 furnished)

FUEL TANK

One 50-gallon 20'' diameter steel tank under cab on left-hand side (painted)

Heavy-duty steel fuel tank brackets and straps

MODEL 387 STANDARD SPECIFICATIONS

BATTERY BOX

Steel battery box with stirrup step under cab on right-hand side

Bumper step plates
Narrow steel bumper with center tow hook

Bumper step plates
Heavy-duty bumper mounted radiator guard (painted)

ELECTRICAL SYSTEM

"Pop-out" style manual-reset circuit breakers; crosslinked polyethelene insulated wiring harnesses with braided covering; all circuits numbered, color-coded, and routed through "hardshell" connectors in weather-proof enclosure; automatically actuated back-up light; four-way emergency flasher switch.

CAB & HOOD

Severe service cab; all aluminum construction with steel back panels, roof panels, and windshield mask; fully insulated with foam and lined with embossed aluminum; three point rubber mounting; extruded aluminum door frames; heavy-duty piano-type hinges; tinted safety glass throughout; dual air operated windshield wipers and washers; interior lining beige; tilt-out instrument panel; coat hooks.

126" B.B.C. steel butterfly type hood with removable side panels; flat steel fenders with "safety walk" surface

Stepboards to back of cab

Single rubber hood latches

SEATS

Driver-Peterbilt/Anchorlock Earl with seatbelt.

PASSENGER - None furnished
Vinyl upholstery

CAB ACCESSORIES

Black upholstery
Rubber floor mats
Padded doors with carpet inserts
41-7/8" heavy-duty stainless steel grab handle on left and 27½" heavy-duty stainless steel grab handle on right side

19-1/2" x 36" fixed rear window

Fresh air heater, 40,000 BTU, with integral windshield defroster, and central controls.
Dual padded interior sunvisors
Dual 7" x 16" adjustable, stainless steel rear view mirrors
Electric horn

Single Grover 1024 air horn with chrome finish
Cigar lighter and ashtray

INSTRUMENTS

Speedometer, 0 to 80 MPH with odometer

Tachometer, 0 to 3500 RPM
Engine oil pressure gauge
Water temperature gauge
Fuel level gauge
Ammeter
Dual air pressure gauge

Low air pressure warning light
Rheostat controlled lighting for all instruments
High beam indicator

LIGHTS

Single headlights

Headlight guards
Double faced front directional signals located on fenders
Directional light guards

Five ICC-type marker lights
Single dome light in cab
Combination stop, turn, and tail lights

PAINT

DuPont Thermosetting Acrylic enamel (TAE) paint

One solid color or two solid colors applied separately on cab, chassis, or wheels

MISCELLANEOUS

Wheel wrench
Operator's manual

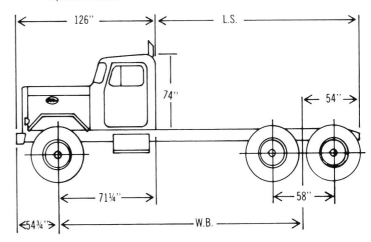

WHEELBASE & LOADSPACE DETERMINED TO EACH CUSTOMER'S REQUIREMENTS. /STANDARD TRACTOR OVERHAND DEPENDS UPON SUSPENSION—CONSULT ENGINEERING DATA BOOK.

MODEL 387
OPTIONAL COMPONENTS
AND EQUIPMENT

ENGINES

Caterpillar	3406 Series	280-400 HP
Cummins	NTC & KT Series	230-600 HP
Detroit Diesel	6V92 Series	270-335 HP
	8V92 Series	365-435 HP
	8V71 Series	305-370 HP

TRANSMISSIONS

Allison	Virtually all popular main and auxiliary
Fuller	transmissions are available to match engine
Spicer	torque and vehicle application.

FRONT AXLES

| Rockwell | 20,000 lb. or 28,000 lb. capacity (with radius rod suspension) |
| Eaton | 20,000 lb. capacity (with radius rod suspension) |

REAR AXLES

Rockwell	58,000 lb. thru 150,000 lb. capacity.
Eaton	65,000 lb. capacity.
Clark	80,000 thru 120,000 lb. capacity.

SUSPENSIONS

| Peterbilt | 6 rod 58,000 lb. thru 100,000 lb. capacity. |
| Hendrickson | RT, RS and R series 50,000 lb. thru 150,000 lb. capacity. |

FUEL TANKS
20″ diameter steel in various gallonages.

FRAME
Double or triple channel heat treated alloy steel.

MISC.
A wide choice of instruments, mirrors, seats, air equipment, electrical equipment, and severe service options. Choose from a variety of factory designed paint schemes or design your own; customer specifies colors. Paint available in either Dupont TAE or Imron.

BBC
126 in BBC with 54¾ inch SBFA.

Peterbilt Model 310

STANDARD SPECIFICATIONS

MODEL 310 STANDARD SPECIFICATIONS

The above illustration may include optional equipment and accessories and may not include all standard equipment.

FRAME
Heat-treated, 110,000 PSI yield, steel.
10-3/4" frame depth with 3-1/2" flange width and 3/8" web thickness.
Square rear frame.

FRONT AXLE
Rockwell FF941TW, 12,000-lb. rated capacity.
Forged aluminum hubs, 11-1/4" bolt circle for disc wheels.
Oil seals.

FRONT SUSPENSION
12,000-lb. nominal capacity constant rate leaf spring 4" wide x 64" long.
Chrome vanadium steel, shot-peened on tension side.
Threaded steel spring pins and bushings.

STEERING SYSTEM
Ross manual steering gear with triple roller contact and aluminum housing.
22" steering wheel.

REAR AXLE
Rockwell SQ100, hypoid single reduction tandem axle.
38,000 lb. rated capacity.
Forged aluminum hubs for disc wheels, 11-1/4" bolt circle.
Inter-axle differential lock-out.
Oil seals.

REAR SUSPENSION
Hendrickson RS-380 suspension.
38,000-lb. rated capacity.

SERVICE BRAKES
Rockwell cam air brakes: 15" x 4", front, 16-1/2" x 7" rear.
Cast drums.
Nylon air piping.

TIRES
11.00" x 24.5", 14-ply rated radial (10 furnished).

WHEELS
24.5" x 8.25" disc. high tensile lightweight steel (10 furnished).

MODEL 310 STANDARD SPECIFICATIONS

ENGINE

Cummins NTC 240 (power torque).
855 cu. in. displacement.
240 HP (S.A.E.) at 2100 RPM.
900 foot pounds maximum torque at 1300 RPM.
Water-cooled with 180° ventless thermostat.
Turbocharged, aftercooled.
28″ diameter high-mounted fan.
Alum. flywheel housing.
F/G spin-on fuel filter.
F/G spin-on bypass oil filter
Cummins 13.2 CFM air compressor.
Horton automatic fan hub.

ENGINE ELECTRICAL

12-volt lighting system with automatic reset circuit breakers.
Circuits number and color coded.
Quick-disconnect modular type harnesses.
12-volt starting system with automatic circuit breaker.
Four 6-volt, Group 4 batteries.
90-amp Leece-Neville belt driven alternator.
Cab mounted self-canceling directional signals with all-flash control.
Single headlamps.
Five marker lights in ICC location (nonpedestal).
Dual stop and taillights/back-up lights.
Front-side marker lights and reflector.
Key start switch.

COOLING SYSTEM.

1200H radiator with 1200 sq. in. frontal area.
Removable top and bottom tanks.
Top tank baffled for deaeration.
Remote coolant recovery tank.
10-lb. pressure relief cap.
Full fan shroud.
Shutterless cooling.
Permanent-type anti-freeze.

EXHAUST SYSTEM/AIR CLEANER

Single vertical exhaust system with muffler, stainless steel flex section for vibration isolation, and wide band clamps.
Exhaust stack height 10′8″.
Donaldson 11″ EBA dry-type air cleaner with filter restriction indicator, automatic moisture ejector.
Molded rubber sleeves and stainless steel clamps at all connections.

MAIN TRANSMISSION

Fuller RT11610, 10-speed twin-countershaft.

CLUTCH

Spicer angle spring 14″ dampened hub clutch assembly, self-adjusting with sealed bearings.

DRIVELINES

Standard duty series with single center bearing and needle-bearing universal joints.

CAB

53″ low cab forward style with back of cab on centerline of the front axle.
Steel frame with aluminum and fiberglass panels with all aluminum doors and continuous piano-type hinges.
Hydraulic cab latch and lift providing 53° tilt.

CAB FEATURES

ABS autumn smoke headliner and rear panel.
Fresh air heater, and integral adjustable defrosters.
Windshield: tinted, laminated safety glass.
Door windows: tinted, tempered safety glass, manual slide.
View window in right door.
Two-way vent in left door.
Stationary rear cab window.
Left and right inside door locks.
Full floor mat.
Insulation in cab roof, doors, side and rear panels.
Removable instrument panel.
Aluminum Grille.
Vernier type hand throttle.

MODEL 310 STANDARD SPECIFICATIONS

SEATS

DRIVER—Bostrom Delux Thin-Line.
RIDER—Seats, Inc. Model 970-20.

ACCESSORIES

Dual air-operated variable speed windshield wipers with separate
motors, heavy duty nonglare arms and parking control.
Electric windshield washers.
Cab dome light.
Dual electric horns.
6" x 16" dual polished stainless steel mirrors on stainless steel
brackets.
Inside sunvisor, driver's side.
Inside sunvisor, rider's side.
Cigarette lighter and one ashtray.
Arm rest on doors.
Black vinyl hood blanket.
Driver and rider side grab handle.
Seat belts.

WARNING DEVICES

Low air pressure warning light and buzzer.
High beam indicator.
High water temperature (210° F.) and low oil pressure warning
light and buzzer.
Inter-axle differential warning light.
Electric back-up alarm wiring installed to end of frame.
Low coolant indicator.

INSTRUMENTS

Voltmeter.
Electronic speedometer, with odometer.
Electronic tachometer.
Engine oil pressure gauge.
Water temperature gauge.
Reservoir air pressure gauges.
Electric fuel gauge.
Air application gauge.

PARKING BRAKE

MGM brake—dual axle, spring applied/air release.

FUEL TANK

One 80-gallon 22"-diameter steel tank behind the cab on right-
hand side.

STANDARD EQUIPMENT

Steel bumper 58" setting.
Front mud flaps.
Two mud flaps at rear.
Aluminum parallel battery box, LH back of cab.
Operator's Manual.
Removable front tow hook.

PAINT

Cab Exterior—DuPont Code 21667: White.
Cab Interior—Sherwin Williams: Flat Black F65-82.
Frame: DuPont Code 005: Black.

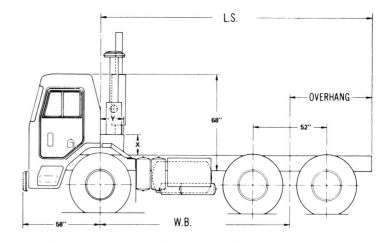

X = 14.0 For 6V92 Series   *Y = 17   For NTC Series
X = 18.5 For NTC Series   Y = 25   For 6L71 Series
X = 15.5 For 6L71 Series   Y = 20   For 6V92 Series

*DIMENSION FROM BACK-OF-CAB TO CLEAR EXHAUST MUFFLER, RADIATOR SURGE
TANK, AND AIR CLEANER SYSTEM, AND TO SERVICE THESE COMPONENTS, IS 20".

WHEELBASE & LOADSPACE DETERMINED TO EACH CUSTOMER'S REQUIREMENTS.
/STANDARD TRACTOR OVERHANG DEPENDS UPON SUSPENSION—CONSULT ENGINEERING
DATA BOOK.

MODEL 310
OPTIONAL COMPONENTS
AND EQUIPMENT

ENGINES

Caterpillar	3208 Series	210-250 HP
Caterpillar	3306 Series	245-270 HP
Cummins	NTC Series	240-350 HP
Detroit Diesel	6V92 Series	270-330 HP
	6L71 Series	230-275 HP

TRANSMISSIONS

Allison	Virtually all popular main and auxiliary
Fuller	transmissions are available to match engine
Spicer	torque and vehicle application.

FRONT AXLES

Rockwell	12,000 to 20,000 lb. capacity.
Ross	Single and dual integral power steering.

REAR AXLES

Rockwell	Single drive 18,000 to 23,000 capacity.
Eaton	Single drive 23,000 thru 26,000 capacity.
Rockwell	Tandem drive 38,000 thru 46,000 lb. capacities.
Eaton	Tandem drive 38,000 thru 48,000 lb. capacity.

SUSPENSIONS

Reyco	Single-drive:	Multi-leaf 18,000 lb.-26,000 lbs.
Peterbilt	Single-drive:	Air Trac 20,000 lb. capacity.
	Tandem:	Air Trac 38,000 lb. capacity.
Reyco		102-4-Spring 36,000 lb. capacity.
Hendrickson	Tandem:	RT, RS Series 38,000 thru 50,000 lb. capacity.

FUEL TANKS 22" diameter steel.

FRAME 10⅛" steel channel with steel crossmembers. Steel inserts also available.

MISC. Front engine PTO provisions with 78" bumper setting, fifth wheels, instruments and trailer connections. Paint available in either Dupont TAE or Imron.

Peterbilt Model

362

STANDARD SPECIFICATIONS

MODEL 362 STANDARD SPECIFICATIONS

The above illustration may include optional equipment
and may not include all standard equipment.

FRAME

Heat-treated, 110,000 P.S.I. yield, alloy steel with SAE Grade 8
flanged heat treated bolts, and flanged nuts.

10-3/8" frame depth with 3-1/2" flange width and 1/4" web thickness, up to 324", with steel crossmembers and gussets.

Tractor-tapered end of frame.

Peterbilt rear mudflaps with straight hangers.

FRONT AXLE

Rockwell FF931TW, 12,000 lb. capacity 15" x 4" cam brakes.

12,000 lb. capacity chrome vanadium split - progressive eight
leaf steel springs.
NSK recirc. ball type manual steering gear with 32.16 to 1 ratio;
22" diameter steering wheel.

Forged aluminum hubs, 11-1/4" bolt circle and 1-1/8" studs.
Centrifuse brake drums.

Stemco oil seals with "Grit Guard" deflector ring.

REAR AXLE

Rockwell SQHD hypoid single reduction tandem axle; 38,000 lb.
capacity.

Forged aluminum hubs, 11-1/4" bolt circle and 1-1/8" studs.
Centrifuse brake drums.

Eaton 16-1/2" x 7" "S" Cam Service Brakes.

Anchorlok 30" parking brake on one axle.
Manual slack adjusters.

Stemco oil seals with "Grit Guard" deflector ring.
Inter-axle differential lock-out with dash mounted warning light.
Iron differential carrier housings.

REAR SUSPENSION

Peterbilt tandem four-spring suspension; six point frame attachment, longitudinal torque arms to center frame bracket, center
equalizer beam for 50/50 load distribution, 52" axle spacing;
34,000 lb. capacity.

MODEL 362 STANDARD SPECIFICATIONS

ENGINE
Cummins Form. NTC 300 Big Cam.
855 cu. in. displacement.
300 BHP (S.A.E.) at RPM 1800.
1000 lb. feet maximum torque at 1300 RPM.
Water-cooled with 180° ventless thermostat.
Six cylinder – Turbocharged.
32" diameter high-mount fan.
Oil cooler.
PTG fuel system.

ENGINE ELECTRICAL
Leece-Neville 90 amp (crank-shaft/belt driven) 12 volt alternator with integral regulator.

12 volt starter.

Peterbilt Ether Injection system.
Push button start switch.
Key ignition.

Four Peterbilt 6 volt, Group 4 low-maintenance batteries rated at 800 cold cranking amps each.

FAN CLUTCH
Horton automatic fan clutch with override switch.

AIR COMPRESSOR
Cummins 13.2 CFM air compressor.

FILTERS
Integral spin-on full-flow oil filter.

Peterbilt (painted) remote mounted bypass oil filter.
Spin-on fuel filter.

Peterbilt spin-on water filter.

COOLING SYSTEM
Standard core radiator with 1470 in² frontal area.
Aluminum sidemembers.
Removable aluminum top tank.
Removable aluminum bottom tank.
Peterbilt "Air sweep".
10-lb. pressure relief cap.
Full fan shroud.
Dynacraft "B" ("Kevlar" aramid fiber) radiator hoses.
Shutterless cooling.
Permanent-type anti-freeze effective to –20°F below zero.
Chrome stainless steel bugscreen.

AIR CLEANER
Fram FA2550 engine mounted air cleaner with frontal air intake.

Air restriction indicator.

EXHAUST
Single 5" vertical exhaust system with 10" muffler, stainless steel flex tubing and clamps, and automatic cab tilt release with reseal connection.
Ceramic coated standpipe with 45° cut-off.

12' – 3" exhaust height from ground.

Standard aluminum full round muffler guard.

TRANSMISSION
Fuller "Roadranger" RT-9509A; twin-countershaft, 9-speed, iron case and cover, 950 lb.–ft. nominal torque capacity.

DRIVELINES
1710 series with needle bearing and glidecote spline.

CLUTCH
Spicer 14" 2-plate asbestos damp. disc, angle spring clutch.

Manually-adjustable clutch with greasable bearing.

AIR SYSTEM
Peterbilt dual air system.
Dynacraft 3069 rubber chassis hose.

Trailer hand valve located on console.
Combination tractor and trailer parking valve.
Tractor protection valve.
Trailer charge valve.

TIRES
11.00" x 24.5" 14 ply steel radial tread.

WHEELS
24.5" x 8.25" disc, high tensile lightweight steel (10 furnished).

FUEL TANK
One 60-gallon 23" diameter aluminum tank behind the cab on left-hand side (unpainted).

Heavy duty aluminum fuel tank brackets and straps.

MODEL 362 STANDARD SPECIFICATIONS

BATTERY BOX

Aluminum battery box with diamondette step under cab on left-hand side.

BUMPER

Deep tapered aluminum with recessed center tow pin.

ELECTRICAL SYSTEM

"Pop-out" style manual-reset circuit breakers; cross-linked polyethylene insulated wiring harnesses with braided covering all circuits numbered, color-coded, and routed through "hard-shell" connectors in weather-proof enclosure; automatically actuated back-up light; four-way emergency flasher switch.

CAB & SLEEPER

90" sleeper cab.
86° tilt with independent hydraulic system.
Aluminum construction, fully insulated with foam and lined vinyl, with positive dual locking cab hold-down devices; extruded aluminum door frames; heavy duty piano-type hinges; tinted safety glass throughout; triple air-operated windshield wipers and washers; tilt-out instrument panel; coat hooks.

825 mm x 2030 mm polyurethane sleeper mattress.
Vinyl sleeper curtain.

Safety net.
Single luggage compartment left and right.

SEATS

Driver-Peterbilt Air Ride (low-back) with seatbelt.

PASSENGER – Peterbilt bucket type with lower storage compartment and seat belt (low-back).

CAB ACCESSORIES

Black Upholstery.

Rubber floor mats.

Padded doors with carpet inserts.
Padded engine tunnel.

Cab entry system R&L.

Fresh air heater, 48,000 BTU with auxiliary blower to sleeper, integral windshield defroster, and central controls.
Triple padded interior sunvisors.
Dual 7" x 16" adjustable, stainless steel rear view mirrors.
Electric Horn.

Single Grover 1024 air horn with chrome finish.

Cigar lighter and 2 ashtrays.

INSTRUMENTS

Speedometer, 0–80 MPH with odometer (electric).

Tachometer, 0–3500 RPM (electric).
Engine oil pressure gauge.
Water temperature gauge.
Fuel level gauge.
Ammeter.
Dual air pressure gauge.

Low air pressure warning light.
Rheostat controlled lighting for all instruments.
High beam indicator.

LIGHTS

Dual rectangular headlights.

Double faced front directional signals.

Five ICC-type marker lights.
Single dome light in cab door actuated.
Combination stop, turn, and tail lights.

PAINT

DuPont Thermosetting Acrylic Enamel (TAE) paint.

One solid color or two solid colors applied separately on cab, chassis, or wheels.

MISCELLANEOUS

Wheel wrench.
Operator's manual.

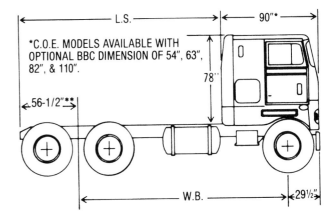

WHEELBASE & LOADSPACE DETERMINED TO EACH CUSTOMER'S REQUIREMENTS. **STANDARD TRACTOR OVERHANG DEPENDS UPON SUSPENSION — CONSULT ENGINEERING DATA BOOK. ENGLISH DIMENSIONS ARE NOMINAL.

MODEL 362
OPTIONAL COMPONENTS
AND EQUIPMENT

ENGINES

Caterpillar	3400 Series	280-450 HP
Cummins	NTC & KT Series	230-600 HP
	V Series	300-350 HP
Detroit Diesel	6V92 Series	270-335 HP
	8V92 Series	365-435 HP
	8V71 Series	305-370 HP

TRANSMISSIONS

Allison
Fuller
Spicer

{ Virtually all popular main and auxiliary transmissions are available to match engine torque and vehicle application.

FRONT AXLES

| Rockwell | 12,000 to 18,000 lb. capacity. |
| Eaton | 12,000 lb. capacity. |

REAR AXLES

Rockwell	Single drive 23,000 lb. capacity
Eaton	Single drive 23,000 thru 26,000 and 35,000 lb. series.
Rockwell	Tandem drive 38,000 thru 50,000 lb. capacities.
Eaton	Tandem drive 38,000 thru 48,000 lb. capacity.

SUSPENSIONS

Peterbilt	Single drive:	Air Trac 20,000 lb. capacity
		Leaf Spring 23,000 to 35,000 lb. capacity
	Tandem:	Air Trac 38,000 lb. capacity
		Air Leaf 38,000 lb. capacity
		4-Spring 34,000 and 38,000 lb. capacity.
		6 rod 44,000 lb. capacity.
Hendrickson	Tandem:	U, RT, RS Series 34,000 thru 50,000 lb. capacity.

FUEL TANKS 23 inch diameter in steel and 23, 26, or 29 inch aluminum in various gallonages.

FRAME Aluminum or steel channel with aluminum or steel crossmembers.

MISC. A wide choice of interiors, instruments, mirrors, seats, air equipment, electrical equipment, and radios and CB installation packages. Choose from a variety of factory designed paint schemes or design your own; customer specifies colors. Paint available in either Dupont TAE or Imron.

BBC Available in non-sleeper 54 and 63 inch BBC and 82, 90, and 110 inch sleeper cabs. (Note: All engines are not available in all cab lengths.)

FRAME AND EQUIPMENT

362 TANDEM STEER

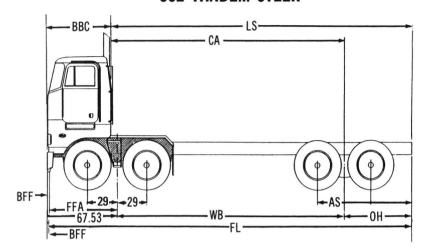

WB	Wheelbase **variable**	FFA	Front of frame to axle **66.53"**
LS	Loadspace **variable**	OH	Frame overhang **variable**
BBC	Bumper to back of cab **54", 63", 76", 82", 90", 110"**	AS	Tandem axle spacing **variable**
CA	Cab to C/L of axle(s) **variable**	FL	Frame length **variable**
		BFF	Bumper to front of frame **1"**

Model 362 Air Force Missile Carrier

Photo courtesy Bob A. Ray

Model 320 Commercial Front Loader

Model 378 Transfer Tractor

Model 320 Automated Side Loader

Model 357 Roll-Off

Model 357 Rear Loader

Model 379 Roll-Off

Model 357 Roll-Off

COME TO THE SOURCE.

Whether it's commercial or residential pickup, roll-off or transfer operations – Peterbilt offers a full line of proven refuse trucks. Trucks that help you answer your every need with workhorse durability. Low maintenance. Maneuverability. Power.

And no one offers you more choice in design, more flexibility when working with your body manufacturer.

In fact, no matter what body style your operation requires, Peterbilt has a model that will fit right in. Premium trucks that can be tailored to meet individual specifications – helping you achieve what may well be the lowest life cycle cost of any truck you've ever operated.

Need a tough truck that can handle tight situations? A truck that can be custom-built for specific jobs? A truck proven to deliver a long, reliable service life? A truck that drivers prefer?

Then come to the source.

For the name of the Peterbilt dealer nearest you call: 1-800-447-4700.

A DIVISION OF PACCAR

CLASS ATTRACTS CLASS

Peterbilt Model 362 D/F

STANDARD SPECIFICATIONS

362D   362F

The above illustration may include optional equipment and may not include all standard equipment.

FRAME

10⅜" x 3½" x ¼" steel rails, steel crossmembers and gussets, tapered end of frame

FRONT AXLE

Rockwell FF941 12,000 lb. front axle, 15" x 4" cam brakes, manual slack adjusters, iron hubs, cast brake drums, oil seals, manual steering, 12,000 lb. rolled eye springs

REAR AXLE

362D: Rockwell R-170 23,000 lb. rear axle, 16½" x 7" cam brakes, manual slack adjusters, iron hubs, cast brake drums, oil seals, parking brakes, Peterbilt split-progressive spring suspension, 20,000 lb. capacity

362F: Rockwell SQ100 38,000 lb. rear axle, 16½" x 7" cam brakes, manual slack adjusters, iron hubs, cast brake drums, oil seals, parking brakes on one axle, Peterbilt four-spring 34,000 lb. suspension, 52" axle spacing

ENGINE

Cummins Formula NTC 300, 300 HP @ 1800 RPM, 1000 lb-ft @ 1300 RPM

ENGINE ELECTRICAL

Delco 12 volt starter, key ignition with push button start switch, Leece-Neville 65 amp alternator, three 12 volt maintenance-free batteries (1875 CCA)

FILTERS

Spin-on fuel filter, spin-on oil filter, Fleetguard LF777 bypass oil filter

COOLING SYSTEM

Standard core (70mm) radiator with 1470 in² frontal area, shutterless cooling, Peterbilt "Air Sweep," Nalcool cooling system treatment, chrome stainless steel bugscreen, full fan shroud, Horton automatic fan clutch with override switch

AIR CLEANER

Donaldson "Custom" ECG11-2403 engine mounted air cleaner with frontal air intake, air restriction indicator

EXHAUST

Single 5" cab mounted vertical exhaust with 10" muffler, stainless steel flex tubing and clamps, automatic cab tilt release with reseal connection, 34" aluminum standpipe

TRANSMISSION

Fuller RT-11609A, 9-speed, 1150 lb-ft

DRIVELINES

1710 type

CLUTCH

Spicer 14" 2-plate non-asbestos dampened disc angle spring clutch, torque limiting clutch brake, manual adjust clutch cover with greasable bearing

Peterbilt

A DIVISION OF PACCAR

MODEL 362D/F STANDARD SPECIFICATIONS

AIR SYSTEM

Cummins 13.2 CFM air compressor, Peterbilt dual air system, steel air tanks, nylon chassis hose, two valve parking systems

TRAILER OPERATION

Hand valve mounted on console, 12 foot trailer air and electric lines, center mounted hose tenna (pogo stick)

TIRES

Goodyear G159 295/75R 22.5 14-ply radial tires.

WHEELS

Firestone 27404 22.5" x 8.25" steel disc wheels

FUEL TANK

60 gallon 23" diameter (unpainted) aluminum fuel tank mounted LH back of cab, heavy-duty aluminum brackets and straps

BATTERY BOX

Aluminum battery box with non-skid step mounted LH under cab

BUMPER

Bobbed minimum (unpainted) aluminum bumper

ELECTRICAL SYSTEM

Manual-reset circuit breakers, insulated wiring harnesses with braided covering, numbered and color-coded circuits

CAB

362D: 63" BBC non-sleeper cab, 86° tilt with independent hydraulic system, aluminum construction, positive dual locking cab hold-down devices, extruded aluminum door frames, heavy-duty piano-type door hinges, tinted safety glass throughout

362F: 90" BBC sleeper cab, 86° tilt with independent hydraulic system, aluminum construction, positive dual locking cab hold-down devices, extruded aluminum door frames, heavy-duty piano-type door hinges, tinted safety glass throughout, two luggage compartments

CAB EXTERIOR

Three air operated windshield wipers with washers, cab entry system on each side, 6" x 16" painted rear view mirrors, convex mirror over RH door

CAB INTERIOR

362D: Foam insulation, rubber floor mats in cab, engine tunnel cover and kick panel carpeting, padded vinyl sunvisor, black vinyl headliner and back of cab, 48,000 BTU fresh air heater with integral windshield defroster, 22" beige steering wheel, single electric horn, vent window locks, cigarette lighter and ashtray

362F: Foam insulation, rubber floor mats in cab, engine tunnel cover and kick panel carpeting, padded vinyl sunvisor, black vinyl headliner and sleeper walls, 48,000 BTU fresh air heater with integral windshield defroster, 22" beige steering wheel, single electric horn, vent window locks, cigarette lighter and two ashtrays, polyurethane sleeper mattress, vinyl sleeper curtain, bunk restraint

DRIVER SEAT

Peterbilt UltraRide™ vinyl low-back air suspension seat with seatbelt

PASSENGER SEAT

Peterbilt UltraRide™ vinyl low-back non-suspension seat with storage compartment and seatbelt

LIGHTS

Single round headlights with halogen high beam, cab mounted double-faced front directional signals, rear combination stop- turn- and tail-lights, five ICC type marker lights, dome light in cab

INSTRUMENTS

Tilt-out instrument panel, rheostat controlled lighting, high beam indicator, warning light on low air pressure (and inter-axle differential lock-out with 362F), Dixson electric speedometer (0-80 MPH) and electric tachometer (0-3500 RPM), ammeter, dual air pressure gauge, engine oil pressure gauge, water temperature gauge, fuel level gauge

PAINT

DuPont TAE paint, one color cab

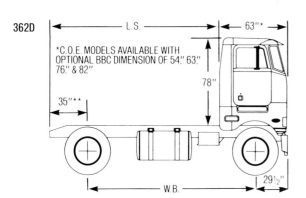

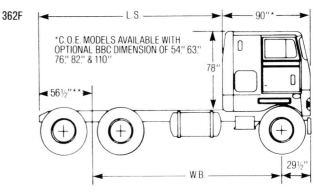

WHEELBASE & LOADSPACE DETERMINED TO EACH CUSTOMER'S REQUIREMENTS.
**STANDARD TRACTOR OVERHANG DEPENDS UPON SUSPENSION — CONSULT ENGINEERING DATA BOOK. ENGLISH DIMENSIONS ARE NOMINAL.

A DIVISION OF **PACCAR**

Peterbilt Model 397

Peterbilt's largest conventional, the Model 397 offers an added dimension of strength to off-highway trucking. From the ground up, the 397 will out-muscle, out-power and out-live just about any rig off the road.

Custom built to take the punishment of the heavy load, the 397 is designed to house bigger engines and carry bigger payloads. There's more steel and heavy-duty components to stand up to the job longer. There's better suspension and shock absorption to cut wear and tear, increase road life and smooth out the ride. And there's power steering and heavy springs for easy handling.

For additional load carrying capacity, the backbone of this heavy hauler is a triple channel steel frame. The rails run from the bumper under the radiator and cab. There are no frame add-ons or extensions: it's a single integral unit from front to rear. It's got a beefy front end protection system—grille and headlight guards; belly pan; short, rugged bumper—that's all heavy steel.

Under the butterfly hood there's a choice of engines rated up to 600 horse-power. You also get heavy-duty rear axles rated up to 150,000 pounds carrying capacity and 500,000 pounds gross combination weight.

Setting high off the ground, Peterbilt's severe service cab is standard. The heavy aluminum cab is bolted, riveted and steel skinned with extruded aluminum door frames and heavy-duty piano type hinges on both doors. Large windows are tinted safety glass throughout.

A typical example of Peterbilt quality engineering is in the cab support system for the 397. It reduces the cab stress all off-highway rigs are subject to when rolling over frame twisting, cab wrenching, uneven ground. Since it gets less wear and tear, the cab stays in shape longer. And the driver gets a smoother, more stable ride.

We know that a truck that is well built to begin with will last longer on the job with less maintenance and give better performance day after day. The result is Class—and at Peterbilt we're dedicated to it.

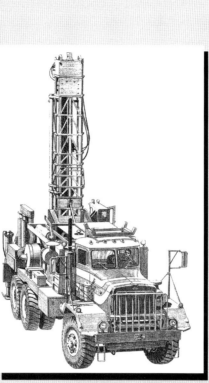

397 Base Model

Frame and Equipment

11½" triple stl rails/steel cross-
   members
Steel front spring brackets
Severe service front cab mount brkt
Steel front cab support
40" frame width
Square EOF

Front Axle and Equipment

DCB-SC4 wide track
24,000 lb. springs w/torque rods
Sheppard 592 power steering
6-spoke 24" hubs
Grease seals

Rear Axle and Equipment

Rockwell SPR-270
20x7 brakes
Grease seals
36" park brake—2 axles
Peterbilt 5" (80,000 #) suspension

Engine and Engine Equipment

NTC350 350HP @ 2100 rpm
Oil pan guard
Leece-Neville 85 amp alternator
Peterbilt ether injection
12-volt starter
(4) 6-volt H.D. Prestolite batteries

Fan clutch—none furnished
Cummins 13.2 CFM compressor
Peterbilt bypass oil filter
Spin-on fuel filter
Spin-on water filter
Iron flywheel housing
Deep core radiator
H.D. radiator support
Steel radiator sidemembers
Steel radiator bottom tank
Cowl mounted radiator tie rods
(1) FVG16-0152 air cleaner
Single 5" exhaust
H.D. stainless full round guard—single
Hand throttle

Transmission and Clutch

Allison CLBT 750 w/retarder 5-speed
1810 series driveline

Tires and Wheels

Front: Mich. XRB 14x24 ***ply
Rear: Mich. XRB 14x24 ***ply
Front: Goodyear 1024MD (24x10.0) rims
Rear: Goodyear 1024MD (24x10.0) rims

Fuel Tanks and Accessories

20" dia. stl. 50 gal: L/H under cab

Battery Box and Bumper

Steel battery box w/stirrup step
Narrow steel bumper w/center tow hook

H.D. radiator guard (bumper mtd)

Cab and Equipment

Severe service cab
141" steel butterfly hood
Single rubber hood latches
Stepboards to back of cab
Driver: Peterbilt/Anchorlok Earl
Passenger: none furnished
Black upholstery
Padded doors w/carpet inserts
Grab handles: 41⅞" l/h, 27½" r/h
Fixed rear window boc—std tint
Fresh air heater
Fender mtd rear view mirrors
(1) 1024 air horn
Reinforced windshield mask
Dual rear cab mounts

Instrument Lights

Low air warning light
Peterbilt speedometer 0-80 mph
   w/odometer
Peterbilt tachometer, 0-3500 rpm
Single headlights—painted shell
(5) ICC type Marker lights
Mirror mtd front directionals

Paint

Dupont TAE paint

397 Model Options

Front Axles

	Capacity
Eaton DCB-S (spoke wheels w/brakes)	20,000 lb.
Rockwell FL-951 (w/o brakes)	22,000 lb.
(w/brakes)	
FU-910P (w/brakes)	28,000 lb.

Rear Axles

Clark BD-71000	80,000 lb.
BD-91000	100,000 lb.
BD-101000	100,000 lb.
BD-121000	120,000 lb.
Rockwell SPR-440	100,000 lb.
SPR-570	150,000 lb.

Suspensions

Peterbilt 6"	100,000 lb.
Hendrickson R-700 Series	80,000 lb.
R-1000 Series	100,000 lb.
R-1500 Series	150,000 lb.

Engines

Cummins NTC-400-475
         KT   450-525-600
CAT 3406
      3408
DDAD 8V-92 Series

Transmissions

Allison CLBT 6061 & CLBT 5960
   remote mtd.

Tires

14x24 (25)   18x25
16x24 (25)

Wheels/Rims

Goodyear (demountable rims)

Fuel Tanks

20" diam steel
(70 and 100 gallon)

Miscellaneous

Consult your dealer
for availability.

Air Cleaner

Restricted to two-stage
Donaclone SBG series

Specifications are subject to change without notice. See your Peterbilt Dealer for latest prices and adjustments.

Peterbilt Model

349

STANDARD SPECIFICATIONS

Peterbilt

MODEL 349 STANDARD SPECIFICATIONS

The above illustration may include optional equipment
and may not Include all standard equipment.

OPTIONAL CONFIGURATIONS

349A   6x4 set-forward front axle chassis

349B   6x4 set-back front axle chassis

349W   6x6 set-back front axle chassis

FRAME

349A & 349B — 10-5/8" x 3-5/8" x 3/8" steel rails,
steel crossmembers and gussets, square end of frame,
suspension channel inserts, steel front cab support
crosstie.

349W — 10-3/8" x 3-1/2" x 1/4" steel rails, with full
length 9-13/16" x 3-1/4" x 1/4" steel liner, steel crossmembers and gussets, square end of frame, 8" guppy
belly suspension outsert, steel front cab support crosstie.

FRONT AXLE

349A & 349B — Rockwell FL941RDA 18,000 lb. front axle,
15" x 6" wedge brakes, manual slack adjusters, iron
hubs, cast brake drums, oil seals, TRW power steering with
right hand assist, 18,000 lb. cast eye springs.

349W — Rockwell RDS 1808RSA 18,000 lb. front axle,
17" x 6" wedge brakes, manual slack adjusters, iron hubs,
cast brake drums, grease seals, TRW power steering with
right hand assist, front axle drive shaft, 21,000 lb. cast
eye springs.

REAR AXLE

All configurations — Rockwell SQR-100 44,000 lb. rear
axle, 16-1/2" x 7" cam brakes, manual slack adjusters,
iron hubs, cast brake drums, oil seals, parking brakes on
both axles, brake dust shields, Hendrickson RT-440
suspension.

MODEL 349 STANDARD SPECIFICATIONS

ENGINE
All configurations — Caterpillar 3306 DITA, 245 HP @ 2100 RPM, 860 lb.-ft. @ 1350 RPM.

ENGINE ELECTRICAL
Leece-Neville 12 volt starter, key ignition switch with push button start switch, Leece-Neville 65 Amp alternator, four 6-volt low maintenance batteries (1600 CCA).

AIR COMPRESSOR
All configurations — Bendix "Tu-Flo 501" 12 CFM air compressor.

FILTERS
All configurations — Integral spin-on full flow oil filter, spin-on fuel filter, spin-on water filter.

COOLING SYSTEM
All configurations — Standard core (3 in.) radiator with 1270 in.^{2} frontal area, shutterless cooling, Peterbilt "Air Sweep," anti-freeze effective to −20°F, stainless steel bugscreen, full fan shroud, Horton automatic fan clutch with override switch, steel radiator sidemembers, aluminum radiator bottom tank, heavy-duty radiator crosstube, cowl mounted radiator tie rods.

AIR CLEANER
All configurations — Donaldson EBA 13-0049, 13" cowl mounted dry air cleaner with vacuator, air restriction indicator.

TRANSMISSION
All configurations — Fuller RTO-11608LL, 10 speed, 1150 lb.-ft.

349W — Dana 738 transfer case.

DRIVELINES
All configurations — Heavy-duty 1710 type main and 1710 type interaxle.

CLUTCH
All configurations — Spicer 14" 2-plate non-asbestos rigid disc angle spring clutch, torque limiting clutch brake, manual adjust clutch cover with greasable bearing.

AIR SYSTEM
All configurations — Peterbilt dual air system, steel air tanks, nylon chassis hose, spring brake modulator valve.

TIRES
Front — 349A & 349B — 11" x 22" 14-ply bias ply.
349W — 15" x 22.5" 16-ply bias ply.
Rear — All configurations — 11" x 22" 14-ply bias ply.

WHEELS
Front — 349A & 349B — 22" x 8" steel disc.
349W — 22.5" x 12.25" steel disc.
Rear — All configurations — 22" x 8" steel disc.

FUEL TANK
All configurations — One 50-gallon 23" diameter steel fuel tank mounted right hand side under cab, heavy-duty aluminum brackets and straps, full width grip-strut fuel tank step.

BATTERY BOX
All configurations — Steel battery box with grip-strut step mounted left hand side under cab.

BUMPER
All configurations — Tapered steel bumper with dual recessed tow eyes and one tow pin.

ELECTRICAL SYSTEM
All configurations — "Pop-out" style manual-reset circuit breakers; cross-linked polyethylene insulated wiring harnesses with braided covering all circuits numbered, color-coded, and routed through "hard-shell" connectors in weather-proof enclosure; automatically actuated back-up light; four-way emergency flasher switch.

MODEL 349 STANDARD SPECIFICATIONS

CAB AND HOOD

All configurations — Aluminum cab, three point rubber mounting, extruded aluminum door frames, heavy-duty piano-type hinges, door wedges, tinted safety glass throughout, 19-1/2" x 36" fixed rear window, view window in right hand door. Dual air-operated windshield wipers with washers, 6" x 16" painted rear view mirrors, convex mirror over right hand door.

349A — 115-1/4" BBC fiberglass hood with 90° spring assisted tilt, fiberglass fenders, front wheel mudflaps, dual rubber hood latches.

349B & 349W — 115-1/4" BBC fiberglass hood with 90° spring assisted tilt, fiberglass fenders and quarter fenders, front wheel mudflaps, dual rubber hood latches.

CAB INTERIOR

All configurations — Foam insulation, rubber floor mats, one padded sunvisor left hand side, formed ABS headliner with black vinyl inserts, black padded vinyl cab, back wall, 28,000 BTU fresh air heater with integral windshield defroster, 20" beige steering wheel, single electric horn, door actuated light switch, window vent locks, cigarette lighter and ashtray, Peterbilt "Cruise-Air" black vinyl low-back air suspension seat with seatbelt.

INSTRUMENTS

All configurations — Tilt-out instrument panel, rheostat controlled lighting, high beam indicator, warning light on low air pressure and inter-axle differential lock-out, Dixson electric speedometer (0-80 MPH) and electric tachometer (0-3500 RPM), ammeter, dual air pressure gauge, engine oil pressure gauge, water temperature gauge, fuel level gauge.

LIGHTS

All configurations — Single round sealed beam headlights with painted shell, fender mounted double faced front directional signals, rear combination stop-turn and tail lights, five ICC type marker lights, one dome light in cab.

PAINT

All configurations — Dupont TAE paint, one color cab.

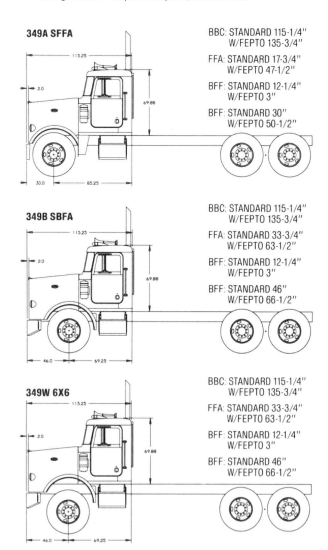

349A SFFA

BBC: STANDARD 115-1/4"
W/FEPTO 135-3/4"

FFA: STANDARD 17-3/4"
W/FEPTO 47-1/2"

BFF: STANDARD 12-1/4"
W/FEPTO 3"

BFF: STANDARD 30"
W/FEPTO 50-1/2"

349B SBFA

BBC: STANDARD 115-1/4"
W/FEPTO 135-3/4"

FFA: STANDARD 33-3/4"
W/FEPTO 63-1/2"

BFF: STANDARD 12-1/4"
W/FEPTO 3"

BFF: STANDARD 46"
W/FEPTO 66-1/2"

349W 6X6

BBC: STANDARD 115-1/4"
W/FEPTO 135-3/4"

FFA: STANDARD 33-3/4"
W/FEPTO 63-1/2"

BFF: STANDARD 12-1/4"
W/FEPTO 3"

BFF: STANDARD 46"
W/FEPTO 66-1/2"

MODEL 349
OPTIONAL COMPONENTS
AND EQUIPMENT

ENGINES

Caterpillar	3306B	270 HP
Cummins	NTC&PT Series	240-400 HP
Cummins	LTA 10 Series	240-270 HP
Detroit Diesel	6L71 Series	230-275 HP
Detroit Diesel	6V92 Series	270-330 HP
Detroit Diesel	8V92 Series	355-400 HP

TRANSMISSIONS

Allison	Virtually all popular main and auxiliary
Fuller	transmissions are available to match engine
Spicer	torque and vehicle application.

FRONT AXLES

349A & 349B:
Rockwell	14,600 to 20,000 lb. capacity.

349W (Front Drive Axles):
Rockwell	18,000 to 21,000 lb. capacity.
Fabco	16,000 to 23,000 lb. capacity.

REAR AXLES

Rockwell	Single drive 23,000 to 30,000 lb. capacity.
Eaton	Single drive 23,000 to 35,000 lb. capacity.
Rockwell	Tandem drive 38,000 to 58,000 lb. capacity.
Eaton	Tandem drive 38,000 to 58,000 lb. capacity.
Rockwell	Non-driving up to 20,000 lb. capacity.

SUSPENSIONS

Peterbilt	Single Drive:	Leaf Spring 23,000 to 35,000 lb. capacity.
	Tandem Drive:	6-rod 44,000 lb. capacity.
Hendrickson	Tandem Drive:	R, RS, RT Series; 38,000 to 65,000 lb. capacity.

FRAME

Steel channel with steel or aluminum cross-members; heavy-duty aluminum channel with aluminum crossmembers; front engine power take-off provisions with extended frame.

FUEL TANKS

20" or 23" diameter steel or aluminum in various gallonages.

MISC.

Wheels and tires up to 12" x 24" and 18" x 22.5," a wide choice of interiors, instruments, seats, electrical equipment and severe service options.

PETERBILT MODEL 320 STANDARD SPECIFICATIONS

MODEL 320 STANDARD SPECIFICATIONS

The illustration may include optional equipment and accessories and may not include all standard equipment.

FRAME
10-3/4″ x 3-1/2″ x 3/8″ steel rails, steel crossmembers and gussets, square end of frame without crossmember, front wheel mudflaps, one front tow eye with pin

FRONT AXLE
Rockwell FL941 20,000 lb. front axle, 16-1/2″ x 6″ cam brakes, iron hubs, cast brake drums, oil seals, dual TRW power steering with 9 quart reservoir, 18,000 lb. rolled eye springs

REAR AXLE
Eaton DS451 45,000 lb. rear axle, 16-1/2″ x 7″ cam brakes, manual slack adjusters, iron hubs, cast brake drums, oil seals, parking brakes on both axles, Hendrickson RT440 44,000 lb. suspension, 52″ axle spacing

ENGINE
Cummins L10-240, 240 HP @ 2100 RPM, 900 lb-ft @ 1300 RPM

ENGINE ELECTRICAL
Delco 12 volt starter, key ignition with push button start switch, L-N 100 amp alternator, three 12 volt maintenance free batteries (1875 CCA)

FILTERS
Fleetguard FS1212 spin-on fuel filter/water separator, spin-on oil filter, Fleetguard LF777 bypass oil filter

COOLING SYSTEM
High-capacity core radiator with 1154 in² frontal area, 10 psi relief cap, removable top and bottom tanks, top tank baffled for deaeration, shutterless cooling, anti-freeze effective to — 20 °, full fan shroud, stainless steel grille, Horton automatic fan clutch with override switch, remote mounted coolant recovery tank

AIR CLEANER
Donaldson 11″ ECG horizontal mounted air cleaner with vacuator, air restriction indicator

EXHAUST
Single vertical exhaust with muffler located behind cab on right hand side, stainless steel flex tubing, wide band clamps

TRANSMISSION
Fuller RTO-11708LL, 10 speed, 1150 lb-ft

DRIVELINE
1710 type main and interaxle

CLUTCH
Spicer 14″ 2-plate non-asbestos dampened disc angle spring clutch, torque limiting clutch brake, manual adjust clutch cover with greasable bearing

MODEL 320 STANDARD SPECIFICATIONS

AIR SYSTEM
Cummins 13.2 CFM air compressor, Peterbilt dual air system, steel air tanks, Nylon chassis hose, (2) valve parking system, SBM valve

TIRES
Front: Michelin Pilot XZZ 14/80R20 18 ply radial
Rear: Michelin XDHT 11″x22.5″ 14 ply radial

WHEELS
Front: Budd R92060-2; 20″x10.0″ steel disc
Rear: Budd R87460; 22.5″x8.25″ steel disc

FUEL TANK
50 gallon 23″ diameter (painted) steel fuel tank, heavy-duty aluminum brackets and straps

BATTERY BOX
Steel COE type battery box mounted LH back of cab

BUMPER
Steel channel (painted) bumper

ELECTRICAL SYSTEM
Automatic-reset circuit breakers, insulated wiring harnesses with braided covering, numbered and color-coded circuits, back-up alarm wiring to end of frame

CAB
53″ LCF (58″ BBC) LH drive cab with 53° hydraulic tilt, steel frame with aluminum and fiberglass panels, all aluminum doors with piano type hinges and roll-down windows, view window in RH door, two-way vent in LH door, door locks, 17″x38″ fixed rear window, tinted safety glass throughout, bright finish grille

CAB EXTERIOR
Electric windshield washers, dual air-operated variable speed windshield wipers with separate motors, cab entry system on each side, 7″x16″ stainless steel rear view mirrors, dual rear cab fenders, service module back of cab

CAB INTERIOR
Foam insulation, rubber floormats, ABS autumn smoke headliner and rear cab panel, black vinyl engine tunnel cover, (2) sunvisors, 41,000 BTU fresh air heater with integral adjustable defrosters, 18″ black steering wheel, dual electric horns, door mounted armrests, cigarette lighter and ashtray

MODEL 320 STANDARD SPECIFICATIONS

DRIVER SEAT

Peterbilt non-suspension seat with retractable seat belt

PASSENGER SEAT

Peterbilt non-suspension seat with retractable seat belt

INSTRUMENTS & CONTROLS

Removable instrument panel, engine tunnel mounted control console, vernier type hand throttle, cab mounted cable style transmission shifter, low air pressure warning light and buzzer, low oil pressure and high water temperature warning lights and buzzers, interaxle differential lockout warning light, parking brake control valve, headlight switch with beam indicator, directional signal controls with headlight dimmer switch, water temperature gauge, engine oil pressure gauge, dual air pressure gauge, fuel level gauge, voltmeter, electric speedometer (0-80 mph), electric tachometer (0-3500 rpm)

LIGHTS

Dual rectangular headlights, (5) ICC type marker lights, cab mounted front directionals, (1) dome light in cab

PAINT

DuPont Imron solid color

One color on cab, chassis, bumper and fuel tank; white wheels

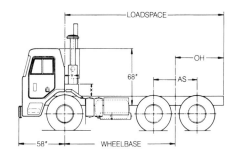

320 MODEL CHASSIS DIMENSIONS

	C-Series	L-10	3306
X	12.0"	7.0"	9.25"
Y	9.0"	19.0"*	19.5"*

*Dimension from back of cab to clear exhaust muffler, radiator surge tank, and air cleaner system and to service these components is 20"

MODEL 320 OPTIONAL SPECIFICATIONS*

FRAME
Steel Inserts
Aluminum Crossmembers

FRONT AXLES
Eaton	EFA12F4	12,000 lbs.
Rockwell	FG941	14,600 lbs.
Rockwell	Tandem FL941	36,000 lbs.

REAR AXLES
Rockwell & Eaton
23,000-30,000 lbs.	single drive
40,000-52,000 lbs.	tandem drive

REAR SUSPENSIONS
Single Drive	Peterbilt Air Trac	20,000 lbs.
	Peterbilt Spring	23,000-35,000 lbs.
	Reyco Spring	29,000 lbs.
Tandem Drive	Hendrickson	38,000-52,000 lbs.
	Peterbilt Air Trac	38,000-44,000 lbs.
	Reyco Spring	44,000 lbs.
	Ridewell Dynalastic	44,000 -50,000 lbs.

ENGINES
Caterpillar	3306 Series	245-270 HP
Cummins	C-Series	240-250 HP
	L10 Series	240-300 HP

*Consult your Dealer for additional optional specifications

TRANSMISSIONS
Allison	MT653, MT654, HT740, HT754, HT750
Fuller	5, 7, 9, 10 and 13 speed
Spicer	5, 6, 7 and 10 speed
ZF	5HP600, 6HP600

TIRES
General, Goodyear, Michelin

WHEELS/RIMS
Accuride, Alcoa, Budd, Motorwheel, Peterbilt

FUEL TANKS
Aluminum and steel 40-100 gallon capacity

CABS
Right Hand Drive
Dual Drive with low-entry RH Stand-Up
Left Hand Drive with 3-man seating

CAB EQUIPMENT
Air Suspension Driver Seat
Air Conditioning
Wheel Well Fenders
Diamond Plate Roof Cover
Front Cab Guard

PETERBILT MODEL 357 STANDARD SPECIFICATIONS

MODEL 357 STANDARD SPECIFICATIONS

The illustration may include optional equipment and accessories and may not include all standard equipment.

FRAME

Heat-treated, 110,000 P.S.I. yield, alloy steel with SAE Grade 8 bolts and nuts

10.625″ frame depth with 3.625″ flange width and .375″ web thickness with steel crossmembers and gussets

Square end of frame

Suspension channel inserts

Front wheel mudflaps

FRONT AXLE

Eaton EFA18F3; 18,000 lb. capacity; 16.5″ x 6″ cam brakes

18,000 lb. split-progressive springs

TRW power steering with right hand assist and cowl mounted reservoir

Iron Hubs

Cast brake drums

Manual slack adjusters

REAR AXLE

Eaton DS451P 45,000 lb. capacity

16.5″ x 7″ cam brakes; brake chambers mounted for additional suspension clearance

Cast brake drums

Iron Hubs

Parking brakes on both axles

Manual slack adjusters

Oil seals

Brake dust shields

REAR SUSPENSION

Hendrickson RT440, 44,000 lb. capacity

ENGINE

Caterpillar 3306B (ATAAC)

285 BHP (SAE) at 2000 RPM

1050 lb. feet maximum torque at 1350 RPM

ENGINE ELECTRICAL

Delco 80 amp alternator

Leece-Neville 12 volt starter

Push button start switch-key ignition

Three Peterbilt 12 volt, low maintenance batteries rated at 1875 cold cranking amps

FAN CLUTCH

Horton automatic fan clutch with override switch

FILTERS

Integral spin-on full flow oil filter

Frame-mounted spin-on fuel filter

Radiator-mounted spin-on water filter

MODEL 357 STANDARD SPECIFICATIONS

COOLING SYSTEM
Standard core radiator with 1270 sq. in. frontal area

Peterbilt Air Sweep®

Full fan shroud

Shutterless cooling

Permanent-type anti-freeze effective to 20° below zero

Polished outer radiator shell and stainless steel grille

AIR CLEANER
Donaldson 13″ dry-type air cleaner cowl mounted with vacuator

Stainless steel brackets and straps

EXHAUST
Single 5″ vertical exhaust system with resilient-mounted 10″ muffler on cab

Stainless steel flex tubing and clamps

Aluminum standpipe with 45° cut-off

TRANSMISSION
Fuller RT011609B; 9 speed; 1150 lb.-ft. nominal torque capacity

DRIVELINES
Spicer heavy-duty 1710 type main and 1710 type interaxle

CLUTCH
Spicer 14″ 2-plate non-asbestos dampened disc angle spring clutch

Torque-limiting clutch brake

Manually-adjustable clutch with greasable bearing

AIR SYSTEM
Bendix "Tu-Flo 501" 12CFM air compressor

Peterbilt dual air system

Nylon chassis hose

Steel air tanks

Spring brake modulator valve

Two valve parking system

TIRES
Super Hi Miler, 11″ x 22″; 14-ply (10 furnished)

WHEEL
22″ x 8″ steel disc (10 furnished)

FUEL TANK
50 gallon 20″ diameter aluminum fuel tank mounted right-hand side under cab

Aircraft style fuel cap

Heavy-duty aluminum fuel tank brackets and straps

Full-width non-slip fuel tank step

BATTERY BOX
Steel battery box with non-slip step mounted left-hand side under cab

BUMPER
Tapered painted aluminum bumper with center tow hook

ELECTRICAL SYSTEM
Manual reset circuit breakers and auto fuses with braided covering on harnesses; all circuits numbered and routed through "hard shell" connectors in weather-proof enclosure; automatically actuated back-up light; four-way emergency flasher switch; power distribution center in cab

CAB & HOOD
Aluminum cab fully insulated with foam; three-point rubber mounting; extruded aluminum door frames; heavy-duty piano-type hinges; tinted safety glass throughout; fixed rear window; view window in right-hand door; lift out instrument panel. 111″ BBC fiberglass hood with 90° spring assisted tilt; single hood latches; fiberglass fenders; polished hood crown

SEAT
Peterbilt UltraRide™ air suspension low-back driver's seat with retractable seat belts

CAB FEATURES
Vantage interior includes:

    Padded vinyl upholstery panels and headliner

    Vinyl door pads

    Padded interior sunvisor

    Black rubber floor mats

36″ heavy-duty stainless steel grab handle mounted left hand side

Vent window locks

Fresh air heater with integral windshield defroster

Dual 6″ x 16″ painted rear view mirrors

MODEL 357 STANDARD SPECIFICATIONS

Convex mirror over right-hand door

Electric horn

Single Grover 1024 air horn with chrome finish

Cigarette lighter and ashtray

20″ black 2 spoke steering wheel

INSTRUMENTS

Speedometer, 0-80 MPH with odometer (electric)

Tachometer, 0-3000 RPM (electric)

Voltmeter

Engine oil pressure gauge

Water temperature gauge

Fuel level gauge

Dual air pressure gauge

Low air pressure warning light

High water temperature warning light

Low oil pressure warning light

High beam indicator

LIGHTS

Single pod mounted rectangular halogen high beam headlights with integral turn signals

Five rectangular ICC-type marker lights

Dome light in cab

Rear combination stop, turn and tail lights

PAINT

Dupont Imron solid color

One solid color applied on cab and chassis; white wheels

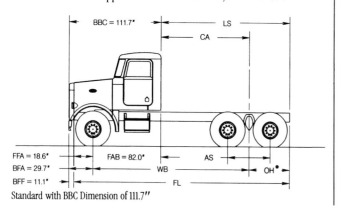

Standard with BBC Dimension of 111.7″

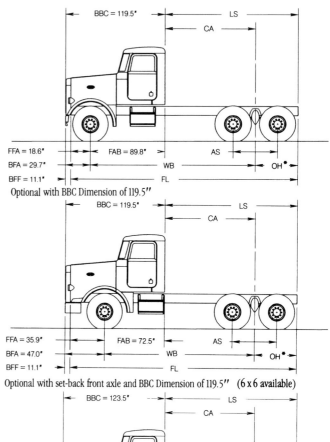

Optional with BBC Dimension of 119.5″

Optional with set-back front axle and BBC Dimension of 119.5″   (6 x 6 available)

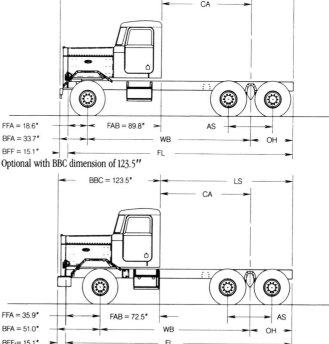

Optional with BBC dimension of 123.5″

Optional with set-back front axle and BBC dimension of 123.5″   (6 x 6 available)

Wheel base & load space determined to each customer's requirements

*Standard tractor overhang depends upon suspension Consult engineering data book

MODEL 357 OPTIONAL COMPONENTS AND EQUIPMENT

ENGINES

Caterpillar	3306B	285-300 HP
	3406B	310-425 HP
Cummins	LTA 10 Series	250-300 HP
	NTC Series	300-444 HP

TRANSMISSIONS

Fuller	Virtually all popular main and auxiliary
Spicer	transmissions are available to match
	engine torque and vehicle application

FRONT AXLES

Rockwell & Eaton	12,000-20,000 lbs.	Non-Driving
Rockwell	21,000 lbs.	Driving
Fabco	23,000 lbs.	

REAR AXLES

Rockwell	40,000-46,000 lbs.	tandem drive
Eaton	40,000-52,000 lbs.	tandem drive

REAR SUSPENSIONS

Tandem Drive	Peterbilt Air Trac	38,000-44,000 lbs.
	Hendrickson	
	R, RS, RT Series	38,000-65,000 lbs.

FRAME

Steel channel with steel or aluminum crossmembers;
heavy-duty aluminum channel with aluminum crossmembers;
forward extension of frame for mixer and snow plow service

FUEL TANKS

20", 23" and 26" aluminum and 23" steel in various gallonages

BBC

Available with a 111" BBC, a 119" BBC with a set-forward or set-back front axle, or a 123" BBC with a set-forward or set-back front axle and steel butterfly hood (Note: Not all engines are available in all BBC's)

MISCELLANEOUS

Wheels and tires up to 12" x 24" and 18" x 22.5", a wide choice of interiors, instruments, seats, electrical equipment and severe service options. Consult applications engineering for other optional components

PETERBILT MODEL 375 STANDARD SPECIFICATIONS

MODEL 375 STANDARD SPECIFICATIONS

The illustration may include optional equipment and accessories and may not include all standard equipment.

FRAME

Heat-treated, 110,000 P.S.I. yield, alloy steel with SAE Grade 8 flanged heat treated bolts, and flanged nuts

10.375″ frame depth with 3.5″ flange width and .25″ web thickness with steel crossmembers and gussets

Tractor-tapered end of frame

Peterbilt rear mudflaps with straight hangers

Front wheel mudflaps

FRONT AXLE

Eaton EFA12F4; 12,000 lb. capacity 15″ x 4″ cam brakes

10,000 lb. capacity taper leaf springs with tubular shocks

Iron hubs, 11.25″ bolt circle and standard studs

Cast brake drums

Oil seals

REAR AXLE

Eaton DS402 single reduction tandem axle; 40,000 lb. capacity

Iron hubs, 11.25″ bolt circle and standard studs

Cast brake drums

Eaton 16.5″ x 7″ "S" cam service brakes

30″ parking brake on one axle

Manual slack adjusters

Oil Seals

Inter-axle differential lock-out with dash mounted warning light

REAR SUSPENSION

Peterbilt tandem four spring suspension; six point frame attachment, longitudinal torque arms to center frame bracket, center equalizer beam for 50/50 load distribution, 52″ axle spacing, 34,000 lb. capacity

ENGINE

Caterpillar 3306B (ATAAC)

285 BHP (SAE) at 1900 RPM

950 lb. feet maximum torque at 1350 RPM

ENGINE ELECTRICAL

Delco 80 amp 12 volt alternator

12 volt starter

Ether injection system

Push button start switch — key ignition

Three Peterbilt 12 volt, maintenance-free batteries rated at 1875 cold cranking amps

FAN CLUTCH

Horton automatic fan clutch with override switch

MODEL 375 STANDARD SPECIFICATIONS

FILTERS
Integral spin-on full flow oil filter

Frame-mounted spin-on fuel filter

Radiator-mounted spin-on water filter

COOLING SYSTEM
Standard core radiator with 1270 sq. in. frontal area

Aluminum sidemembers

Removable aluminum top tank

Removable aluminum bottom tank

Peterbilt Air Sweep®

10 lb. pressure relief cap

Full fan shroud

Dynacraft "B" ("Kevlar" aramid fiber) radiator hoses

Shutterless cooling

Permanent-type anti-freeze effective to 20° below zero

Polished outer radiator shell and stainless steel grille

Flex-a-lite plastic fan

AIR CLEANER
Donaldson 11" dry-type under hood mounted with vacuator

Air restriction indicator in cab

Stainless steel clamps at all air intake connections

EXHAUST
Single 5" horizontal exhaust system with 10" muffler, stainless steel flex tubing and clamps

TRANSMISSION
Fuller T8607A: 7 speed, iron case and cover, 975 lb.-ft. nominal torque capacity

DRIVELINES
Spicer 1710 type main and interaxle

CLUTCH
Spicer 14" 2-plate non-asbestos dampened disc, angle spring clutch

Torque-limiting clutch brake

Manually-adjustable clutch with greasable bearing

AIR SYSTEM
Bendix 12 CFM air compressor

Stainless steel/teflon discharge line

Peterbilt dual air system

Nylon chassis hose

Steel air tanks

Two valve parking system

TRAILER OPERATION
Trailer hand valve located on steering column

Tractor protection valve

Trailer charge valve

12' trailer air and electric lines

Center mounted hose tenna

TIRES
22.5", 14-ply, low profile radial tread (10 furnished)

WHEELS
22.5" x 8.25" disc, high tensile lightweight steel (10 furnished)

FUEL TANK
One 80-gallon 26" diameter aluminum tank under cab on right-hand side (unpainted)

Aircraft style fuel cap

Heavy-duty aluminum fuel tank brackets and straps

Non-slip fuel tank step

BATTERY BOX
Aluminum battery box with non-slip step under cab on left-hand side

BUMPER
Cycolac® aerodynamic bumper with center tow hook

ELECTRICAL SYSTEM
Manual reset circuit breakers and auto fuses with braided covering on harnesses; all circuits numbered, color-coded, and routed through "hard shell" connectors in weather-proof enclosure; automatically actuated back-up light; four-way emergency flasher switch; power distribution center in cabs

CAB & HOOD
Aluminum cab fully insulated with foam; three-point rubber mounting; extruded aluminum door frames; heavy-duty piano-type hinges; tinted safety glass throughout; electric windshield wipers and washers with intermittent feature; lift-out instrument panel; fixed rear window. 114" BBC with fiberglass hood and fenders with 90° spring assisted tilt; single hood latches, polished hood crown

MODEL 375 STANDARD SPECIFICATIONS

SEATS

Driver: Peterbilt/UltraRide™ air-suspension seat (low back with retractable seatbelt)

Passenger: Peterbilt/UltraRide™ non-suspension seat (low back with retractable seatbelt and storage compartment)

Vinyl upholstery

CAB FEATURES

Vantage interior includes:

    Padded vinyl headliners, back panels and doors

    Rubber floor mats

    Padded interior sunvisor

    2 coat hooks

    20″ black 2 spoke steering wheel

36″ heavy-duty stainless steel left hand and right hand cab mounted grab handles

Vent window locks

Fresh air heater with integral windshield defroster

Dual 6″ x 16″ painted rear view mirrors

Electric horn

Cigarette lighter and ashtray

Convex mirror over right hand door

INSTRUMENTS

Speedometer, 0-80 MPH with odometer (electric)

Tachometer, 0-3000 RPM (electric)

Voltmeter

Engine oil pressure gauge

Water temperature gauge

Fuel level gauge

Dual air pressure gauge

Low air pressure warning light

High water temperature warning light

Low oil pressure warning light

Electronically controlled lighting for all instruments

High beam indicator

LIGHTS

Fender mounted composite halogen high beam headlights; bumper mounted directional signals

Five rectangular ICC-type marker lights

Single dome light in cab

Rear combination stop, turn, and tail lights

PAINT

DuPont Imron solid color

One solid color or two solid colors applied separately on cab, chassis, white wheels

MISCELLANEOUS

Operator's Manual

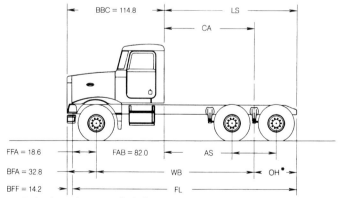

Standard with BBC dimension of 114.8″

Wheel base & load space determined to each customer's requirements

*Standard tractor overhang depends upon suspension Consult engineering data book

MODEL 375 OPTIONAL COMPONENTS AND EQUIPMENT

ENGINES

Caterpillar	3306 Series	270-300 HP
Cummins	L10 Series	240-300 HP

TRANSMISSIONS

Fuller	Many popular main transmissions are
Spicer	available to match engine torque and vehicle application

FRONT AXLES

Rockwell & Eaton	12,000 lb. capacity

REAR AXLES

Rockwell & Eaton	23,000 lbs.	single drive
Rockwell	40,000-46,000 lbs.	tandem drive
Eaton	40,000-48,000 lbs.	tandem drive

SUSPENSIONS

Single Drive	Peterbilt Air Trac	20,000 lbs.
	Peterbilt Leaf Spring	20,000-23,000 lbs.
Tandem Drive	Peterbilt Air Trac	38,000-40,000 lbs.
	Peterbilt Air Leaf	38,000 lbs.
	Peterbilt Leaf Spring	38,000 lbs.

Hendrickson U, RT, RS Series	34,000-44,000 lbs.
Reyco 101, 102 Series	34,000-44,000 lbs.

FUEL TANKS

23", steel; 23", 26" aluminum in various gallonages

FRAME

Aluminum or steel channel with aluminum or steel crossmembers

MISCELLANEOUS

A wide choice of interiors, instruments, mirrors, seats, air equipment, electrical equipment, severe service options, radios and CB installation packages. Choose from a variety of factory designed paint schemes or design your own (customer specifies colors). Paint available in DuPont Imron.

BBC

Available in 114" BBC with a 33" axle setting

SLEEPER BOX

36" walk-thru sleeper box

PETERBILT MODEL 377 STANDARD SPECIFICATIONS

MODEL 377 STANDARD SPECIFICATIONS

The illustration may include optional equipment and accessories and may not include all standard equipment.

FRAME

Heat-treated, 110,000 P.S.I. yield, alloy steel with SAE Grade 8 bolts and nuts

10.375" frame depth with 3.5" flange width and .25" web thickness with steel crossmembers and gussets

Tractor-tapered end of frame

Peterbilt rear mudflaps with straight hangers

Front wheel mudflaps

FRONT AXLE

Eaton EFA12F4; 12,000 lb. capacity 15" x 4" cam brakes

12,000 lb. capacity taper leaf springs with tubular shocks

TRW HFB64 power steering with engine compartment mounted reservoir

Iron hubs, 11.25" bolt circle and standard studs

Cast brake drums

Oil seals

REAR AXLE

Eaton DS402 single reduction tandem axle; 40,000 lb. capacity

Iron hubs, 11.25" bolt circle and standard studs

Cast brake drums

16.5" x 7" "S" cam service brakes

30" parking brake on one axle

Manual slack adjusters

Oil seals

Inter-axle differential lock-out with dash mounted warning light and buzzer

REAR SUSPENSION

Peterbilt tandem four spring suspension; six point frame attachment, longitudinal torque arms to center frame bracket, center equalizer beam for 50/50 load distribution, 52" axle spacing, 34,000 lb. capacity

ENGINE

Caterpillar 3406B (ATAAC)

310 BHP (SAE) at 1800 RPM

1150 lb. feet maximum torque at 1100 RPM

Oil cooler

ENGINE ELECTRICAL

Leece-Neville 100 amp 12 volt alternator with integral regulator

12 volt starter

Ether injection system

Push button start switch — key ignition

Three Peterbilt 12 volt, maintenance-free batteries rated at 1875 cold cranking amps

MODEL 377 STANDARD SPECIFICATIONS

FAN CLUTCH
Horton automatic fan clutch with override switch

FILTERS
Integral spin-on full flow oil filter

Engine mounted spin-on fuel filter

Radiator mounted spin-on water filter

COOLING SYSTEM
Standard core radiator with 1270 sq. in. frontal area

Peterbilt Air Sweep®

Full fan shroud

Permanent-type anti-freeze effective to 20° below zero

Polished outer radiator shell and stainless steel grille

Flex-a-lite plastic fan

AIR CLEANER
Donaldson 11″ dry type air cleaner mounted under hood with vacuator

Stainless steel clamps at all air intake connections

EXHAUST
Single 5″ vertical exhaust system with resilient mounted 10″ muffler on cab, stainless steel flex tubing and clamps

Chrome steel standpipe with 45° cut-off

Aluminum full round muffler guard

TRANSMISSION
Fuller "Roadranger" RT 11609A; 9 speed, iron case and cover, 1150 lb.-ft. nominal torque capacity

DRIVELINES
Spicer 1710 type main and interaxle

CLUTCH
Spicer 14″ super-duty ceramic dampened disc clutch

Torque-limiting clutch brake

Manually-adjustable clutch with greasable bearing

AIR SYSTEM
Peterbilt dual air system

Nylon chassis hose

Bendix 12 CFM air compressor

Steel air tanks

Stainless steel/teflon discharge line

Two valve parking system

TRAILER OPERATION
Trailer hand valve located on steering column

Tractor protection valve

Trailer charge valve

Center mounted hose tenna

12′ trailer air and electric lines

TIRES
24.5″ 14-ply, low profile radial tread (10 furnished)

WHEELS
24.5″ x 8.25″ disc, high tensile lightweight steel (10 furnished)

FUEL TANKS
Two 100-gallon 26″ diameter aluminum tanks mounted right and left hand back of cab

Aircraft style fuel cap

Heavy-duty aluminum fuel tank brackets and straps

Single draw/single return with crossover and guard

BATTERY & TOOL BOX
Aerodynamic battery box with non-slip step under cab on left-hand side

Aerodynamic tool box with non-slip step under cab on right-hand side

BUMPER
Black molded aerodynamic bumper fairing with center tow hook

ELECTRICAL SYSTEM
Manual reset circuit breakers and auto fuses with braided covering on harnesses; all circuits numbered and routed through "hard shell" connectors in weather-proof enclosure; automatically actuated back-up light; four-way emergency flasher switch; power distribution center in cab

CAB & HOOD
Aluminum cab fully insulated with foam; three-point rubber mounting; extruded aluminum door frames; heavy-duty piano-type hinges; tinted safety glass throughout; electric windshield wipers and washers with intermittent feature; lift out instrument panel; fixed rear window. 122″ BBC fiberglass hood with 90° spring assisted tilt; fiberglass fenders. Polished hood crown

MODEL 377 STANDARD SPECIFICATIONS

SEATS

Driver: Peterbilt UltraRide™ air-suspension seat (low back with retractable seatbelt)

Passenger: Peterbilt UltraRide™ non-suspension seat (low back with retractable seatbelt and storage compartment)

Vinyl upholstery

CAB FEATURES

Accent interior includes:

  Padded vinyl upholstery panels and headliner

  Vinyl door pads with carpet inserts and manifest pouch

  Dual padded interior sunvisors

  Black rubber floor mats

  2 coat hooks

36″ heavy-duty stainless steel grab handle mounted left hand side

44″ heavy-duty stainless steel grab handle exhaust guard mounted right hand side

Vent window locks

Combination fresh air heater/air conditioner with integral windshield defroster

Dual 7″ x 16″ stainless steel rear view mirrors with heat elements

Electric horn

Single Grover 1024 air horn with chrome finish

Cigarette lighter and ashtray

20″ black 2 spoke wheel

Convex mirror over right hand door

INSTRUMENTS

Speedometer, 0-80 MPH with odometer (electric)

Tachometer, 0-3000 RPM (electric)

Voltmeter

Engine oil pressure gauge

Engine oil temperature gauge

Water temperature gauge

Fuel level gauge

Dual air pressure gauge

Low air pressure warning light

High water temperature warning light

Low oil pressure warning light

High beam indicator

LIGHTS

Fender mounted composite halogen high beam headlights

Bumper mounted directional signals

Five rectangular ICC-type marker lights

Two combination dome/reading lights in cab

Rear combination stop, turn, and tail lights

PAINT

DuPont Imron solid color

One solid color applied on cab and chassis; white wheels

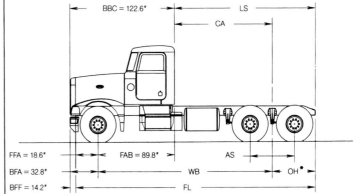

Standard with BBC dimension of 122.6″

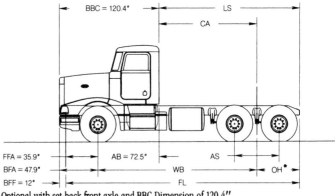

Optional with set-back front axle and BBC Dimension of 120.4″

Wheel base & load space determined to each customer's requirements

*Standard tractor overhang depends upon suspension Consult engineering data book

MODEL 377 OPTIONAL COMPONENTS AND EQUIPMENT

ENGINES

| Caterpillar | 3406 Series | 310-425 HP |
| Cummins | NTC Series | 300-444 HP |

TRANSMISSIONS

Fuller	Virtually all popular main and auxiliary
Spicer	transmissions are available to match
	engine torque and vehicle application

FRONT AXLES

| Rockwell & Eaton | 12,000-14,600 lb. capacity |

REAR AXLES

Rockwell & Eaton	23,000 lbs.	single drive
Rockwell	40,000-44,000 lbs.	tandem drive
Eaton	40,000 lbs.	tandem drive

SUSPENSIONS

Single Drive	Peterbilt Air Trac	20,000 lbs.
	Peterbilt Leaf Spring	23,000 lbs.
Tandem Drive	Peterbilt Air Trac	38,000-44,000 lbs.
	Peterbilt Air Leaf	38,000 lbs.
	Peterbilt Leaf Spring	38,000 lbs.

Hendrickson	38,000-44,000 lbs.
RT, RS Series	
Reyco 101, 102 Series	34,000-44,000 lbs.

FUEL TANKS

23", 26", and 29" aluminum in various gallonages

FRAME

Aluminum or steel channel with aluminum or steel crossmembers

MISCELLANEOUS

A wide choice of interiors, instruments, mirrors, seats, air equipment, electrical equipment, service options, radios and CB installation packages. Choose from a variety of factory designed paint schemes or design your own (customer specifies colors). Paint available in DuPont Imron

BBC

Available in 122" BBC with a 33" axle setting and 120" with a 48" set-back front axle. (Note: Not all engines are available with all BBC's)

SLEEPER BOX

36" and 63" Walk-thru sleeper boxes; 63" stand-up sleeper box

PETERBILT MODEL 379 STANDARD SPECIFICATIONS

MODEL 379 STANDARD SPECIFICATIONS

The illustration may include optional equipment and accessories and may not include all standard equipment.

FRAME

Heat-treated, 110,000 P.S.I. yield, alloy steel with SAE Grade 8 bolts and nuts

10.625″ frame depth with 3.45″ flange width and .31″ web thickness with steel crossmembers and gussets

Tractor-tapered end of frame

Peterbilt rear mudflaps with straight hangers

Front wheel mudflaps

FRONT AXLE

Eaton EFA12F4; 12,000 lb. capacity 15″x4″ cam brakes

12,000 lb. capacity taper leaf springs with tubular shocks

TRW TAS65 power steering with engine compartment mounted reservoir

PHP-10 Hub-Pilot Iron hubs, 11.25″ bolt circle and standard studs

Cast brake drums

Eaton automatic slack adjusters

Oil seals

REAR AXLE

Eaton DS402 single reduction tandem axle; 40,000 lb. capacity

PHP-10 Hub-Pilot Iron hubs, 11.25″ bolt circle and standard studs

Cast brake drums

16.5″x7″ "S" cam service brakes

30″ parking brake on one axle

Eaton automatic slack adjusters

Oil seals

Inter-axle differential lock-out with dash mounted warning light

REAR SUSPENSION

Peterbilt tandem Quadraflex taper leaf suspension; six point frame attachment, longitudinal torque arms to center frame bracket, center equalizer beam for 50/50 load distribution, 52″ axle spacing, 38,000 lb. capacity

ENGINE

Detroit Series 60

320 BHP (SAE) at 1800 RPM

1250-ft-lb maximum torque at 1200 RPM

Oil cooler

ENGINE ELECTRICAL

Delco 100 amp 12 volt alternator

Delco 12 volt starter

Ether injection system

Push button start switch — key ignition

Three Champion 12 volt, maintenance-free batteries rated at 1875 cold cranking amps

MODEL 379 STANDARD SPECIFICATIONS

FAN CLUTCH
Horton automatic fan clutch with override switch

FILTERS
Frame-mounted spin-on fuel filter

Engine-mounted spin-on water filter

COOLING SYSTEM
Standard core radiator with 1270 sq. in. frontal area

Full fan shroud

Permanent-type anti-freeze effective to 20° below zero

Polished outer radiator shell and stainless steel grille

Flex-a-lite plastic fan

AIR CLEANER
Donaldson 13″ dry-type air cleaner cowl mounted with vacuator

Stainless steel brackets and clamps

EXHAUST
Single 5″ vertical exhaust system with resilient-mounted 10″ muffler on cab, stainless steel flex tubing and clamps

Chrome steel standpipe with 45° cut-off

Aluminum full round muffler guard

TRANSMISSION
Fuller "Roadranger" RT12609A; 9 speed, iron case and cover, 1250 lb.-ft. nominal torque capacity

DRIVELINES
Spicer 1710 HD main and 1710 interaxle

CLUTCH
Spicer 14″ flat ceramic dampened disc clutch

Torque-limiting clutch brake

Manually-adjustable clutch with greasable bearing

AIR SYSTEM
Bendix 13.2 CFM air compressor

Stainless steel/teflon discharge line

Peterbilt dual air system

Nylon chassis hose

Three steel air tanks

Two valve parking system

Bendix BPR-1 brake proportioning valve

TRAILER OPERATION
Trailer hand valve located on steering column

Tractor protection valve

Trailer charge valve

Center mounted hose tenna

12′ trailer air and electric lines

TIRES
24.5″ 14-ply, low profile radial tread (10 furnished)

WHEELS
24.5″ x 8.25″ disc, high tensile lightweight steel (10 furnished)

FUEL TANKS
Two 100-gallon 26″ diameter aluminum tanks mounted right and left-hand back of cab

Aircraft style fuel cap

Heavy-duty aluminum fuel tank brackets and straps

Single draw/single return with crossover and guard

BATTERY & TOOL BOX
Aluminum battery box with non-slip step under cab on left-hand side

Aluminum tool box with non-slip step under cab on right-hand side

BUMPER
Deep tapered chromed aluminum with center tow hook

ELECTRICAL SYSTEM
Manual reset circuit breakers and auto fuses with braided covering on harnesses; all circuits numbered and routed through "hard shell" connectors in weather-proof enclosure; automatically actuated back-up light; four-way emergency flasher switch; power distribution center in cab

CAB & HOOD
Aluminum cab fully insulated with foam; three-point rubber mounting; extruded aluminum door frames; heavy-duty piano-type hinges; tinted safety glass throughout; electric windshield wipers and washers with intermittent feature; lift out instrument panel; fixed rear window; right-hand door view window; 119″ BBC aluminum hood and fenders with 90° spring assisted tilt; single hood latches; polished hood crown; fender liners.

MODEL 379 STANDARD SPECIFICATIONS

SEATS

Driver: Peterbilt UltraRide™ air-suspension seat (low back with 3-point retractable seatbelt)

Passenger: Peterbilt UltraRide™ non-suspension seat (low back with 3-point retractable seatbelt and storage compartment)

Vinyl upholstery

CAB FEATURES

Accent interior includes:

Padded vinyl upholstery panels and headliner

Vinyl door pads with carpet inserts and manifest pouch

Dual padded interior sunvisors

Black rubber floor mats

2 coat hooks

36″ heavy-duty stainless steel grab handle mounted left-hand side

44″ heavy-duty stainless steel grab handle exhaust guard mounted right-hand side

Vent window locks

Combination fresh air heater/air conditioner with integral windshield defroster

Dual 7″ x 16″ stainless steel rear view mirrors

Electric horn

Single Grover 1024 air horn with chrome finish

Cigarette lighter and ashtray

20″ black 2-spoke wheel

Convex mirror over right-hand door

INSTRUMENTS

Speedometer, 0-80 MPH with odometer (electric)

Trip odometer

Tachometer, 0-3000 RPM (electric)

Voltmeter

Engine oil pressure gauge

Engine oil temperature gauge

Water temperature gauge

Fuel level gauge

Dual air pressure gauge

Low air pressure warning light

High water temperature warning light

Low oil pressure warning light

High beam indicator

LIGHTS

Dual pod-mounted rectangular halogen high beam headlights with integral turn signals

Five rectangular ICC-type marker lights

Two combination dome/reading lights in cab

Rear combination stop, turn, and tail lights

PAINT

DuPont Imron solid color

One solid color applied on cab and chassis, white wheels

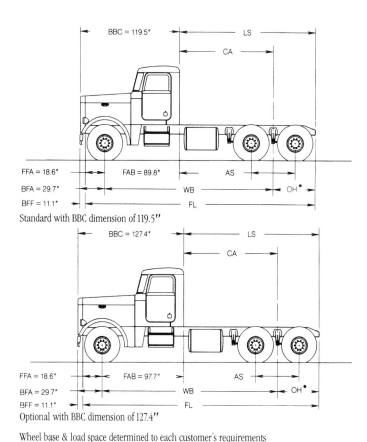

Standard with BBC dimension of 119.5″

Optional with BBC dimension of 127.4″

Wheel base & load space determined to each customer's requirements

*Standard tractor overhang depends upon suspension Consult engineering data book

MODEL 379 OPTIONAL COMPONENTS AND EQUIPMENT

ENGINES

Caterpillar	3406 Series	310-460 HP
	3176 Series	250-325 HP
	3306 Series	300 HP
Cummins	N14 Series	310-460 HP
Detroil Diesel	60 Series	320-450 HP

TRANSMISSIONS

Fuller	Virtually all popular main and auxiliary
Spicer	transmissions are available to match
	engine torque and vehicle application

FRONT AXLES

Rockwell & Eaton   12,000-18,000 lb. capacity

REAR AXLES

Rockwell & Eaton	23,000 lb.	single drive
Rockwell	40,000-46,000 lb.	tandem drive
Eaton	40,000-52,000 lb.	tandem drive

SUSPENSIONS

Front	Peterbilt Front Air	12,000 lb.
Rear Single Drive	Peterbilt Air Trac	20,000 lb.
	Peterbilt Leaf Spring	23,000 lb.
Rear Tandem Drive	Peterbilt Air Trac	38,000-44,000 lb.
	Peterbilt Air Leaf	38,000 lb.
	Peterbilt Quadraflex	
	Two-stage Multileaf	38,000 lb.

Peterbilt Low Air Leaf	38,00 lb.
Hendrickson	38,000-44,000 lb.
RT, RS Series	
Reyco 101, 102 Series	34,000-44,000 lb.

FUEL TANKS

23," 26," and 29" aluminum in various gallonages

FRAME

Aluminum or steel channel with aluminum or steel crossmembers

MISCELLANEOUS

A wide choice of interiors, instruments, mirrors, seats, air equipment, electrical equipment, severe service options, radios and CB installation packages. Choose from a variety of factory designed paint schemes or design your own (customer specifies colors). Paint available in DuPont Imron.

BBC

Available in 119" and 127" BBC with a 30" axle setting (Note: Not all engines are available with all BBC's).

SLEEPER BOX

36," 48" and 63" walk-thru sleeper boxes; 48" and 63" stand-up sleeper boxes.

PETERBILT MODEL 376 STANDARD SPECIFICATIONS

MODEL 376 STANDARD SPECIFICATIONS

The illustration may include optional equipment and accessories and may not include all standard equipment.

FRAME

Heat-treated, 110,000 P.S.I. yield, alloy steel with SAE Grade 8 bolts and nuts

10.5″ frame depth with 3.4″ flange width and .25″ web thickness with steel crossmembers and gussets

Tractor-tapered end of frame

Peterbilt rear mudflaps with straight hangers

Front wheel mudflaps

FRONT AXLE

Eaton EFA12F4; 12,000 lb. capacity 15″ x 4″ cam brakes

12,000 lb. capacity taper leaf springs with tubular shocks

Iron hubs, 11.25″ bolt circle and standard studs

Cast brake drums

Oil seals

REAR AXLE

Eaton 23070 S single reduction axle; 23,000 lb. capacity

Iron hubs, 11.25″ bolt circle and standard studs

Cast brake drums

Eaton 16.5″ x 7″ "S" cam service brakes

30″ parking brake on one axle

Manual slack adjusters

Oil Seals

REAR SUSPENSION

Peterbilt split-progressive single drive suspension 20,000 lb. capacity

ENGINE

Cummins C-Series (6CTA8.3)

250 BHP (SAE) at 2200 RPM

728 lb. feet maximum torque at 1500 RPM

ENGINE ELECTRICAL

Delco 80 amp 12 volt alternator

12 volt starter

Push button start switch — key ignition

Two Peterbilt 12 volt, maintenance-free batteries rated at 1850 cold cranking amps

FAN CLUTCH

Eaton viscous fan clutch

MODEL 376 STANDARD SPECIFICATIONS

FILTERS
Integral spin-on full flow oil filter

Frame-mounted spin-on fuel filter

Radiator-mounted spin-on water filter

COOLING SYSTEM
Standard core radiator with 1000 sq. in. frontal area

Peterbilt Air Sweep®

Full fan shroud

Permanent-type anti-freeze effective to 20° below zero

Polished outer radiator shell and stainless steel grille

Flex-a-lite plastic fan

AIR CLEANER
Donaldson 9″ dry-type under hood mounted with vacuator

Stainless steel clamps at all air intake connections

EXHAUST
Single 5″ horizontal exhaust system with 10″ muffler, stainless steel flex tubing and clamps

TRANSMISSION
Fuller T8607B: 7 speed, iron case and cover, 975 lb.-ft. nominal torque capacity

DRIVELINES
Spicer 1710 type

CLUTCH
Spicer 14″ 2-plate non-asbestos rigid disc, angle spring clutch

Torque-limiting clutch brake

Manually-adjustable clutch with greasable bearing

AIR SYSTEM
Cummins 13.2 CFM air compressor

Stainless steel/teflon discharge line

Peterbilt dual air system

Nylon chassis hose

Steel air tanks

Two valve parking system

TRAILER OPERATION
Trailer hand valve located on steering column

Tractor protection valve

7-way socket frame mounted back of cab

TIRES
22.5″ 12-ply, bias ply (6 furnished)

WHEELS
22.5″ x 8.25″ disc, high tensile lightweight steel (6 furnished)

FUEL TANKS
One 50-gallon 23″ diameter aluminum tank under cab on right-hand side (unpainted)

Aircraft style fuel cap

Heavy-duty aluminum fuel tank brackets and straps

Non-slip fuel tank step

BATTERY BOX
Aluminum battery box with non-slip step under cab on left-hand side

BUMPER
Painted tapered steel bumper

ELECTRICAL SYSTEM
Manual reset circuit breakers and auto fuses with braided covering on harnesses; all circuits numbered and routed through "hard shell" connectors in weather-proof enclosure; automatically actuated back-up light; four-way emergency flasher switch; power distribution center in cab

CAB & HOOD
Aluminum cab fully insulated with foam; three-point rubber mounting; extruded aluminum door frames; heavy-duty piano-type hinges; tinted safety glass throughout; electric windshield wipers and washers with intermittent feature; lift-out instrument panel; fixed rear window; 114″ BBC with fiberglass hood and fenders with 90° spring assisted tilt; single hood latches, polished hood crown

MODEL 376 STANDARD SPECIFICATIONS

SEAT

Driver: Peterbilt UltraRide™ air-suspension seat
(low back with retractable seatbelt)

Vinyl upholstery

CAB FEATURES

Vantage interior includes:

    Padded vinyl headliners, back panels and doors

    Rubber floor mats

    Padded interior sunvisor

    2 coat hooks

20″ black 2 spoke steering wheel

36″ heavy-duty stainless steel left hand cab mounted
grab handle

Vent window locks

Fresh air heater with integral windshield defroster

Dual 6″ x 16″ painted rear view mirrors

Electric horn

Cigarette lighter and ashtray

Convex mirror over right hand door

INSTRUMENTS

Speedometer, 0-80 MPH with odometer (electric)

Tachometer, 0-3000 RPM (electric)

Voltmeter

Water temperature gauge

Fuel level gauge

Dual air pressure gauge

Low air pressure warning light

High water temperature warning light

Low oil pressure warning light

High beam indicator

LIGHTS

Fender mounted composite halogen high beam
headlights; bumper mounted directional signals

Five rectangular ICC-type marker lights

Single dome light in cab

Rear combination stop, turn, and tail lights

Auxiliary door mounted turn signals

PAINT

DuPont Imron solid color

One solid color applied on cab, black chassis
and bumper, white wheels

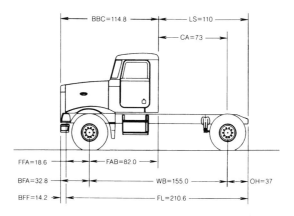

Tractor

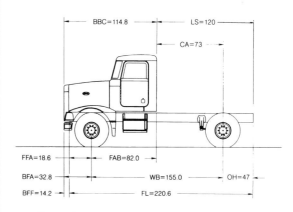

Full Truck

Peterbilt

MODEL 376 OPTIONAL SPECIFICATIONS

FIFTH WHEELS
Fontaine and Holland Fixed

POWER STEERING
TRW   TAS65

TIRES
11″ x 22.5″   Radial

MISCELLANEOUS
UltraRide™ Passengers Seat

Combination fresh air heater/air conditioner

Peterbilt Roof Fairing

Cab Extenders

TRUCK WHEELBASE OPTIONS

Wheelbase	C/A	O/H W/O Tag	O/H W/Tag	Loadspace W/O Tag	Loadspace W/Tag
155″	73″	47″	95″	120″(10′)	168″(14′)
166″	84″	60″	108″	144″(12′)	192″(16′)
190″	108″	60″	108″	168″(14′)	216″(18′)
202″	120″	72″	102″	192″(16′)	222″(18.5′)
220″	138″	84″	84″	222″(18.5′)	222″(18.5′)

PETERBILT MODEL 378 STANDARD SPECIFICATIONS

MODEL 378 STANDARD SPECIFICATIONS

The illustration may include optional equipment and accessories and may not include all standard equipment.

FRAME
Heat-treated, 110,000 P.S.I. yield, alloy steel with SAE Grade 8 bolts and nuts

10.625″ frame depth with 3.45″ flange width and .31″ web thickness with steel crossmembers and gussets

Tractor-tapered end of frame

Peterbilt rear mudflaps with straight hangers

Front wheel mudflaps

FRONT AXLE
Eaton EFA12F4; 12,000 lb. capacity 15″x4″ cam brakes

12,000 lb. capacity taper leaf springs with tubular shocks

TRW TAS65 power steering with engine compartment mounted reservoir

PHP-10 Hub-Pilot Iron hubs, 11.25″ bolt circle and standard studs

Cast brake drums

Eaton automatic slack adjusters

Oil seals

REAR AXLE
Eaton DS402 single reduction tandem axle; 40,000 lb. capacity

PHP-10 Hub-Pilot Iron hubs, 11.25″ bolt circle and standard studs

Cast brake drums

16.5″x7″ "S" cam service brakes

30″ parking brake on one axle

Eaton automatic slack adjusters

Oil seals

Inter-axle differential lock-out with dash mounted warning light

REAR SUSPENSION
Peterbilt tandem Quadraflex taper leaf suspension; six point frame attachment, longitudinal torque arms to center frame bracket, center equalizer beam for 50/50 load distribution, 52″ axle spacing, 38,000 lb. capacity

ENGINE
Cummins N14-310P

310 BHP (SAE) at 1700 RPM

1250 lb. feet maximum torque at 1100 RPM

Cummins PT pacer road speed governor

Oil cooler

ENGINE ELECTRICAL
Delco 100 amp 12 volt alternator

Delco 12 volt starter

Ether injection system

Push button start switch — key ignition

Three Champion 12 volt, maintenance-free batteries rated at 1875 cold cranking amps

MODEL 378 STANDARD SPECIFICATIONS

FAN CLUTCH
Horton automatic fan clutch with override switch

FILTERS
Fleetguard engine-mounted spin-on combination full flow/bypass oil filter

Engine-mounted spin-on fuel filter

Engine-mounted spin-on water filter

COOLING SYSTEM
Standard core radiator with 1270 sq. in. frontal area

Full fan shroud

Permanent-type anti-freeze effective to 20° below zero

Polished outer radiator shell and stainless steel grille

Flex-a-lite plastic fan

AIR CLEANER
Donaldson 13″ dry-type air cleaner cowl mounted with vacuator

Stainless steel brackets and clamps

EXHAUST
Single 5″ vertical exhaust system with resilient-mounted 10″ muffler on cab, stainless steel flex tubing and clamps

Chrome steel standpipe with 45° cut-off

Aluminum full round muffler guard

TRANSMISSION
Fuller "Roadranger" RT12609A; 9 speed, iron case and cover, 1250 lb.-ft. nominal torque capacity

DRIVELINES
Spicer 1710 HD main and 1710 interaxle

CLUTCH
Spicer 14″ flat ceramic dampened disc clutch

Torque-limiting clutch brake

Manually-adjustable clutch with greasable bearing

AIR SYSTEM
Cummins 13.2 CFM air compressor

Stainless steel/teflon discharge line

Peterbilt dual air system

Nylon chassis hose

Three steel air tanks

Two valve parking system

Bendix BPR-1 brake proportioning valve

TRAILER OPERATION
Trailer hand valve located on steering column

Tractor protection valve

Trailer charge valve

Center mounted hose tenna

12′ trailer air and electric lines

TIRES
24.5″ 14-ply, low profile radial tread (10 furnished)

WHEELS
24.5″ x 8.25″ disc, high tensile lightweight steel (10 furnished)

FUEL TANKS
Two 100-gallon 26″ diameter aluminum tanks mounted right and left-hand back of cab

Aircraft style fuel cap

Heavy-duty aluminum fuel tank brackets and straps

Single draw/single return with crossover and guard

BATTERY & TOOL BOX
Aluminum battery box with non-slip step under cab on left-hand side

Aluminum tool box with non-slip step under cab on right-hand side

BUMPER
Deep tapered chromed aluminum with center tow hook

ELECTRICAL SYSTEM
Manual reset circuit breakers and auto fuses with braided covering on harnesses; all circuits numbered and routed through "hard shell" connectors in weather-proof enclosure; automatically actuated back-up light; four-way emergency flasher switch; power distribution center in cab

CAB & HOOD
Aluminum cab fully insulated with foam; three-point rubber mounting; extruded aluminum door frames; heavy-duty piano-type hinges; tinted safety glass throughout; electric windshield wipers and washers with intermittent feature; lift out instrument panel; fixed rear window; right-hand door view window; 119″ BBC fiberglass hood and fenders with 90° spring assisted tilt; single hood latches; polished hood crown

MODEL 378 STANDARD SPECIFICATIONS

SEATS

Driver: Peterbilt UltraRide™ air-suspension seat (low back with 3-point retractable seatbelt)

Passenger: Peterbilt UltraRide™ non-suspension seat (low back with 3-point retractable seatbelt and storage compartment)

Vinyl upholstery

CAB FEATURES

Accent interior includes:

  Padded vinyl upholstery panels and headliner

  Vinyl door pads with carpet inserts and manifest pouch

  Dual padded interior sunvisors

  Black rubber floor mats

  2 coat hooks

36″ heavy-duty stainless steel grab handle mounted left-hand side

44″ heavy-duty stainless steel grab handle exhaust guard mounted right-hand side

Vent window locks

Combination fresh air heater/air conditioner with integral windshield defroster

Dual 7″x 16″ stainless steel rear view mirrors

Electric horn

Single Grover 1024 air horn with chrome finish

Cigarette lighter and ashtray

20″ black 2-spoke wheel

Convex mirror over right-hand door

INSTRUMENTS

Speedometer, 0-80 MPH with odometer (electric)

Trip odometer

Tachometer, 0-3000 RPM (electric)

Voltmeter

Engine oil pressure gauge

Engine oil temperature gauge

Water temperature gauge

Fuel level gauge

Dual air pressure gauge

Low air pressure warning light

High water temperature warning light

Low oil pressure warning light

High beam indicator

LIGHTS

Dual pod-mounted rectangular halogen high beam headlights with integral turn signals

Five rectangular ICC-type marker lights

Two combination dome/reading lights in cab

Rear combination stop, turn, and tail lights

PAINT

DuPont Imron solid color

One solid color applied on cab and chassis, white wheels

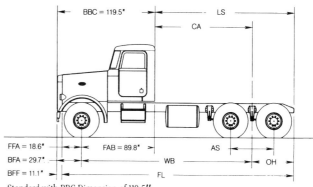

Standard with BBC Dimension of 119.5″

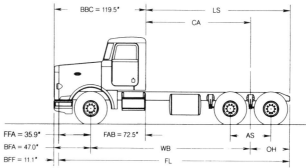

Optional with set-back front axle and BBC Dimension of 119.5″

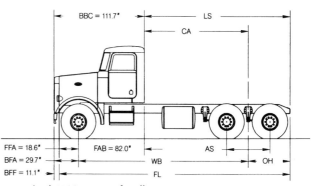

Optional with BBC Dimension of 111.7″

Wheel base & load space determined to each customer's requirements
*Standard tractor overhang depends upon suspension Consult engineering data book

MODEL 378 OPTIONAL COMPONENTS AND EQUIPMENT

ENGINES

Caterpillar	3406 Series	310-460 HP
	3176 Series	250-325 HP
	3306 Series	300 HP
Cummins	N14 Series	310-460 HP
Detroit Diesel	60 Series	320-450 HP

TRANSMISSIONS

Fuller	Virtually all popular main and auxiliary
Spicer	transmissions are available to match
	engine torque and vehicle application

FRONT AXLES

Rockwell & Eaton 12,000-18,000 lb. capacity

REAR AXLES

Rockwell & Eaton	23,000 lb.	single drive
Rockwell	40,000-46,000 lb.	tandem drive
Eaton	40,000-52,000 lb.	tandem drive

SUSPENSIONS

Front	Peterbilt Front Air	12,000 lb.
Rear Single Drive	Peterbilt Air Trac	20,000 lb.
	Peterbilt Leaf Spring	23,000 lb.
Rear Tandem Drive	Peterbilt Air Trac	38,000-44,000 lb.
	Peterbilt Air Leaf	38,000 lb.
	Peterbilt Quadraflex	
	Two-stage Multileaf	38,000 lb.
	Peterbilt Low Air Leaf	38,000 lb.
	Hendrickson	38,000-44,000 lb.
	RT, RS Series	
	Reyco 101, 102 Series	34,000-44,000 lb.

FUEL TANKS

23," 26," and 29" aluminum in various gallonages

FRAME

Aluminum or steel channel with aluminum or steel crossmembers

MISCELLANEOUS

A wide choice of interiors, instruments, mirrors, seats, air equipment, electrical equipment, severe service options, radios and CB installation packages. Choose from a variety of factory designed paint schemes or design your own (customer specifies colors). Paint available in DuPont Imron

BBC

Available in 111" and 119" BBC with a 30" axle setting and 119" with a 47" set-back front axle

SLEEPER BOX

36," 48" and 63" walk-thru sleeper boxes; 48" and 63" stand-up sleeper boxes

MODEL 13-210 TRACTOR CONVERSION SPECIFICATIONS

ENGINE AND ENGINE EQUIPMENT
- Engine Cummins 6CT8.3, 210 hp at 2200 rpm, 605 lb.-ft. torque@1500 rpm
- Air Cleaner — Dry-type
- Radiator — 540 sq. in. single pass, 50% antifreeze
- Exhaust System — Single 4 in. under frame
- Alternator — 60 amp, "Poly-V" belt drive
- Batteries — Two 12 volt, group 31, low maintenance
- Starter — 12 volt, negative ground
- Fan — Eaton 240 drive with Kysor Alu-Metal blade (reinforced nylon)
- Bosch Fuel Pump — Sealed and tamper proof

TRANSMISSION AND CLUTCH
- Transmission — Fuller "Synchro-6", 605 lb-ft input torque capacity
  - RATIOS: 1st 9.08   5th 1.36
  - 2nd 5.27   6th 1.00
  - 3rd 3.25   Rev 8.63
  - 4th 2.04
- Clutch — Spicer 14 inch, two plate self-adjusting organic dampened

DRIVELINE
- Spicer 1610 series noise dampened

FRONT AXLE AND EQUIPMENT
- Axle — Rockwell FDB931 rated at 9700 lbs.
- Brakes — Rockwell 16-1/2 x 5 inch S-cam full air
- Iron Hubs — I.S.O. mount 10-stud type, 11-1/4 inch bolt circle
- Front Springs — 9700 lbs. rolled eye with tuned shocks and sway bar
- Power Steering — Integral gear type

REAR AXLE AND EQUIPMENT
- Axle — Rockwell RS-20-145 rated at 20,000 lbs.
- Suspension — 20,000 lbs. constant rate spring suspension with rear sway bar
- Ratio — 4.10
- Brakes — Rockwell 16-1/2 x 6 inch S-cam full air
- Iron Hubs — I.S.O. mount 10-stud type, 11-1/4 inch bolt circle
- Emergency Brakes — Air operated spring brakes

ELECTRICAL SYSTEM
- 12-volt negative ground

TIRE AND WHEELS
- Tires — Goodyear G-159 front, G-124 rear, 11R22.5G (14ply)
- Wheels — Steel Disc 7.5 in. x 22.5

FRAME AND EQUIPMENT
- Frame — Riveted ladder design, 54,000 psi yield strength steel
- 758,000 lb.-in. RBM per rail, (at back of cab)
- 34 in. frame width
- Reinforcement — Inverted "L" type
- Bumper — Stamped steel with center tow hitch
- Battery Box — Steel cantilever type
- Wheelbase - 126"

TRACTOR EQUIPMENT
- Hosetenna LH rail back of cab
- Coiled trailer brake lines
- Coiled 7-way trailer light cord

FUEL TANK AND EQUIPMENT
- Tank — Single 50 gallon rectangular steel tank right side (42 imperial gallons)

CAB AND EQUIPMENT
- Cab — Stamped and welded steel design, Low Cab Forward type, torsion bar cab tilt mechanism
- Heater — High output with heavy-duty blower motor
- Gauges — Fuel, engine temperature, oil pressure, air pressure
- Buzzers — Low air pressure, low oil pressure, high water temperature, low water level cab latch
- Speedo/Tach — Mechanical speedo, electronic tachometer
- Sunvisor — Dual interior
- Sound System — Standard with speaker, antenna and power lead, Radio not included
- Drivers Seat — Heavy-duty vinyl, 6-way adjustable with headrest
- Rider Seat — Heavy-duty vinyl 2-man bench
- Heavy-duty electric wiper motor
- Roof vent
- Breakaway style mirrors
- Storage/tool box inside cab

LIGHTS AND SIGNALS
- Headlights — Single rectangular
- Turn Signals — Cab mounted
- Combination stop, turn, tail and backup lights

MIDRANGER™

MODEL 200-33 33,000-LBS. GVWR

Engine and Engine Equipment	**Engine:** Cummins C8.3, 210 hp @ 2200 rpm, 605 lb.-ft. torque @ 1300 rpm. Includes 13.2 cfm Cummins air compressor. **Air Cleaner:** Donaldson radial seal dry air cleaner with frontal intake. **Radiator:** 765 sq. in. single pass. Includes air-to-air heat exchanger/aftercooler. **Exhaust System:** Single 4-in. under frame. **Fan:** Kysor on/off drive with Kysor nylon fan (reinforced nylon). **Bosch Fuel Pump:** Sealed and tamper-proof. **Optional Engines:** Cummins B5.9, 210 hp @ 2500 rpm, 520 lb.-ft. torque @ 1600 rpm. Includes 8.5 cfm air compressor, 685 sq. in. radiator, Eaton viscous fan drive, Delco 12-volt 28 MT starter. Or Cummins C8.3 250 hp @ 2000 rpm, 800 lb.-ft. torque @ 1300 rpm.
Transmission and Clutch	**Transmission:** Fuller FS6206A, "Synchro-6" 605 lb.-ft. input torque capacity. (Fuller FS5106A standard with Cummins B5.9, 210 hp engine. Fuller RT8609 9-speed standard with Cummins C8.3, 250 hp engine.) **Ratios:** 1st 9.01; 2nd 5.27; 3rd 3.22; 4th 2.04; 5th 1.36; 6th 1.00; Rev. 8.63. **Clutch:** Eaton Valeo 14-in., 1-plate, ceramic clutch facing. **Optional Transmissions:** Allison MT643 4-speed automatic or Allison MT653DR 5-speed automatic.
Driveline	**Spicer 1610 Series:** Noise dampened shaft, quick-disconnect U-joint (SPL90 series standard with Cummins B5.9, 210 hp engine).
Front Axle and Equipment	**Axle:** Eaton EFA-12F5, 12,000-lb. capacity front axle. **Brakes:** Eaton S-cam EB1655L full air brakes. 16.5-in. x 5-in. Automatic slack adjusters. **Hubs:** Iron hub/cast brake drum. Hub-piloted 10-bolt wheel mounting. 11¼-in. bolt circle. **Front Springs:** Taper leaf, 12,000-lb. capacity. Shock absorbers. **Power Steering:** Shepherd M100 power steering gear, single.
Rear Axle and Equipment	**Axle:** Eaton 21065S, single reduction, single drive rear axle, 21,000-lb. capacity. **Axle Ratio:** 4.33. **Optional Ratios:** 3.90; 4.11; 4.63; 4.88; 5.29. **Suspension:** Reyco 79KB taper leaf rear suspension, 21,000-lb. capacity. **Brakes:** Eaton S-cam EB1657L full air brakes. 16.5-in. x 7-in. Automatic slack adjusters. **Hubs:** Iron hub/cast drum. Hub piloted 10-bolt wheel mounting. 11¼-in. bolt circle. **Emergency brake:** MGM tamper-resistant parking brake. Spring applied, air release.
Electrical System	12-volt negative ground, centralized power distribution with plug-in style relays and circuit protection. Circuits numbered and color coded. **Alternator:** Delco-Remy 21SI 100-amp alternator, Poly-V belt drive, with spring-loaded tensioner. **Batteries:** Two GNB Champion 12-volt, Hi cycler, maintenance-free batteries. Total 1250 cca. **Starter:** Delco-Remy 12-volt, 37 MT starter.
Tires and Wheels	**Tires:** Bridgestone R187 295/75R22.5 (14 ply). **Wheels:** Accuride 28408NE, 22.5-in. x 8.25-in. disc high-tensile light-weight steel wheels.
Frame and Equipment	**Frame:** Steel frame rails: 9.5-in. x 3.5-in. x .25-in., 80,000 psi yield strength, 835,000 in.-lb. RBM, 34-in. frame width. **Bumper:** Channel bumper with composite end caps. Center-mounted tow pin. **Battery box:** Aluminum with composite cover, mounted on left hand frame rail. **Wheelbase:** 190-in. standard. **Optional wheelbases:** 140-in., 160-in., 175-in., 205-in., 225-in., 240-in.
Fuel Tank	**Tank:** Single 50-gallon (42 Imperial gallon) rectangular steel fuel tank mounted behind cab on right hand side.
Cab and Equipment	**Cab:** Stamped and welded steel design, low cab forward type, torsion bar cab tilt mechanism, tilts 45 degrees. **Heater:** Fresh air heater with integral defrosters, 3-speed blower. **Gauges:** Fuel, engine coolant temperature, oil pressure, air pressure. **Warning Light & Alarm:** Low air pressure, low oil pressure, high coolant temperature, low coolant level, cab latch. **Warning Light Only:** Low battery charge. **Speedo/Tachometer:** Electronic speedometer and tachometer. **Driver's Seat:** Bostrom 900R adjustable, orthopedic driver's seat with lumbar support, vinyl-trimmed, high back. Retractable 3-point attachment seat belts. **Passenger's Seat:** Bench style 2-passenger seat, vinyl-trimmed. Center lap belt. **Miscellaneous:** Dual sunvisors, locking glovebox, cab storage pocket, roof vent, heavy duty two-speed wiper motor, aerodynamically-styled break-away mirrors.
Lights and Signals	**Headlights:** Single rectangular, mounted behind bumper. **Turn Signals:** Cab-mounted. Stop, tail, directional and backup lamp unit, right and left-mounted. **Wiring:** Chassis harness wiring numbered and color coded.
Options*	**A wide range,** including: · Several rear axle ratios · Air suspension & stabilizer bars · Air conditioning · Many wheelbases · Dual fuel tanks · Air dryer · Cold weather starting kit, block heater · Heated mirrors. *Some options may not be available at time of publication; contact your Peterbilt dealer for availability.
Warranty**	**Basic Vehicle:** 12 months, unlimited mileage. **Major Components:** 24 months, unlimited mileage. **Cab:** 36 months, unlimited mileage on corrosion perforation and cab structural defects. **Framerail, Cross-members, Suspension:** 36 months unlimited mileage (except springs, bushings and shock absorbers). **See the Peterbilt 200-Series warranty for complete details. Restrictions and other limitations apply.

Peterbilt Motors Company, 38801 Cherry St., Newark, CA 94560.
Call 1-800-447-4700 for the location of your nearest dealer.

563-3505   20M   7/92   Printed in U.S.A.

Peterbilt

CLASS PAYS

A DIVISION OF **PACCAR**

PETERBILT MODEL 372 STANDARD SPECIFICATIONS

MODEL 372 STANDARD SPECIFICATIONS

The illustration may include optional equipment and accessories and may not include all standard equipment.

FRAME

Heat-treated, 110,000 P.S.I. yield, alloy steel with SAE Grade 8 bolts and nuts

10.375″ frame depth with 3.5″ flange width and .25″ web thickness with steel crossmembers and gussets

Tractor-tapered end of frame

Peterbilt rear mudflaps with straight hangers

FRONT AXLE

Eaton EFA12F4; 12,000 lb. capacity 15″ x 4″ cam brakes

12,000 lb. capacity taper leaf springs with tubular shocks

TRW TAS65 power steering with engine compartment mounted reservoir

Iron hubs, 11.25″ bolt circle and standard studs

Cast brake drums. Non-asbestos brake linings

Oil seals

REAR AXLE

Eaton DS402 single reduction tandem axle; 40,000 lb. capacity

Iron hubs, 11.25″ bolt circle and standard studs

Cast brake drums. Non-asbestos brake linings

16.5″ x 7″ "S" cam service brakes

30″ parking brake on one axle

Manual slack adjusters

Oil seals

Inter-axle differential lock-out with dash mounted warning light

REAR SUSPENSION

Peterbilt tandem four spring suspension; six point frame attachment, longitudinal torque arms to center frame bracket, center equalizer beam for 50/50 load distribution, 52″ axle spacing, 34,000 lb. capacity

ENGINE

Cummins FNTC315 Big Cam IV (OAC)

315 BHP (SAE) at 1800 RPM

1150 lb. feet peak torque at 1300 RPM

Oil cooler

ENGINE ELECTRICAL

Leece-Neville 100 amp 12 volt alternator with integral regulator

12 volt starter with integral relay and thermal overload protection switch

Ether injection system

Push button start switch — key ignition

Three Peterbilt 12 volt, maintenance-free batteries rated at 1875 cold cranking amps

MODEL 372 STANDARD SPECIFICATIONS

FAN CLUTCH
Horton automatic fan clutch with override switch

FILTERS
Fleetguard spin-on combination full flow/bypass oil filter

Engine mounted spin-on fuel filter

Engine mounted spin-on water filter

COOLING SYSTEM
Standard core radiator with 925 sq. in. frontal area

Full fan shroud

Permanent-type anti-freeze effective to 20° below zero

Polished aluminum grille

AIR CLEANER
Donaldson ECG11-2403 air cleaner mounted back of engine

EXHAUST
Single 5" vertical exhaust system outboard frame mounted with 10" muffler, stainless steel flex tubing and clamps

54" chrome square-cut standpipe

Aluminum full round muffler guard

TRANSMISSION
Fuller "Roadranger" RT11609A; 9 speed, iron case and cover, 1150 lb.-ft. nominal torque capacity

DRIVELINES
Spicer 1710 type main and interaxle with half-round end yokes

CLUTCH
Spicer 14" flat ceramic dampened disc clutch

Torque-limiting clutch brake

Manually-adjustable clutch with greasable bearing

AIR SYSTEM
Cummins 13.2 CFM air compressor

Peterbilt dual air system

Nylon chassis hose

Steel air tanks

Two valve parking system

TRAILER OPERATION
Trailer hand valve located on console

Tractor protection valve

Trailer charge valve

Left-hand mounted hose tenna

12' trailer air and electric lines

TIRES
24.5" 14-ply, low profile radial tread (10 furnished)

WHEELS
24.5" x 8.25" disc, high tensile lightweight steel (10 furnished)

FUEL TANKS
Two 100-gallon 26" diameter aluminum tanks mounted right and left hand back of cab

Aircraft style fuel cap

Heavy-duty aluminum fuel tank brackets and straps

Single draw/single return with crossover and guard

BATTERY & TOOL BOX
Aluminum battery box mounted over rails behind engine

BUMPER
Black molded aerodynamic bumper fairing with center tow hook

ELECTRICAL SYSTEM
"Pop-out" style manual-reset circuit breakers; cross-linked polyethylene insulated wiring harnesses with braided covering all circuits numbered, color-coded, and routed through "hard-shell" connectors in weather-proof enclosure; automatically actuated back-up light; four-way emergency flasher switch

CAB & SLEEPER
108" sleeper cab
62° tilt with independent hydraulic system
Aluminum and fiberglass construction, fully insulated with foam and lined with vinyl; one-piece fiberglass roof with integral outside visor and removable roof fairing; cab side extenders; positive dual locking cab hold-down devices; extruded aluminum door frames; heavy duty piano-type hinges; tinted safety glass throughout; dual electric windshield wipers and washers; tilt-out instrument panel; large overhead storage compartment with padded carpet and cargo net

MODEL 372 STANDARD SPECIFICATIONS

SEATS

Driver: Peterbilt UltraRide™ air-suspension seat (low back with 3 point retractable seatbelt)

Passenger: Peterbilt UltraRide™ non-suspension seat (low back with 3 point retractable seatbelt and storage compartment)

Vinyl upholstery

CAB FEATURES

Accent interior includes:

Padded vinyl upholstery panels and headliner

Vinyl door pads with carpet inserts and manifest pouch

Padded vinyl tunnel cover

Three padded interior sunvisors

Black rubber floor mats

2 coat hooks

Kick panel carpeting

Polyurethane sleeper mattress

Vinyl sleeper curtain

Bunk restraint

Bunk partition carpeting

Combination fresh air heater/air conditioner with integral windshield defroster and auxiliary blower to sleeper

Vent window locks

Dual 7″ x 16″ stainless steel rear view mirrors

Electric horn

Single Grover 1022 air horn

Cigarette lighter and two ashtrays

18″ black 2-spoke wheel

Convex mirror over RH door

INSTRUMENTS

Speedometer, 0-80 MPH with odometer (electric)

Tachometer, 0-3000 RPM (electric)

Voltmeter

Engine oil pressure gauge

Engine oil temperature gauge

Water temperature gauge

Fuel level gauge

Dual air pressure gauge

Low air pressure warning light

High water temperature warning light

Low oil pressure warning light

High beam indicator

LIGHTS

Single rectangular halogen headlights

Cab mounted aerodynamic front directional signals

Five flush mounted ICC-type marker lights

Two combination dome/reading lights in cab

Rear combination stop, turn, and tail lights

PAINT

DuPont Imron solid color

One solid color applied on cab and chassis, white wheels

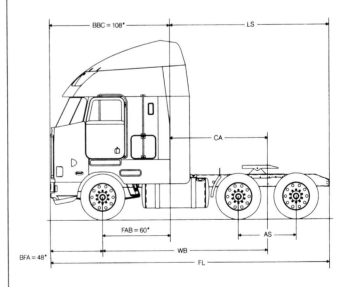

Wheel base & load space determined to each customer's requirements

*Standard tractor overhang depends upon suspension. Consult engineering data book

MODEL 372 OPTIONAL COMPONENTS AND EQUIPMENT

ENGINES

Caterpillar	3406 Series	310-425 HP
Cummins	NTC Series	300-444 HP
Detroit Diesel	Series 60	285-400 HP

TRANSMISSIONS

Fuller	Virtually all popular main and auxiliary
Spicer	transmissions are available to match engine torque and vehicle application

FRONT AXLES

Rockwell & Eaton   12,000-18,000 lb. capacity

REAR AXLES

Rockwell & Eaton	23,000 lbs.	single drive
Rockwell	38,000-46,000 lbs.	tandem drive
Eaton	38,000-46,000 lbs.	tandem drive

SUSPENSIONS

Single Drive	Peterbilt Air Trac	20,000 lbs.
	Peterbilt Leaf Spring	23,000 lbs.
Tandem Drive	Peterbilt Air Trac	38,000-44,000 lbs.
	Peterbilt Air Leaf	38,000 lbs.
	Peterbilt 4-Spring	34,000 and 38,000 lbs.
	Hendrickson RT, RS Series	38,000-44,000 lbs.
	Reyco 102 Series	38,000-44,000 lbs.

FUEL TANKS

26" diameter aluminum in various gallonages

FRAME

Aluminum or steel channel with aluminum or steel crossmembers

MISCELLANEOUS

A wide choice of interiors, instruments, mirrors, seats, air equipment, electrical equipment, radios and CB installation packages. Choose from a variety of factory designed paint schemes or design your own (customer specifies colors). Paint available in DuPont Imron.

* FUEL EFFICIENT	The Peterbilt 320 gives you all the features you're looking for in a rugged, dependable low cab forward heavy duty truck, including fuel efficient engines. The Caterpillar 3306, a 300 horse power engine, is standard equipment. The Cummins L10 Mechanical and the C-series engines are popular options.
* GREAT STYLING	Our Model 320 shares the Peterbilt tradition of custom-built heavy duty trucks, combining low operating costs and rock-solid reliability with an image that tells customers you do things right.
* DRIVER COMFORT	When a truck has a spacious interior and comfortable seating, drivers tend to work smarter and job loyalty improves. The Peterbilt 320 is designed for driver comfort. Built wider than most LCFs, the cab is a full eight feet in width, offering plenty of operating room for drivers. Comfortable Peterbilt non-suspension seats are standard. Air suspension driver and passenger seats are popular options.
* CONFIGURATION	You won't find an OEM better able to customize a heavy duty low cab forward truck to meet your needs. For example, you have your choice of front and rear axles rated at various load capacities. Other options include a right-hand drive and a dual drive with stand-up right hand drive and low entry. Also available is a front end power takeoff option.
* LOW COST OF OWNERSHIP	Routine maintenance can be quick and easy due to the convenient oil, coolant and transmission fluid check and fill module at the back of the cab. The cab tilts a full 53 degrees for easy access to engine and drivetrain.

A DIVISION OF **PACCAR**

* FUEL EFFICIENT

The Peterbilt Model 385 is engineered to answer the needs of the short-to-medium haul fleet operator. Available with a full range of ten and eleven liter engines, the Peterbilt 385 is a highly efficient performance vehicle.

* GREAT STYLING

Like all other Peterbilts, the 385 is a real eye-catcher on the road. Its road worthy lineage is unmistakable. And everything about its styling says "Class." The contemporary design of the dramatically sloped hood provides fuel efficient aerodynamics and a 28% increase in driver forward visibility. Peterbilt continues to exceed customer expectations with products that deliver quality and timeless beauty.

* PERFORMANCE

The 385 is engineered for optimum performance for both city and highway transport, with a 112″ BBC and set-back front axle. All of which, when combined with your drivers, equals a money making formula.

* EASE OF MAINTENANCE

Full engine access, along with components designed to Truck Maintenance Council standards, are features that help reduce maintenance headaches.

* VOCATIONAL SPECING

The Model 385 is engineered for bulk and regional haulers that require a medium length hood with a set-back front axle for better maneuverability and weight distribution. For the weight conscious customer, the 385 can be specified with numerous lightweight options that increase payload. When specified for light weight, it delivers one of the lowest tare weights of any conventional on the road today.

A DIVISION OF **PACCAR**

* **PETERBILT "CLASS" DESIGN:** The 330 carries the same innovations that have distinguished Peterbilt's for generations. Like our corrosion-resist cab - made of lightweight, high strength aluminum and huck bolted for maximum durability and a unique 2-piece flat windshield, which keeps replacement costs to a minimum.

* **SERVICEABILITY:** The hood tilts 90° for easy engine access. The bumper has a three piece design for quick and easy repair. The steering gear is mounted outside the frame rail for easy access.

* **DRIVER COMFORTS:** Doors open a full 90° for easy entry. Optimal engine in chassis mounting eliminate excessive intrusion in the cab provision. Both the driver and the passenger have abundant leg room. The fiberglass hood slopes 15° for greater driver visibility. Gauges are within easy view.

* **FUEL EFFICIENT POWER:** The fuel efficient Caterpillar 3126 @ 210 HP is standard: Also available are other Caterpillar engines from 185 HP to 300 HP and Cummins engines from 210 HP to 300 HP.

* **CONFIGURATION:** The 4 x 2 configuration is standard with Eaton 10,000 F/A, with options currently up to 12,000 lbs. Rear axles are available up to 40,000 lbs. to meet a variety of vocational needs.

A DIVISION OF **PACCAR**

COMING SOON...

THE CLASS OF 2000.

Model 387

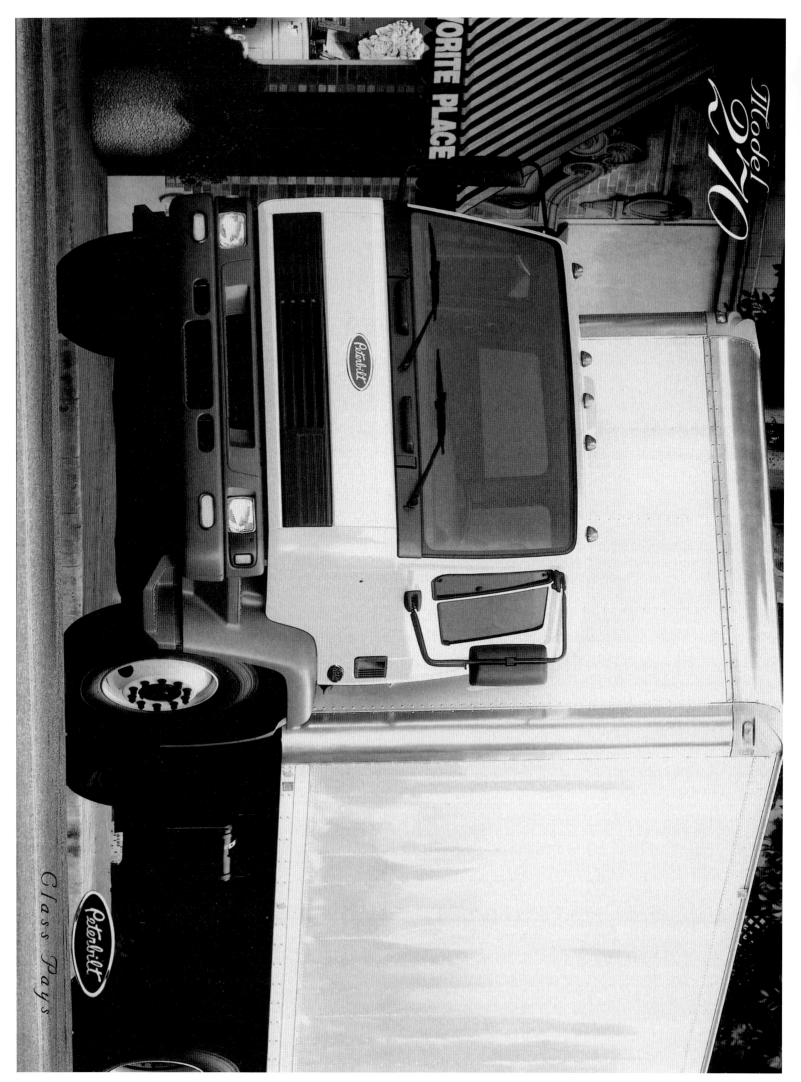

The Evolution of the Loggers

Peterbilt's history was born in the Western United States when, in 1934, Al Peterman purchased 30,000 acres of forest land near Tacoma, Washington. He modified a fleet of White trucks to meet his needs to harvest that forest. In 1939 Peterman purchased the Fageol Truck Factory, then went on to build his legacy. Peterman envisioned the answer to his truck needs in Fageol's Model 10-66 off-road logger. This would lead to the Models' 354, 355, 370, 380, 390, 381, 383, and the 387.

1938 Fageol, Model 10-66 off-road logger.

Peterbilt engineer drawing SK102, dated May 2, 1940.

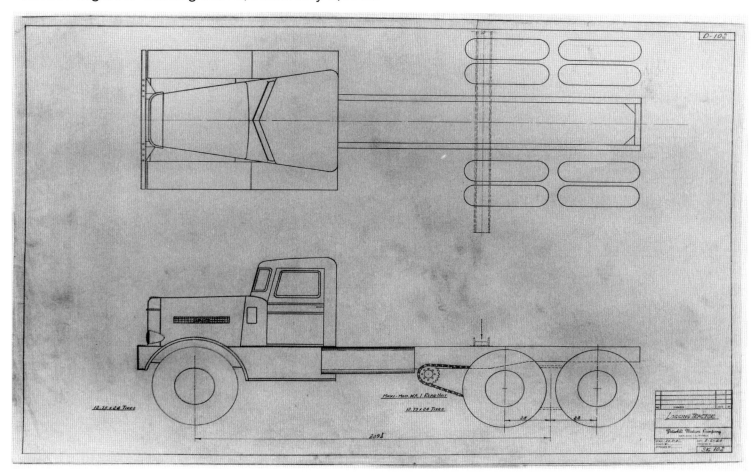

Peterbilt Loggers

Owner HILDEBRANDS' INC.
UKIAH~CALIF.
PETERBUILT TRUCK ~ RELIANCE TRAILER
300 hp. CUMMINS MOTOR   12 Ft. BUNKER
TIRES - 12 x 24 FRONT - REAR & TRAILER 14 x 24
28/126 Ft. 332760 Estimated Weight of Load
CUT FROM MASONITE TIMBER
SELECT LOGGING for HOLLOW TREE LBR. Co.

Peterbilt Model 381 off-road logger St. Regis Paper Co., July, 1960.

Peterbilt Model 355 with Hall Scott Power.

When he's all alone.

Like the man said: if you can't haul 'em out,
might just as well leave 'em on the stump.
And it's your rigs that do the hauling.

You don't boss a trucking outfit
without making a lot of lonely decisions.
From taking on drivers. To buying rolling stock.
You're putting money on the line.

And out there is where it all pays off. That's where class counts.
And that's why we build our trucks the way we do.

We build 'em
for the guys
who drive 'em.

Peterbilt Model 359, Circa 1973.

The Evolution of the Cabovers

Peterbilt's design and engineering department was looking at the cabover market from the onset as evidenced in these early engineer drawings. The early proposals were takeoffs of Fageol's cabover, then took on a look of their own with the first production trucks, the Models 280, 350, and 360 of 1949.

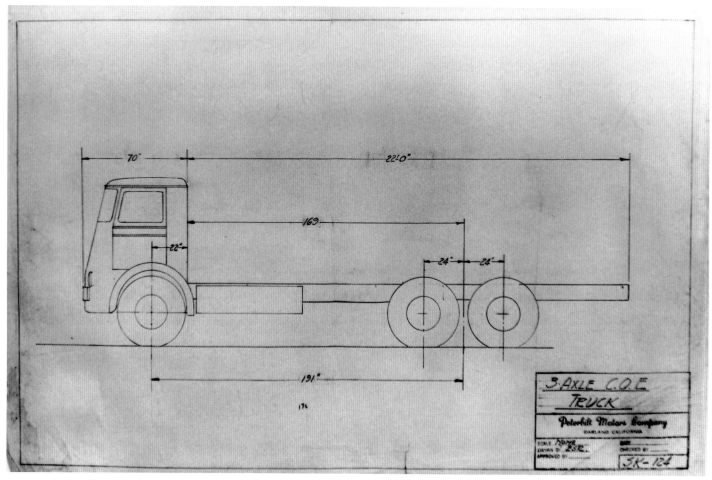

Peterbilt engineer drawing SK124, circa July, 1940.

Proposed cabover engine truck, November 23, 1945. Drawing SK332.

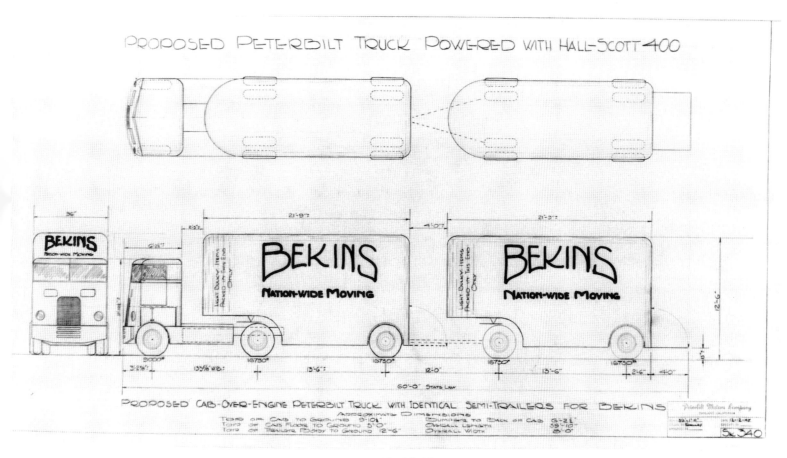

Peterbilt engineer drawing SK340, dated December 12, 1945.

Peterbilt Model 350 with full trailer.

The Evolution of Aerodynamics

With the fuel crunch of the 70's aerodynamics would come to the forefront of design technology.

Peterbilt Model 362, aerodynamic drag reduction experimentation.

Peterbilt experimental Model P-12.

The evolution of the Peterbilt Model 372.

The Evolution of Peterbilt Logos

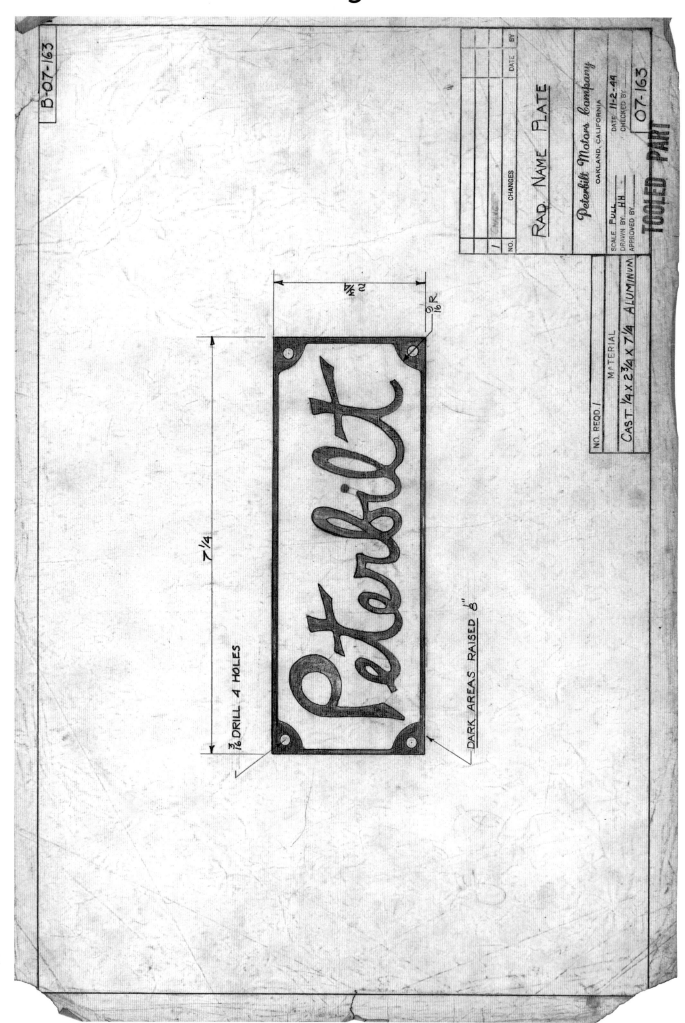

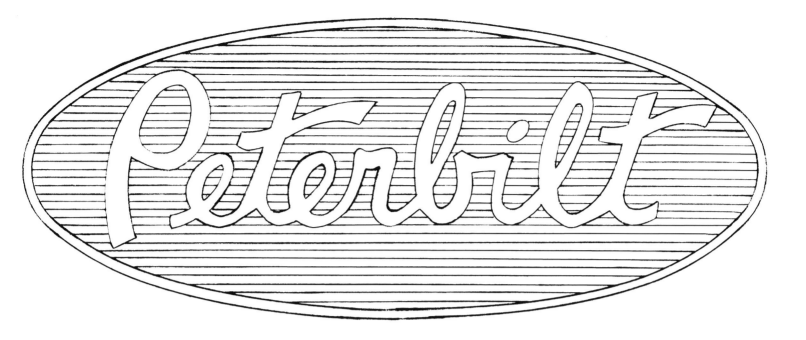

Current production: Chrome border and lettering – maroon background, Circa 1951.

Model	From-To	Units	First Sales Order#	Build Date	Remarks
120	1939-1942	6	5001	6-39	Chassis Only
334	1939-1941	53	5002	8-2-39	
260	1939-1942	79	5003	8-18-39	
344	1941-1949	344	5117	1-16-41	
345	1945-1949	487	5646	3-6-45	
354	1940-1948	225	5094	9-13-40	
364	1941-1943	40	5146	6-25-41	
270	1941-1949	323	5177	8-21-41	
355	1945-1949	136	5707	5-18-45	
280	1949-1957	387	6673	3-23-49	
350	1949-1957	847	6772	4-18-49	
380	1949-1954	86	6854	4-25-49	
360	1949-1956	198	6889	1-11-49	
390	1949-1953	38	6993	7-25-49	
370	1949-1955	53	6978	7-27-49	
360C.O.	1949-1952	14	7002	10-5-49	First 2 Had Trussed Frame
280C.O.	1950-1956	117	7061	7-19-50	
350C.O.	1950-1959	299	7086	2-24-50	
351	1954-1976	7,089	8542	3-18-54	
381	1954-1974	391	8555	3-22-54	
281	1954-1975	2,790	8559	3-30-54	
361	1955-Only	1	8940	11-1-55	

Model	From-To	Units	First Sales Order#	Build Date	Remarks
351C.O.	1955-1959	197	9245	12-22-55	
281C.O.	1956-1959	123	9371	5-2-56	
451C.O.	1956-1957	39	9671	8-1-56	4 Axle Drom
356C.O.	1957-Only	21	10196	7-18-57	3 Axle Drom
352C.O.	1959-1980	(28,897)	10805	3-14-59	352/282 Combined 56,300 Through 1980
282C.O.	1959-1980	(4,504)	10986	6-12-59	
371	1959-1965	140	11072	5-22-59	
287	1962-Only	8	13889	8-2-62	
341	1962-1972	779	14490	11-21-62	
383	1964-1975	240	16043	10-22-64	
343	1964-1968	34	17740	9-16-64	
358	1965-1976	2773	20638	11-8-65	First Tilt Hood
288	1965-1975	685	20713	11-24-65	
359	1967-1987	(14,207)	24561	4-21-67	14,207 to 1976 ⟩ Total Run 64,858
289	1967-1986	(1,057)	25624	6-2-67	1,057 to 1976
348	1970-1987	(575)	37525	6-9-70	575 to 1976 Total 348/349 5,152
CB300	1970-1977	638	38656	8-31-70	
CB200	1970-1977	198	37906	9-28-70	
349	1972-1987	5,152	45531	4-17-72	348/349 Total Run 5,152
353	1972-1987	1,843	46831	4-20-72	
346	1972-1974	10	45885	7-3-72	
352	1972-Only	2	45892	7-19-72	Turbine Power
387	1975-1982	181	76595	6-75	
248	1976-Only	1	78439	1-13-76	Single Axle Version of 348
253	1976-Only	1	78435	1-17-76	Single Axle Version of 353
310	1977-1985	1,097			
397	1981-Only	2	134284		
362	1981-Present				
320	1985 Present				
357	1986-Present		205183	10-18-86	
375	1986-1995		205181	10-18-86	376/375 Total run 4,747 units
377	1986-Present		205174	10-18-86	SO# 212092 377 Idea Truck
379	1986-Present		205168	10-18-86	SO# 192942 Prototype 379
376	1988-1991				2 axle version of model 375
378	1986-Present				
372	1988-1993	772			
13-210	1987-Only				Single Axle Cab Forward Midranger
224	1988-1992				29,700 GVW Cab Forward Midranger
227	1988-1992				33,000 GVW Cab Forward Midranger
265	1988-1992				50,000 GVW Cab Forward Midranger
200-30	1992-1999				30,000 GVW Cab Forward Medium Duty
200-33	1992-1999				33,000 GVW Cab Forward Medium Duty
385	1995-Present				
330	1995-Present				
387	1999-Present				
270	1999-Present				
L700R	1986		702539		Cab Forward Right Hand Steer
359	1986		207524	8-15-86	"Classic 359" Prototype
359	1987		211579	1-17-87	Last Ordered 359
359	1987		211472	1-24-87	Last Built 359
359	1987		211386	1-17-87	Last "Classic 359" Built

Numbers in parenthesis are unit counts to 1976

The above chart is a fairly accurate count of the earlier models by verification of each truck built through 1976. Because of typographical errors, only a complete scrutiny of each build sheet would eliminate any mistakes. Truck counts from 1977 forward generally are still considered propietary information by Peterbuilt.